Making Marriage Work For Dummies®

Cheat Sheet

Six Common Marriage Myths

Chapter 1 gives you detailed information about each of the following myths:

- There's only one right person for you.
- Two people in a good marriage automatically grow closer with time.
- When couples argue, it destroys the relationship.
- Pursuing your own individual needs is incompatible with making a marriage work.
- Marriage partners can fill the gaps in one another's makeup.
- The goal of marriage is for both partners to get exactly what they want.

The Do's and Don'ts of Fair Marital Fighting

Flip to Chapter 5 for the low-down on fair fighting.

- Do be clear about what you want.
- Do stick to the issues at hand.
- Do look at both sides of the story.
- Do listen more than you talk.
- Do apologize when you're wrong.
- Don't look for total victory.
- Don't prolong the argument.
- Don't nag or withdraw.
- Don't take the moral high ground.
- Don't go for the jugular.

Ways to Reduce the Stress on Your Marriage

Chapter 13 is chock full of more information about reducing stress in your marriage.

- Talk to a friend.
- Slow down.
- Find time in your day to do something that makes you feel good.
- Keep your sense of humor — even in difficult situations.
- Don't dwell on your mistakes.
- Forgive yourself and your partner.
- Don't expect perfection — from your partner or yourself.
- Find ways to take care of your partner — and yourself.
- Change the scenery.
- Eliminate unnecessary pressure and people.

Making Marriage Work For Dummies®

Cheat Sheet

Prescription for a Sexier, More Exciting Marriage

Take a look at Chapters 6 and 7 for more tips on improving your sex life.

- Show your love every day.
- Touch each other lovingly and sensuously.
- Show and tell your spouse what pleases you.
- Let your fantasies run free.
- Make time to be alone together.
- Play and laugh together.
- Make special time for sex.
- Become an artful kisser.
- Talk sexy to each other.

Ideas for Resolving Money Differences

Chapter 14 helps you pinpoint and resolve money disputes between you and your spouse.

- Sit down with your partner and talk about the way each of your families of origin dealt with money.
- Talk about the effects that past experiences may be having on your present attitudes about money. Ask yourself and your partner if those current attitudes and behaviors make sense.
- Understand each other's short- and long-term financial goals.
- Understand that your different values and ideas about money require constant negotiation.
- Respect each other's values and preferences about spending and saving.
- Brainstorm solutions that make you both feel comfortable.
- Respect each other's contribution to the marriage as equal — even if one partner earns most or all of the money.
- Make sure you and your partner both have access to a significant portion of the money.
- Agree on an amount that each spouse can spend without consulting the other.

For Dummies: Bestselling Book Series for Beginners

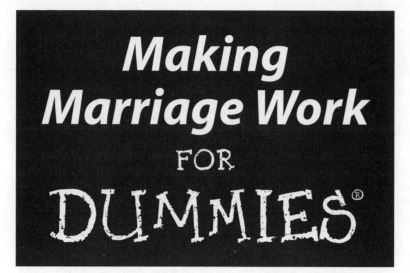

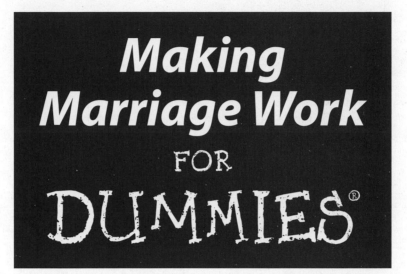

Making Marriage Work

FOR DUMMIES®

**by Dr. Steven Simring and
Dr. Sue Klavans Simring**

with Gene Busnar

WILEY

Wiley Publishing, Inc.

Making Marriage Work For Dummies®

Published by
Wiley Publishing, Inc.
111 River Street
Hoboken, NJ 07030
www.wiley.com

Copyright © 2001 Wiley Publishing, Inc., Indianapolis, Indiana

Published simultaneously in Canada

For general information on our other products and services or to obtain technical support, please contact our Customer Care Department within the U.S. at 800-762-2974, outside the U.S. at 317-572-3993, or fax 317-572-4002.

Wiley also publishes its books in a variety of electronic formats. Some content that appears in print may not be available in electronic books.

Library of Congress Cataloging-in-Publication Data:

Library of Congress Catalog Card No.: 99-66336

ISBN: 0-7645-5173-6

Manufactured in the United States of America

10 9 8

1O/TQ/QZ/QW/IN

About the Authors

Steven Simring, MD, MPH is coauthor of *How to Win Back the One You Love* (Macmillan). He is Associate Professor and Vice Chair of the Department of Psychiatry at New Jersey Medical School. He is the recipient of numerous awards for outstanding teaching. Dr. Steve Simring is a practicing psychotherapist who has served as an expert psychiatrist in numerous highly publicized civil and criminal cases.

Sue Klavans Simring, DSW is a practicing psychotherapist who specializes in working with couples and families. She is a lecturer at the Columbia University School of Social Work. Dr. Sue Simring has conducted independent research on the consequences of divorce, and has presented her findings in the academic literature. She has spoken extensively to professional and lay audiences.

The Simrings are coauthors of *The Compatibility Quotient* (Ballantine), a popular and helpful guide for couples who want to find out if they have made the right choice. Steve and Sue were regular guests on *A.M.-Philadelphia* for five years. They now make frequent appearances on such national TV talk shows as *Oprah*, *Montel Williams*, *Maury Povich*, *Sally Jessy Raphael*, and *Ricki Lake*. They have been married for 30 years and have three children.

Gene Busnar is a respected author and collaborative writer. His books include: *Loving and Leaving: Winning at the Business of Divorce* (The Free Press), *KidBiz* (Warner), *Conquering Corporate Codependence* (Prentice-Hall), *Working for Yourself* (McGraw-Hill), and *The Winds of Turbulence* (HarperBusiness).

Authors' Acknowledgments

We would like to thank our agent, Linda Konner, for all her help and guidance throughout this process; Tami Booth of Hungry Minds, who believed in this book and came through whenever we needed support; and Tere Drenth, for her sensitivity and understanding, and for her skillful hands-on editing. Finally, we would like to express special gratitude to our patients, who continue to make our work as therpists stimulating and worthwhile.

Dedication

For Eric, Kira, and Owen Simring

For Liz and Nadine Busnar

A special dedication to

Minnie Klavans
May 10, 1915 – September 19, 1999

Extraordinary artist, extraordinary mother

Publisher's Acknowledgments

We're proud of this book; please register your comments through our Online Registration Form located at www.dummies.com/register.

Some of the people who helped bring this book to market include the following:

Acquisitions, Editorial, and Media Development

Project Editor: Tere Drenth

Executive Editor: Tammerly Booth

General Reviewer: Riette Thomas Smith, MS, LCSW, LMFT, LMHC

Acquisitions Coordinator: Karen Young

Associate Permissions Editor: Carmen Krikorian

Editorial Director: Kristin A. Cocks

Composition

Project Coordinators: E. Shawn Aylsworth, Amanda Foxworth

Layout and Graphics: Amy M. Adrian, Angela F. Hunckler, Tracy Oliver, Jill Piscitelli, Doug Rollison, Brian Torwelle, Maggie Ubertini, Erin Zeltner

Proofreaders: Laura Albert, John Greenough, Marianne Santy, Susan Sims

Indexer: Steve Rath

Special Help
Mary Goodwin, Jonathon Malysiak

Publishing and Editorial for Technology Dummies

    Richard Swadley, Vice President and Executive Group Publisher

    Andy Cummings, Vice President and Publisher

    Mary Bednarek, Executive Acquisitions Director

    Mary C. Corder, Editorial Director

Publishing for Consumer Dummies

    Diane Graves Steele, Vice President and Publisher

    Joyce Pepple, Acquisitions Director

Composition Services

    Gerry Fahey, Vice President of Production Services

    Debbie Stailey, Director of Composition Services

Contents at a Glance

Table of Contents

Foreword

$\cdots$

*W*hen it comes to marriage, I suppose we're all dummies because we don't have any way to learn the ropes before jumping in. Marriage is the ultimate leap of faith — you have only limited data from which to predict what's going to happen tomorrow, so how can you know what will happen ten or twenty years down the line? So where can a person turn for answers to the everyday complications married couples face — and to the more serious problems that can derail a relationship? This book, that's where.

Making Marriage Work For Dummies is a user-friendly reference that's fun to read. The chapters feature down-to-earth, prescriptive advice from two outstanding and creative therapists who have forged their own successful marriage. Owning a copy of *Making Marriage Work For Dummies* is like having a personal marriage-counseling team at your disposal — it almost feels as if Drs. Steve and Sue Simring are right there talking to you.

The Simrings show you how to approach your partner and your marriage with renewed understanding and sensitivity. They answer questions on virtually every aspect of marriage — from sex and money to children and in-laws. They give you the tools to solve problems on your own, but also show you how to find the right kind of outside help, should that become necessary.

Now when people ask me to recommend a good self-help book on the subject of marriage, I can enthusiastically tell them: "Read *Making Marriage Work For Dummies!*".

June Machover Reinisch, Director Emerita, Kinsey Institute for Research in Sex, Gender, and Reproduction; author of *The Kinsey Institute New Report on Sex: What You Must Know to be Sexually Literate*.

Introduction

*F*or many people, marriage is a given. It's one of many things that people are programmed to do, such as getting your high school diploma. The vast majority of people marry at least once, but enter the waters without a real idea of how and where they're going to paddle. Our purpose in writing this book is to give you some guidelines you can actually use — a place to turn when questions come up or trouble strikes.

Trouble in a marriage can be a battle with your spouse over money, a snag in your sex life, tension with your in-laws, or an argument over how to deal with children. The problem can be something as simple as an argument over household responsibilities or forgetting a birthday. It can complicated as depression, physical or emotional abuse, or an addiction to alcohol, drugs, or gambling.

Making Marriage Work For Dummies deals with the big and small things that come up in the course of day-to-day living — and at all stages of the marriage life cycle. The book addresses the needs of women and men who are thinking about getting married, adjusting to married life, raising children, experiencing the stresses of middle age, or fighting to save a troubled marriage.

Marriage is a never-ending series of challenges, any one of which can throw you for a loop. Some couples go along for ten or twenty years, and then suddenly, something happens that makes one-or both partners feel lost or puts the future of the marriage in doubt. But small changes in what you do and say can often lead to major improvements in your relationship. That's what this book is about: Showing you how to make the small changes that can make a big difference.

While making marriage work is a serious business, it can also be filled with humor and fun. That's also an important part of what this book is about.

Why You Need This Book

Making Marriage Work For Dummies gives you a framework for understanding what it takes to sustain a successful marriage, and shows you how to apply that understanding to your relationship. The book also helps you work on specific areas of your relationship, and deal with problems as they come up. By exploring the chapters, you discover how to do the following:

- ✔ Make your relationship more romantic.
- ✔ Work out big and small differences.
- ✔ Have a more exciting sex life.
- ✔ Argue in ways that strengthen your relationship.
- ✔ Handle a spouse who cheats.
- ✔ Deal with families and in-laws.
- ✔ Reduce the stress on your marriage.
- ✔ Understand your partner's annoying habits and quirks.
- ✔ Balance career and family goals.
- ✔ Seek professional help when you need it.

How This Book Is Organized

We want you to use *Making Marriage Work For Dummies* in the way that's most comfortable for you. You can read the book from cover to cover and refer to relevant sections as the need arises. Or, you can use the book as a marriage fix-it manual, turning to the chapters or sections that answer specific questions or talk about key issues that are important to you.

This book is divided into six parts that make it easy to pinpoint your needs and address them in a direct and constructive way.

Part I: What It Means To Say "I Do!"

This part explores the ingredients for a successful marriage. We help you take a clear-eyed look at the condition of your marriage, and pinpoint the areas where it most needs improvement. We debunk some common marriage myths and replace them with realities you can build on, and also show you strategies that strengthen your relationship.

Part II: Can We Talk?

Part II of *Making Marriage Work For Dummies* begins by describing the causes of marriage problems. We show you different ways to solve problems between you and your partner. We also show you how to recognize ongoing patterns in your relationship that are often obvious to everyone but you.

We give you the tools to negotiate big and small differences in your personal styles and preferences. Finally, we show you how to turn potentially hurtful arguments into win-win situations for both of you.

Part III: Making Marriage Sexy

Sex may not define a good marriage. Still, it's not easy to sustain a vital relationship without a good sex life. In this part, we help you recognize and deal with both expected and unexpected changes in sexual chemistry. We show you how to communicate your needs and wants to your partner — and tell you how to insulate your sex life from career pressures, children, and other stresses. We help you recognize problems that can prevent you and your partner from enjoying sex, and show you how to increase the sexual compatibility between you. We explain male and female sexual problems, and show you how couples can resolve them — either on their own or with the help of a therapist.

Part IV: Examining the Marriage Life Cycle

Every marriage has a life of its own, apart from the lives of the two partners. A wife and husband who marry at a relatively young age and stay together for life will experience numerous personal changes in the course of those 40, 50, or more years. The structure and boundaries of the marriage will change as well.

First, there's an initial adjustment period, during which a newly married wife and husband have to feel their way through a new and unfamiliar world. A few years later, many couples are expanding their families to include children — and dealing with the added challenges that those changes bring. By the time children reach adolescence, many parents are coping with the emotional and physical challenges of midlife. They may also be reassessing their relationship, and thinking of ways to change it. We help you understand and negotiate the many adjustments and challenges you may face during each phase of the marriage cycle.

Because many people find themselves living in a re-married or stepfamily situation at some point in their lives, we also explore the special considerations these families face, and offer guidelines for balancing the needs of children with a husband's and wife's needs as a loving couple.

Part V: Maintaining a Healthy Marriage

A number of factors keep a marriage healthy. In this part, we show you how to reduce negative stress, and how to use positive stress to strengthen your marriage. We explore the role of money in marriage, and show you how to resolve some common financial disputes. We discuss the causes of marital infidelity, so that you recognize your options in handling this delicate issue. We explore a number of alternatives to divorce, and show you the best places to turn for outside help, should that become necessary.

Part VI: The Part of Tens

No ...*For Dummies* book would be complete without this summary of top-ten tips. In this part, we highlight important issues in your marriage: How to put more romance into your relationship, things never to say to your husband or wife, the do's and don'ts of fair fighting, a list of warning signs that your marriage is in trouble, and ways to put more excitement into your sex life.

Icons Used in This Book

Throughout this book, we use *icons* — small markers in the margins — to highlight information that we think is especially important. Here's a rundown of what each icon means.

This icon points out tips, tricks, and techniques that can strengthen your marriage.

When you're looking for step-by-step methods for improving an aspect of your marriage, keep an eye out for this icon. Here, we've earmarked homework for you and your spouse. Don't worry, though, we won't give you an exam!

The individuals and couples that we've counseled through the years have helped us see that the majority of marital problems can be solved — and that most marriages are well worth the effort it takes to keep them afloat. With this icon, we highlight their stories.

Steve and Sue, married to each other for 30 years, use this icon to give you advice from their own practices — and from their own marriage. Like any married couple, though, they don't always agree with each other!

 This icon gives you bits of advice to remember — chances are, they'll come up again.

Caution! Beware! Watch out! This icon points out pitfalls and hazards. Proceed at your own peril.

Where to Go from Here

You don't have to read this book from cover to cover: Simply dive into whichever chapter gives you the information that you need most. To understand how to communicate with your spouse, flip to the chapters in Part II. Chapter 7 gives you tips on improving a faltering sex life. Chapter 10 helps you decide when — and if — to include children in your marriage. In Chapter 15, you find pointers and techniques for managing money as a couple. And Part VI, the Part of Tens, gives you 50 ways to improve your marriage today.

Part I
What It Means To Say "I Do!"

The 5th Wave   By Rich Tennant

@RICHTENNANT

"I knew they were writing their own vows, but I expected quotes from Robert Frost poems, not The Geneva Convention."

In this part . . .

*W*hether you're already married or considering tying the knot, reading this part gives you an eye-opening look at the realities of marriage, and separates these realities from all of the myths and unrealistic expectations that people take for granted. In Chapter 1, you have a chance to compare what you gain to what you give up when you marry. You find out why the fear of being "stuck in a relationship for life" can turn out to be one of the real pluses of choosing marriage over living together or remaining single.

Chapter 2 explores the building blocks of a successful marriage. We describe productive ways in which couples deal with differences and disappointments that erode loving feelings. We show you why no marriage can deliver absolute happiness, and help you assess whether your marriage is good enough to meet you and your partner's emotional needs.

Chapter 1

Taking a Candid Look at Marriage

*I*n this chapter, we talk about the key differences between marriage and other kinds of relationships. We look at some of the tradeoffs women and men face when they decide to marry, and help you take an objective look at the pluses and minuses of your marriage. Don't worry — we don't expect perfection.

We've been counseling married couples and navigating the twists and turns of our own marriage for three decades, so we know better than to expect perfection. Anyone who claims to have a perfect marriage is either clueless or overly attached to the myths that we deflate in this chapter — myths that would have you believe that happy couples should do everything together or that they never argue.

Whether you've been married for decades or are considering tying the knot, we help you take an honest look at your relationship and start pinpointing areas that can use improvement. A successful marriage isn't rocket science. Mostly, it's a matter of commitment to each other, love, mutual respect, and trying to have fun as you work at making it better.

To Marry or Not to Marry?

Many people consider living together to be just like marriage, except without the certificate. In fact, marriage differs from all other forms of pairing (including living together) in one very important way which has nothing to do with a piece of paper.

Living together means that you are free to leave at any time, without going through the hassle and expense of a divorce. Marriage entails a commitment to your partner, a promise that says that you won't just get up and walk out at a moment's notice. When all is said and done, that legal, social, and emotional commitment is the most important difference between marriage and living together. Which, by the way, is the whole point of dragging your families and the rest of the community into the process: To declare to the world that you are making a lifetime pledge to another human being.

After living together for a time, many couples find it difficult to agree on the importance of marriage. Very often, the lack of agreement stems from one or both individuals not wanting to make the commitment that marriage entails.

If you and your partner are debating whether to get married, following these steps may help you come to a decision:

1. **Sit down and have an honest discussion about the way each of you feels about the advantages and disadvantages of marriage.**

   The next section in this chapter, "Understanding Marriage Pluses and Minuses," can prepare you for this discussion.

   Couples marrying for the first time need to recognize that cohabitation doesn't provide the same dedication to each other as does marriage. Researchers have found that married couples who lived together before marriage are twice as likely to divorce as other couples. One explanation for this may be that living together fosters an atmosphere of noncommitment. Couples considering marriage need to recognize that marriage involves the loss of certain freedoms, and that this is part of the tradeoff when you commit to a lifelong bond.

   When people marry for the first time, they cast their lots together for the common good. Even when one spouse has more money than the other, there is a feeling that separate bank accounts or prenuptial agreements may undermine the relationship. The situation is often different for older or previously married couples. People in this position may want companionship, but they find it advantageous to keep finances separate. This makes sense when one or both partners have children and property from an earlier marriage, and don't want to risk jeopardizing them.

   If, after an honest, ongoing discussion, one of you has serious doubts about making a commitment and the other is set on marriage, the two of you have to decide whether you can bridge this difference in the foreseeable future.

2. **Set a timeframe for working out your differences regarding marriage.**

   You can agree to suspend making a decision for a set period of time — say six months or a year. If, at that point, you both still can't decide between living together and marriage, you may want to consider whether your long-term goals will ever be compatible.

If you want a committed lifetime relationship, living together is no substitute for marriage. Sharing an apartment, having sex, and keeping your options open may be fine for a while, but ultimately, most people want to take that next step, into marriage, at least once.

Understanding Marriage Pluses and Minuses

If you and your partner are in the process of deciding whether you should get married, taking a look at the advantages and disadvantages of marriage may help you make your decision. If you're already married, reading this section may remind you of some of the reasons you decided to get married in the first place!

Marriage pluses

We once attended a civil wedding ceremony in which the justice of the peace compared marriage to a business. "If you have more assets than liabilities," he mused, "your marriage will be a success." This struck us as a chilly way of talking to a young couple as they were taking their vows, but it inspired us to create this little balance sheet of the *assets* that marriage can bring you:

- **Marriage can mean long-term emotional commitment and support.** Loving marriage partners have the opportunity to achieve an exceptionally high level of intimacy and trust. Married people take a vow to love, honor, and protect each other. Loving partners take these words quite literally and are there for each other in both good times and bad.

- **Marriage can provide greater financial security.** In most marriages, the partners merge their finances and money-making skills. If one partner becomes ill or is laid off from a job, the other can pick up the slack. Depending on where you live, there may be other financial advantages regarding income taxes, home ownership, healthcare, and estate planning.

- **Marriage is a relationship sanctioned by the community.** In some communities, being married opens many more doors, which may mean a better social life. Married couples are often more comfortable taking part in activities with each other's families and their circle of friends.

- **Marriage makes raising children easier.** Single-parent households have become a great deal more common, and are now well-accepted by society. However, raising children can take a lot less work when two parents are actively involved.

✔ **Marriage promotes good physical health.** The health benefits of marriage seem to be more profound for men. Unmarried and divorced men are twice as likely to die prematurely from cardiovascular disease, and they are four times as likely to die prematurely from certain forms of cancer. Single men also have much higher rates of depression, substance abuse, auto accidents, and suicide. However, research shows that both wives and husbands in a happy marriage derive substantial health benefits.

Marriage minuses

Everything you do in life has tradeoffs. So why should marriage be any different? Here, then, are some items that many people place on the minus side of the marriage balance sheet:

✔ **You can no longer come and go as you please.** You give up some autonomy — how much depends on what each couple works out. For example, you may not be able to hang out with your friends like you used to without first checking with your partner.

✔ **You must accept and adapt to your partner's faults and quirks.** Does he leave his clothes all over the bathroom floor after he takes a shower? Does she insist on throwing out the Sunday paper before you're finished with the sports section? You can get your way on some issues, but you have to learn to live with certain parts of the package.

✔ **You must constantly negotiate and compromise.** When you live on your own, you can do things your way. After you're married, most things have to be negotiated. You and your partner will have to come to an understanding about everything from the color of the kitchen walls to who controls the TV remote to how the family money is spent.

✔ **You can't simply pick up and go when the road gets rocky.** There will be times when you wish you could get unmarried — even for just a night or a weekend. You can certainly negotiate time and space to be alone. But your marriage commitment means that you're locked into working out the rough spots.

✔ **You may be forced to deal with members of your partner's family that you can't stand.** When you marry, you assume an obligation to deal with your spouse's family, including some family members you could easily live without. After you marry, you are no longer an island unto yourself. Your partner's family of origin is an important part of his or her package, so your wisest course is to find some relatives you do like and try your best to tolerate the others. Remember, your husband or wife may not be wild about your mother or sister, either.

THE MARRIAGE DOCTORS SAY

Who gives up what?

As veteran marriage partners, we have a pretty good idea of what the tradeoffs are. When we actually discussed them, however, we were a bit surprised at the feelings and differences that surfaced

Steve: I had to give up a lot of my privacy when we got married.

Sue: I moved into your apartment and I couldn't even find a drawer for my clothes.

Steve: It wasn't just drawer space. There are times when it's enjoyable to be alone, without having to face somebody all of the time. Just before our wedding, a friend warned me: "After you tie the knot, you won't even be able to pick your nose in peace."

Sue: That must have been a tremendous luxury for you to sacrifice!

Steve: Then there's all that freedom you have to give up.

Sue: What freedom is that?

Steve: You know, the old ball and chain. You can't hang out with your friends any more. You can't pick up an attractive woman, even if she makes a pass at you. They say that women are gatherers and men are hunters. When a man gets married, he gives up the freedom to go out and hunt.

Sue: It may surprise you to know that we give up at least as much of our freedom. But for women, the ball and chain often has more to do with being in a less secure financial position than your husband.

Steve: But lots of women make as much or more money as their husbands these days.

Sue: Women have traditionally been thought of as caretakers. Too often that means you're expected to become a servant. And those expectations still hold, even for women who work and bring home substantial paychecks.

Steve: (a little sarcastically) It really sounds like a terrible life!

Sue: You can joke all you want, but many husbands have a hard time understanding the load women carry in a marriage. A single woman doesn't have to worry if there's food in the fridge so her husband and children will have enough to eat. After you're married, it's almost as if your own needs go out the window.

Steve: You have a point, but aren't more men assuming a greater caretaking role in terms of family responsibilities?

Sue: That's true, compared to our parents' and grandparents' generations. However, women are still expected to assume the primary role in taking care of the household, even though they may have to go to work. Once children come into the picture, a woman gives up even more. At that point, a woman really can't separate her childrearing duties from all her other caretaking responsibilities.

Why Marriage Isn't for Everyone

Marriage is a great institution, but I'm not ready for an institution.

— Mae West, actress

Most people are told at a very young age that someday you're going to get married and have children. That's the way many people are taught to lead their lives, and it's constantly reinforced by movies, popular songs, and TV commercials. It's natural to assume that marriage is inevitable. But marriage isn't for everybody — even if people sometimes have to get married to figure that out.

Some men and women don't want the closeness or the commitment that comes with matrimony. These people should not get married — at least not until their mindset changes.

 If your partner says that she doesn't want to get married at a particular point in time, don't ignore those words. Such feelings may or may not change later on. No matter how difficult this decision may be for you to accept, remember that this is a valid and very personal decision that must be respected.

Knowing that Unrealistic Expectations Cause Problems

Marriage is not supposed to make you happy. It is supposed to make you married.

— Frank Pittman, family therapist and author

Many of the ideas people have about marriage come from the images they see in movies and TV. Not surprisingly, these images give a distorted picture of marriage, because couples are usually depicted as completely harmonious or fighting like cats or dogs. We also get ideas about marriage from other biased sources, including our families, friends, and communities. Despite good intentions, this kind of advice may lead you to very unrealistic expectations about marriage.

Because you're so often bombarded with these warped images of marriage, it pays to spend some time to deprogram your notions about what a good marriage is and isn't.

Take a few minutes to answer each of the following ten questions with a "yes" or "no."

- Do you believe that there is only one person in the world for you?
- Do you believe that true soulmates never have major differences?
- Do you believe that partners in a good marriage rarely argue?
- Do you believe that husbands and wives must each have specific roles in a marriage?
- Do you believe that happily married couples should do everything together?
- Do you believe that your partner's strengths can make up for your shortcomings?
- Do you believe that your strengths can make up for your partner's shortcomings?
- Do you believe you can choose to ignore either of your families of origin, and it will not affect your marriage?
- Do you believe that people can resolve their differences without much effort as long as they are in love?
- Do you believe you can make your husband or wife change bad habits after you marry?
- Do you believe two people who love each other will automatically grow closer with time?

A "yes" answer to each of the above questions indicates that you may be harboring an unrealistic expectation that is bound to lead to feelings of disappointment about the state of your marriage. Instead of allowing those feelings to get you down, we urge you to take advantage of the mythbusters we offer in the following section.

Deflating Six Common Marriage Myths

The only thing perfect about marriage is the airbrushed wedding photo.

— Anonymous

Rather than allowing myths about marriage to undermine your relationship, we want to help you find those truths that help keep relationships strong. That doesn't mean settling for less. Our purpose is to guide you through this journey so that you can make your marriage all that it can be.

A good marriage is a long-term process — not an overnight miracle. Still, you may be pleasantly surprised at how examining these myths can help you see your marriage more clearly.

Finding Mr. or Ms. Right

Spouses who are having problems in their marriage sometimes complain that their partner turned out not to be Mr. or Ms. Right. Surely, there are couples that really don't belong together. However, the majority of these not-the-right-person complaints are rooted in unrealistic expectations.

Two people in a good marriage automatically grow closer with time

In fact, a good marriage is the product of constant care and nurturing. If you think about it, this myth goes against what we know about achieving anything good in life. For example, how do people stay physically fit? Certainly not by fantasizing. A healthy body takes constant attention and work. The same is true for healthy relationships.

Marriage is very much like a living organism, which means that it is constantly changing. As the years pass, partners are not always going to feel close or affectionate toward one another. There are times when you will be very angry at your spouse, times when you may even question why the two of you married in the first place.

Getting past those rough spots is an important part of growing closer. But there is nothing automatic about the process.

When couples argue, it destroys the relationship

Couples often enter a marriage believing that arguing is bad. They expect things to go smoothly, with maybe a few minor bumps along the way. Then they run into the familiar struggles over money, sex, children, or sharing responsibilities.

If you don't recognize that all couples confront these problems, you may feel that something is wrong with your marriage. Quite possibly, the main problem has to do with harboring unrealistic expectations and therefore feeling vaguely disappointed.

For example, a couple we know let their marriage fall apart because they felt that they should never fight. Dave was devastated when Jessica filed for divorce after they were married for seven years. "We were always so civil to each other," he told us. "We never even had an argument."

This left us wondering about what kind of marriage these people really had. Spouses have to maintain an incredible amount of distance to always be "civil." The more distance people have from each other, the less opportunity there is for conflict.

It turned out that Dave and Jessica both had very demanding jobs that required working twelve hour days. But even when they were together, neither was very open when it came to sharing thoughts and feelings. Things may have worked out differently had they butted heads once in a while.

In the end, arguing can be a positive force in a marriage. What matters most is how you argue. You can read more about effective arguing in Chapter 5.

Pursuing your own individual needs is incompatible with making a marriage work

The happiest couples are those who have spent a lot of time together — and a lot of time apart.

— Phoebe Prosky, family therapist

This myth comes from the expectation that happily married couples must do everything together. Not so. A good marriage is bigger than what the two partners bring to it. That means both partners have to maintain a certain amount of separateness.

Each spouse has a separate life apart from that as a marriage partner. What you do with that separate life is something you must work out, even as you dedicate yourself to building a stronger relationship with your husband or wife.

When two people marry, they become integral parts of each other's world. That means, among other things, taking an interest in your partner's personal goals, and doing your best to have amicable dealings with his or her family of origin. Still, that's a lot different than feeling compelled to do everything together. Spouses who buy into that myth soon find that one or both partners feel trapped.

We've often heard a good marriage compared to the merging of two streams into a river that is stronger and wider than its original sources. We've always had a problem with that comparison, since the new river tends to conceal the identities of those two sources. But several years ago, on a trip to the Amazon, we saw a combining of two rivers that captured the essence of a good marriage. In one of the rivers, the water was a grayish-brown; in the other, a bluish-green. When the two rivers merged, the result was something more powerful and impressive. However, the color of each river was not lost in the merger. One half remained gray-brown, the other blue-green. The newly created body of water did not obscure the separate contributions of its two original sources.

Some marriages require more togetherness; others, more independence. Each couple needs to have a sense of how these domains overlap. The trick is finding a balance of togetherness and self reliance that works for you.

Marriage partners can fill the gaps in one another's makeup

> *In love, the paradox occurs that two beings become one and yet remain two.*
>
> — Erich Fromm, psychoanalyst

One of the great joys of marriage is the ability to pool your strengths and special gifts. So if one of you is physical and the other intellectual, you can help expand one another's horizons. However, if one spouse is painfully shy and relies on the other to do all the talking, you're bound to feel an imbalance.

A similar kind of imbalance can occur when partners assume rigid roles based on gender: the husband who refuses to help with chores like cooking or cleaning because those tasks are "a woman's work" or the wife who refuses to pick up a hammer or screwdriver because "that's the husband's job." For a marriage to succeed in the 21st century, spouses need to be flexible in their roles, and willing to work together at all sorts of tasks.

Strong marriages are collaborative efforts in which both partners are dedicated to improving — as individuals *and* as a couple. Each marriage partner brings a unique package of strengths and weaknesses to the table, and each has a separate timetable for growth. But, if one partner's development or contribution is way out of proportion to the other's, the imbalance can undermine the marriage.

The goal of marriage is for both partners to get exactly what they want

The notion that marriage is a way to achieve fulfillment is relatively new. For a long time, people married out of economic necessity and to have children. Now, many people think of it as a road to personal satisfaction.

Many of the complaints we hear about marriage go something like this: "I am not happy with him anymore. I don't feel fulfilled." We believe that such complaints are a result of overblown and misguided expectations.

You may see signs that this myth is interfering with a marriage. One is when a partner says, "If you loved me you would . . . (check the choice or choices that apply):

- ✔ Spend more time with my family
- ✔ Make love to me more often
- ✔ Take the vacation that I want
- ✔ Not criticize me so much
- ✔ Do more household chores

The message here is, "You don't love me unless you do exactly what I want."

There is also a flip side to this myth that shows up when one partner demands that the other accept his love on faith — even when his words and actions convey the opposite message.

If, for example, your spouse complains because you forgot her birthday, it's not enough to say, "Don't you know I love you?" There is no justification for expecting our partners to forgive our thoughtlessness by simply declaring our love. What that amounts to is just another way of manipulating the situation so you can have things exactly as you please.

All of us have a right to want our needs fulfilled, but it's important to be realistic. Even in the best of marriages, a spouse can provide just so much fulfillment. The rest may have to come from children, from work, from the pursuit of various interests, or from within.

Chapter 2

The Five Building Blocks of a Working Marriage

Half of all marriages end in divorce — and that's not a happy statistic. But when you think about all the hopes and dreams people carry into marriage, it's amazing that the divorce rate isn't even higher. After all, how can any relationship possibly deliver the complete love, great sex, never-ending fun, and permanent security that marriage is supposed to guarantee?

It can take one year, two years, or five years. But, whenever the inevitable disappointments occur, one or both partners may feel tempted to give up on the marriage. More often than not, calling a divorce lawyer is a mistake. A far better course is to figure out strategies that will make your marriage more satisfying.

In this chapter, we show you how to develop the five building blocks of marriage, which can make the difference between a relationship that stays together and one that falls apart.

Developing a Realistic View of Marriage

It may not be that life's purpose is simply . . . to be happy, but rather to be engaged in some rich enterprise with another human.

— Mark S. Goulston, psychiatrist and author

In the Hollywood or TV version of marriage, a couple typically starts out with a passionate love worthy of the kind of emotions expressed in the traditional Inuit love song:

> *You are my soulmate./My feet shall run because of you./My feet dance because of you./My heart shall beat because of you./My eyes see because of you./My mind thinks because of you./And I shall love because of you.*

After a number of years, though, the fairytale life of this once-ecstatic couple can turn into the kind of tired routine that provides material for an endless array of negative jokes — like this one by the late comedian, Henny Youngman:

> *Do you know what it means to come home to a wife who'll give you a little love, a little affection, a little tenderness? It means you're in the wrong house. That's what it means!*

The reality of most enduring marriages lies somewhere between the glorious love song and the cynical joke. Sure, there are bound to be times when things are terrible. However, these are usually balanced by other times when things are going great. Ultimately, the majority of married partners spend most of their time in an emotional space between the two extremes of ecstasy and agony.

When we assess a couple's chances of making their relationship work, this middle ground is where we direct our focus. We're a lot less interested in whether spouses are living up to some fantastic ideal of what marriage is supposed to be. Nor do we buy into the inevitable drudgery and misery that supposedly awaits every married couple. Instead, we ask the question, "Is the relationship *good enough* to meet both partners' emotional needs?" *Good-enough* marriages may not be "made in heaven," but they have a real chance at succeeding for the following two reasons.

- ✔ Both partners have an ongoing stake in making the relationship work.
- ✔ Both partners believe that, in the long run, the positive aspects in their marriage will outweigh the negative.

The number-one reason why marriages last is because the partners take the words "for better or for worse" to heart. They have made a commitment to work things out, to make changes — and not quit when things get tough. As time goes on, these couples often discover that the "better" outweighs the "worse." Sure, there's effort involved; but to a great extent, it's a matter of coming to terms with the reality that no long-term relationship can ever deliver absolute happiness. However, when partners who are meeting enough of each other's emotional needs are determined to work together, a shaky marriage can become *good enough* — and a good-enough marriage can sometimes become great!

There are some instances when the *for worse* becomes bad enough to consider ending the marriage. For example, when a spouse engages in repeated episodes of infidelity or refuses to assume his or her share of family responsibilities. Certainly, any circumstance that endangers the safety of one or both partners is a red flag. Nobody should have to tolerate a physically or emotionally abusive partner. Severe substance abuse and mental illness are also signs that a marriage is in danger of dropping below the *good-enough* level, especially if your spouse refuses to get help.

Instead of dwelling only on the disappointments and problems in your marriage, strive to build a stronger relationship by increasing the number of positive moments between you. The following suggestions can help you accomplish this:

✔ Think back on how you treated each other when you first started dating. Then work on reincorporating those considerate and courtly gestures into your marriage. The following acts of courtesy can go a long way in making your partner feel that you care:

   • Speak with consideration and respect for your partner's opinions and feelings.

   • Listen, without interrupting, when your partner is speaking.

   • Show your affection with flowers, unexpected notes, and thoughtful gifts — which need not be expensive.

   • Dress and groom yourself in ways that are attractive to your partner.

No single small courtesy is likely to generate an earth-shattering improvement in a marriage. However, a considerate, attentive attitude can make an important difference in the overall tone of your relationship.

✔ Take an active interest in your partner.

✔ Make it a point to ask your spouse regularly about what's going on in his or her life. Be sure to ask specific questions such as, "How did your boss like your ideas on that new project?" or "Tell me what you and the children did today?" Generic questions like, "How are things?" will produce generic answers like, "Fine, how are things with you?" Plus, your spouse won't feel that you're really interested in what he or she has to say.

As the ecstasy of the early days of a relationship begins to fade, spouses often become self-involved to the point of tuning out their partners. This indifference can take a variety of forms, including not talking to each other about what's going on in your lives, drowning yourself in work, or spending hours in front of the TV. This kind of detachment creates a tone of apathy that erodes the quality of a marriage.

Be ready for change

There's a saying about the highly changeable weather in New York City: "If you don't like it, just wait a couple of hours." A similar principle applies to the emotional weather conditions of a marriage. If things are stormy now, just give it a little time — you're likely to see some change. If you think of your marriage as being dynamic, not static, you may have an easier time dealing with those periodic storms and cold fronts.

Couples who don't recognize the demands of marriage sometimes feel that things are never going to get better, so they might as well give up. However, partners who take a long-range view of marriage refuse to let their relationship get derailed by such rough spots. That kind of stubborn determination tends to create a positive momentum of its own.

If you catch yourself putting emotional distance between you and your partner, we suggest taking an inventory of the positive qualities of your marriage.

1. **On a sheet of paper, list the ways that you can invest time and energy in optimizing the strengths in your marriage.**

2. **Write down the things that are troubling you, and several different ways you and your partner can work them out.**

3. **Share your thoughts and insights with your partner, and encourage him or her to do the same.**

When things are going smoothly in your relationship, it's tempting to think that they'll stay that way. If you go into marriage expecting mostly smooth sailing with, perhaps, a few minor bumps along the way, you're likely to panic when you run into the inevitable struggles and disappointments that virtually all married couples face.

Most change occurs incrementally, not dramatically. That's why it's important to identify the smallest signs that things are changing for the better, and to encourage these improvements.

Treasuring What the Two of You Have in Common

One of the best ways to become closer with your partner is to value and build on the things the two of you have in common. These common areas can be based on virtually any interest you and your partner share. Your shared interest can be spiritual or cultural. It can be something as profound as a religious conviction, or something as ordinary as playing cards.

Couples who've been married for a number of years often allow the common interests that brought them together to fade into the background. It's important not to become so involved in the details of day-to-day living that you stop investing time in doing things that the two of you enjoy together.

We suggest taking the following steps to start rekindling those common interests:

1. **Sit down by yourself and write out a list of all the interests and activities that you and your partner have enjoyed sharing at various times in your marriage.**

   Writing out this kind of inventory helps you identify areas you may be neglecting.

   Zach was upset because he felt that he and Amanda had stopped doing things together. "I spend my free time reading and going to museums alone, while she's into jogging and playing tennis with a friend," he told us. "It seems like we hardly ever find time to enjoy things together any more."

   We suggested that a good first step for Zach would be to recall the most pleasurable things he and Amanda had shared together over the years. Zach's list included the following areas of common interest: Going to jazz concerts, ballroom dancing, and singing in the church choir.

2. **Think about what caused you to stop doing those things together.**

   Zach realized that he and his wife had relegated their enjoyable joint activities to the back burner for a variety of reasons. He and Amanda had stopped ballroom dancing and going to jazz concerts shortly after their four-year-old daughter Carol was born.

   "Carol was often sick as a baby," Zach recalled. "By the time she was two, Carol's health problems had cleared up, but Amanda and I had fallen out of the habit of doing things together on weekends."

   Amanda and Zach's discontinuing their involvement in church activities was a more complicated matter. Amanda had started working on alternate Sundays, and eventually stopped going to church altogether. "At that point, she started feeling distant toward the pastor and other members of the congregation," Zach told us.

3. **Talk to each other about recapturing the joy of sharing good times and common interests.**

   You may be pleasantly surprised to discover that your spouse also misses those good times, and is interested in finding ways to reincorporate them into your life. At that point, be proactive in coming up with a plan for doing more enjoyable things together.

When you talk to your partner, be careful not to blame him or her for not doing more things together. Assessing blame can only serve to create more distance between the two of you.

We helped Zach recognize that the growing distance between him and his wife was neither of their faults. We then worked with him in coming up with the following way to start reviving their favorite activities. In talking to Amanda, Zach could tell that she really missed the times they had spent ballroom dancing. Even though that particular activity was third on her list (after singing in the church choir and going to jazz concerts), Zach recognized that it was important to begin somewhere. He also understood that their abandonment of church involvement was a more complicated matter, so reinstituting it would take longer.

4. Make your shared activity a priority.

Amanda's face lit up as she and Zach began talking about the fun they used to have when they went dancing. But after a few minutes, that smile disappeared. "Sure, it would be nice to dance," Amanda said, shaking her head. "But we don't have a babysitter for Carol, so I suppose it's not going to happen any time soon."

When the memory of good times reawakens your feelings of excitement, don't allow it to be extinguished by the same mundane concerns that caused you and your partner to abandon the activity in the first place.

Zach anticipated Amanda's objection, so he'd obtained the names of several babysitters beforehand. "I've contacted two sitters who come highly recommended," he announced. "Why don't we meet them and decide which one we want to hire to watch Carol?"

5. Make dates with your partner.

Zach produced a calendar from the Sunday newspaper, and showed Amanda a variety of ads for ballroom dancing events. "There's one next Saturday that looks good. I'd like to call now and make reservations, okay?"

Amanda felt slightly cornered by Zach's direct approach, but she really couldn't offer a good reason not to agree to his suggestion. "I'd like to procrastinate about this for a while," she snickered. "Alright, I guess you'd better call and make those reservations."

Once you fall out of the habit of doing something, there's bound to be some resistance when you try to reactivate it. Initially, your partner may have a positive response to your suggestion. However, unless you both commit to a specific plan, that suggestion can wind up being deferred indefinitely.

6. Emphasize activities that are fun.

The amount of fun a couple has together is one of the most important factors in determining marital happiness. Research by marriage theorist Howard Markman of the University of Denver demonstrates that, aside from making both partners feel good, time spent playing together is an "investment in the relationship that provides a relaxed intimacy that strengthens the bond of marriage."

Married couples can have fun in a variety of ways. Some enjoy biking or playing tennis. Others like to browse through bookstores or take long walks in the woods. After you become accustomed to planning things together, you may find it easier and more natural to add more couple-oriented activities to your schedule.

No matter how busy and frantic your lives are, it's important to make time for the two of you. Don't worry! The kids will do just fine with a sitter. Not only that, your responsibilities and problems will still be waiting for you after you return.

Making Room for Separateness in Your Togetherness

Feeling free to develop on your own creates a sense of loyalty to your mate. Indeed, a relationship should augment self-fulfillment, not limit it.

— David Viscott, psychiatrist and author

Every person needs a certain amount of personal space — and married partners are no exception. Still, some couples feel uncomfortable about doing things without each other. They feel it's a betrayal of the relationship for one partner to engage in any activity without the other.

We disagree with this notion, and always encourage couples to seek out a comfortable degree of separateness in their togetherness. The exact degree of separateness must be negotiated, depending on a couple's comfort level and preferences. We know many couples who pursue separate interests in sports, films, and other hobbies. In many cases, they manage to find ways to work things out so that neither partner feels slighted or threatened, and that their relationship thrives.

Pursuing separate activities alone or with a friend can be more problematic under the following circumstances:

- When the friend is a member of the opposite sex.
- When you don't like or approve of the friend.
- When another couple is involved.
- When the partners have difficulty reaching what both consider a fair compromise.

Not joined at the hip

Cindy and Norman have been happily married for 20 years. They often see films alone or with friends rather than with each other.

"Cindy and I have totally opposite tastes in movies," Norman told us. "She only wants to see period pieces and romantic comedies. If she suspects that a movie will be violent or depressing, she absolutely refuses to go."

Cindy agreed with her husband's assessment of the situation. "I go to the movies to be entertained, not intellectually stimulated," she said. "Norman despises romantic comedies and will only see a period piece if it receives fabulous reviews. For him, films are an art form — not just entertainment."

During the first year or two of their marriage, Cindy and Norman felt funny about going to see movies without each other. But then they came to the realization that there was nothing wrong with each of them pursuing their own tastes and preferences.

"One day, I looked at Norman and said, 'we're not attached at the hip,'" Cindy recalled, "'so what would be wrong with seeing movies alone or with friends who share similar interests?'"

"We do sometimes see movies together," Norman added. "But I'll often go on my own."

"I'm not comfortable going to a movie theater by myself," Cindy admitted. "Fortunately, I have two or three girlfriends I can call when there's a film that I want to see."

We suggest using the following guidelines to find a balance of separateness and togetherness that's right for your relationship:

- ✔ Accept the fact that both of you need a certain amount of personal space.
- ✔ Recognize that your need for separateness may not always be in synch with that of your partner.
- ✔ Express your viewpoint whenever you spot a conflict or imbalance. Ask your spouse to do the same.
- ✔ Negotiate an arrangement that works for both of you. Don't just give in, or you may wind up resenting it.

Even though the relationship with your spouse may be your most important long-term priority, that doesn't necessarily mean that something (or someone) else can't take precedence at any particular time.

For example, if you've made dinner plans with a friend next Wednesday, you have every right to keep that commitment, even if your husband suddenly decides that he wants you to do something with him. This is especially true if he accuses you of caring more about your friend than you do for him.

Some couples have difficulty coming to terms with issues of separateness because of personality clashes that can be hard to negotiate. This was the problem Barbara asked us to help her resolve.

Barbara has an outgoing (or *extroverted*) personality. She loves to go to social events and spend time with lots of different people. Her husband Lee (an *introvert*) would much rather spend time by himself, alone with Barbara, or with one or two close friends. After five years of marriage, Lee and Barbara found themselves at constant loggerheads over their different social needs.

"I feel stifled because I can't attend many of the social events we're invited to," Barbara complained. "Even when I am able to convince Lee to go, it's hard for me to relax because I can tell that he's uptight. I know that Lee won't change, and neither will I. Is there some way we can find a compromise that works for both of us?"

The two following sections give you some of the techniques that we use with couples like Barbara and Lee for effectively accommodating the conflicting needs of extroverts and introverts.

Agree to do some things separately

Doing things separately can only work if both partners understand that it's not a betrayal of the marriage — but rather an attempt to negotiate a better relationship.

What typically happens is that the more social partner has permission to go to certain social functions without the more introverted partner. This gives the extroverted spouse a chance to have a social life that meets her needs. That's fine, as long as the less social spouse doesn't find the arrangement threatening. However, if the less-social partner is still not comfortable, the couple needs to continue discussing ways of resolving this matter.

Barbara agreed to take the initiative. She waited for a time when Lee seemed to be relaxed and in a receptive mood. Then she asked Lee if he'd object to her occasionally going to social functions without him. Lee was open to Barbara's suggestion, so the two of them began to develop the following plan:

- Lee said that there were times when Barbara's going places without him would make him uncomfortable. For example, he didn't want her going to parties alone — especially on weekends.

- If Lee didn't want Barbara to attend a particular gathering without him, she proposed the following two choices. They could either both not attend the function, or they could figure out a way of attending that would address both of their needs.

Who gets stuck at home?

In our own 30-year marriage, we have pursued a number of separate professional and social interests. Here's how we've negotiated (and continue to negotiate) this separateness in our togetherness:

Steve: I've been meeting my friend Paul for dinner twice a month for almost ten years. We've also gotten together with Paul and his wife, yet we never seemed to click as a four-some the way Paul and I do when we're together. I know that you're comfortable with the arrangement, but I suspect that the situation might be more problematic if we were talking about an opposite-sex friendship.

Sue: You're probably right! But other issues come into play. For example, you and Paul always get together on weekdays. That works out well because it never interferes with our weekend plans.

Steve: Did we ever actually agree that week-ends were reserved for us? It's always been a kind of unspoken rule that weekends are sacred. But I remember a time when my going out alone did bother you. Then, we did need to talk about it.

Sue: When the kids were really young, I felt it was unfair. You'd often go out to dinner with a friend or colleague, and I was stuck in the house every night taking care of two small kids. It didn't occur to you that I might also want to go out to dinner or a movie with my friends.

Steve: I was working long hours, while you were staying home with the kids. On some level, I probably didn't believe that your job was as hard or as important as mine. I finally understood that you had as much right as I did to do things on your own, and when we didn't have a babysitter, we started taking turns going out. I wasn't thrilled about the arrangement at first, but that was the fairest way to resolve the situation. In the end, I loved spending so much special time with the kids.

Develop a balance that suits your relationship

It's possible for introvert-extrovert couples to do things together, as long as both are willing to adjust to one another's comfort level. For example, Barbara was invited to a Saturday night cocktail party that she very much wanted to attend. Lee reluctantly agreed to go with her, even though the World Series was on that night, and he wanted to watch the game. Barbara dealt with the situation by proposing the following compromise:

✔ Lee could retreat to another room with a TV set. However, Barbara asked him to do the following:

- Greet the hosts and other guests at the party.

- Spend a half hour with her, talking to a few other guests before going off on his own.

- Join her in saying goodbye to their hosts at the end of the party.

✔ In exchange for accommodating her needs, Barbara agreed to spend the following Saturday doing something alone with Lee.

This kind of trade-off may seem like a forced or extreme solution, but we've helped many couples like Barbara and Lee use these structured compromises to balance their need for separateness and togetherness.

Making the Most of Your Differences

We love because it's the only true adventure.

— Nikki Giovanni, poet

In our practice, we see many couples who have any number of different — often clashing — personality traits. Those differences often fuel the fires of romantic love during the early stages of a relationship. But, in time, the same differences can cause problems.

The courtship or honeymoon phase of a marriage is often replaced by an extended period of fault finding. This is when differences between married partners can overpower the attraction that brought them together. People with different ways of doing things suddenly find themselves constantly clashing over such practical issues as neatness, childrearing, and finances.

The following sections can help couples (even those who have vast differences in several areas) build a loving and enduring marriage.

Combine your strengths

If your husband is all thumbs and you're handy, take the lead in fixing things around the house. If you tend to overspend and he's skillful at balancing family finances, encourage him take the lead in matters of money. By pooling your different strengths in this way, you and your partner can accomplish more as a team than either of you could ever manage alone.

Spouses who capitalize on their differences have the potential to become highly effective in their joint efforts. But, you need to recognize your different skills and strengths, and use them in ways that enhance the marriage rather than tear it apart.

Using your differences to mirror one another's positive traits

Everyone has strengths — as well as frailties and blind spots. The trick is to use your partner's strong points as motivators to stimulate growth in areas where you need improvement.

Unfortunately, many couples don't take advantage of the opportunities for growth that they can achieve by making the most of their differences. In our practice, we often see spouses become overly reliant on their partner's strengths, and neglect their own development in those areas. We urge you to take full advantage of your partner's different characteristics as a potential model for your own self-improvement.

Remember that your differences were once interesting and pleasurable — not sources of conflict

That spark of excitement you and your partner initially felt toward each other can be recaptured — if you remember that the same differences that cause problems now may have played an important part in why you once found each other so attractive.

As you develop a better understanding of the benefits of being married to someone with different personality traits, you may be able to avoid unnecessary conflicts. This is a key to preserving the positive energy and excitement between you.

Accepting That Not All Problems Can Be Solved

Love is what you've been through with somebody.

— James Thurber, humorist and author

Some problems between married partners are relatively simple to resolve; others take a good deal of work; some may never be solved. As you strive to build a stronger marriage, you have to accept that many of your incompatibilities will be constantly recycled in different variations throughout your marriage.

As you and your partner recognize these areas of incompatibility, you can continue to discuss and negotiate your way through those difficulties each time they come up. The following techniques can help you keep marital problems in perspective:

- Identify what's bothering you and communicate those feelings to your partner. Identifying your emotions will help you keep a particular problem from casting a dark shadow on an otherwise solid relationship.

- Be aware of what situations press your partner's hot buttons. Find out what your behavior means to him or her. For example, when you raise your voice, does it remind your husband of the way his mother used to yell at him? When your husband ignores you, do you recall the way your father treated your mother? Putting yourself in your partner's shoes helps you see things from his or her point of view.

- Ask your partner to discuss a particular problem at a time when you're not fighting about it. You and he may not come up with a solution to the problem, but an honest airing of feelings is a display of intimacy that's likely to bring the two of you closer together.

  Don't feel compelled to reveal everything that's on your mind all at one time, especially if those revelations are likely to exacerbate the problem.

- Focus on what's working well in your relationship. Build on those strengths, and use them as a foundation to overcome (or at least de-emphasize) problems.

- Recognize that some problems can be worked out in the long run, even if you don't see an immediate solution. After you and your partner agree that you have an issue requiring work or further discussion, you can make an appointment with him or her to deal with the problem at a later time. But then you have to keep the appointment.

✔ Always encourage positive changes — however small. When you're unhappy about something in your marriage, you can easily fail to see small improvements that can eventually lead to big improvements.

Positive changes need to be encouraged, or they will be quickly extinguished.

✔ Recognize that there's no such thing as a problem-free marriage. Research shows that at least a third of most couples' long-term marital disputes never get resolved to each partner's complete satisfaction. These problems have to be continually negotiated throughout the marriage.

As you accept the fact that not all problems can be solved, you'll be better able to take marital tensions in stride and not allow them to destroy what's good in your relationship.

Part II
Can We Talk?

The 5th Wave   By Rich Tennant

"I heard it was good to use humor when you're having an argument."

In this part . . .

Marriage is a long process of problem solving: Partners who become skilled at the arts of problem solving, conversation, and arguing take a giant step in strengthening their marriage. These are the skills that we explore in this part of the book.

In Chapter 3, we help you recognize and pinpoint the source of marital problems, and give you the tools to begin resolving them. Chapter 4 gives you tools to use for effective communication, including listening, talking, negotiating, and reading body language. In Chapter 5, we explore some of the ongoing battles that most married couples encounter, and give you the tools to referee your arguments. We show you fair and constructive ways to resolve conflicts, so that neither of you ends up feeling like a loser.

Chapter 3

Understanding the Roots of Marital Problems

*P*roblems in a marriage can start with you or your partner. Sometimes, they are rooted in the way the two of you play out the patterns in your relationship. In this chapter, we show you a three-pronged approach to help you understand what contributes to marital conflict.

The process of identifying the source of marital problems is a lot like searching for a malfunction in your computer. The trouble can stem from something you're doing, or it could be a hardware or software defect. Whatever the source, it's important to work to resolve the problem before it crashes the entire system.

Unraveling a Three-Sided Story

> *All marriages are happy. It's trying to live together afterwards that causes all the problems.*
>
> — Shelley Winters, actress

Every marriage is a three-sided story. There's her story, his story, and the story of the relationship. This is our starting point in understanding every marriage — and every marital problem, however big or small.

Rashomon and the three-sided marriage puzzle

Rashomon, an award-winning Japanese film set in 12th-century Kyoto, Japan, talks about the difficulty of discovering which version of a story is true. In the film, three strangers take refuge from a rainstorm beneath some ruins. All three people have witnessed the murder of a samurai lord and the trial of his suspected killer. As they discuss the event, each narrator recounts a different, self-serving version of the same incident. The viewer never finds out whose version of this particular three-sided story is true.

When you try to unravel any couple's marriage, you also never find any absolute truths. That's why we are going to show you how to better understand all three sides of the story and the way they relate to one another.

Before you can get to the bottom of what's taking place in your marriage, you need to look at the situation from three angles: your contribution, your partner's contribution, and your patterns as a couple.

Recognizing what you bring to the mix

When people talk to us about marital problems, they often start out by asking: "How can I correct my partner's faults?" We explain that each of us has the most control over our own behavior. That's why the first step is to implement positive changes in ourselves. "But why should I be the one to change?" people sometimes counter. We explain that the spouse who takes the initiative actually has the most to gain, because he or she is setting the agenda.

When your partner sees you acting in more positive ways, he or she may soon feel inspired to follow suit. Or he may have no choice, because he does not have anyone to fight with. Ultimately, those cumulative changes in how the two of you relate to each other end up strengthening your marriage. And you will feel better and more self-confident, knowing that you were the one who started the ball rolling.

It's only natural to favor your own point of view, but this can make it hard to see what else is going on. When you become overly attached to your side of the story, you may lose sight of other perspectives. This can prevent you from developing the understanding it takes to resolve problems in your marriage.

We suggest taking the following steps to assess what you are bringing to the mix:

1. **Sit down by yourself and write out your viewpoint on the situation. This helps you stay focused on your goals and on the ways that your behavior may be contributing to the difficulties in your marriage.**

Joyce, a high school principal, complained that her husband Frank spent his evenings watching sports on TV instead of doing things with her. Frank, who has a demanding sales job, claimed that he needed to spend "a few hours tuning out" in order to recharge his batteries. Joyce recognized that she was becoming increasingly resentful that Frank watched TV instead of talking to her, and she decided to take some action. She went into the bedroom and quietly wrote out her view of the problem on a piece of notebook paper.

2. **Think about how your past experiences may color how you perceive the problem.**

In telling their story, people often discover that marital difficulties are triggered by something that happened in their childhood or in a previous relationship. This understanding helps you gain a better perspective on what's actually taking place in the here and now.

Shortly after Joyce started writing out her story, it struck her that Frank's tuning her out was reminiscent of what her father used to do when he came home from work.

"My dad would head straight for the TV set. If my mother wanted to talk about a problem that came up with me or my brother, Dad would retreat further into whatever was on that tube. It's not that he didn't love his family. He just didn't seem to have any emotional energy left for us after a hard day's work."

3. **Devise a plan of action that starts with self-change.**

It's not easy to change our own attitudes and behaviors, but trying to effect change in others is far more difficult. Here are some tips that you can use to start solving problems in your marriage:

- **State what you want, what not your partner is doing wrong.** Instead of demanding that he turn off the TV, Joyce sat down next to him and said, "I feel lonely when you watch TV all evening. It reminds me of what my father used to do to my mother. When the show ends, can we talk a little and then play a game of Scrabble?"

- **Exercise patience.** It took a few tries, but Frank soon began responding to Joyce's prodding. At first, he would talk to her with the TV on. Then, he started turning off the sound. In the course of their conversations, Joyce was able to talk about the way she feels when Frank watches TV and tunes her out. Joyce is confident that these are positive signs that Frank is willing to change his behavior because of Joyce's ability to be more explicit about what she wants.

- **Appreciate the benefits of changing your own behavior.** Joyce was pleasantly surprised to discover how quickly things improved after she made a few small behavioral changes. What's more, she now has a template for dealing with problems that may arise in the future.

Recognizing what your partner brings to the mix

When it comes to understanding your partner, knowledge is power. The more you know about what makes your spouse tick, the better able you are to devise effective strategies for making positive changes in your marriage. For example, you're aware that your wife doesn't like to entertain because she feels overwhelmed by having to organize a formal meal for guests. You could just tell her that you want to have some co-workers over for dinner, but she's likely to resist that request. It would be better to let her know that you understand her feelings and respect them. Then, offer to help with the dinner, and ask what else you could do to make this event happen.

You may not always know what's behind your partner's attitudes and behaviors. The best way to find out more about your spouse is to maintain an ongoing dialogue. You don't ever want to come across like a detective or a prosecuting attorney. Still, it's important to have a complete picture of your partner's day-to-day realities, and to understand them in the context of his or her personal history. One of the most effective ways of drawing your spouse into a discussion of personal matters is to talk openly about your own feelings and experiences, and encourage him or her to do the same.

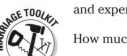

How much do you know about the following background issues:

- ✔ What was your partner's childhood like?
- ✔ Did your spouse grow up in a two-parent, divorced, single-parent, or remarried family?
- ✔ How did his/her parents get along?
- ✔ What were sibling relationships like?
- ✔ What are your spouse's happy or sad childhood memories?
- ✔ Did he or she have many friends?
- ✔ Did he or she have one or more serious love relationships?
- ✔ How would he or she describe those relationships?

How much do you know about your partner's daily life?

- ✔ Have you noticed any recent changes in your partner's mood, stress level, or eating or sleeping patterns?
- ✔ If the answer to any part of the above question is "yes," do you know what is causing the change(s)?
- ✔ Is your partner having trouble at work or in some personal aspect not directly related to your marriage?
- ✔ Does your partner seem distracted or depressed?

✔ Are you aware of events in your partner's life he or she is looking forward to?

✔ Does your spouse have someone (other than you) in whom he or she confides on a regular basis?

✔ Do you believe there are specific things your spouse may be concealing from you?

Answering these questions will help you identify which gaps in your knowledge need to be filled. Then, you can use that information to start making changes in your marriage.

Sometimes, a small piece of information about your spouse can make a big difference in your relationship, as it did with Joe and Patti.

For the past three months, Joe had been coming home from work in an angry mood. He'd been screaming at Patti and their two children for no apparent reason. Patti couldn't get Joe to talk about what was troubling him. Joe's mood change seemed to start two months earlier, shortly after he had received a promotion at work and a substantial pay increase. "But how could that be the problem?" Patti reasoned. "A promotion and a raise is supposed to make you feel good." When she asked Joe, he denied that he was more upset or irritable than usual.

One night, Joe's best friend called while Joe was out. After engaging him in a bit of small talk, Patti casually asked, "Have you noticed that Joe's been kind of irritable lately?"

"Oh sure," the friend replied. "It's that new promotion. He couldn't turn down the money, but the extra pressure has been driving Joe nuts."

Patti thought that the friend made a good point, and she brought it up to Joe. Joe didn't respond immediately, but a couple of days later said, "Maybe that promotion is stressing me out." After that, Joe and Patti were able to talk more openly about his moods.

After you've identified a specific problem that's likely to be contributing to your partner's troubling behavior, you can start making improvements by taking the following steps.

✔ **Put yourself in your partner's shoes.** Close your eyes and imagine how you might feel in your partner's position. Use everything you know about your spouse to visualize the way he or she is reacting.

✔ **Go out of your way to show empathy.** Even if you're uncertain about what's bothering your partner, it always helps to make it clear that you care. Instead of complaining, make it a point to greet your spouse with something that will express your understanding. Prepare a favorite meal or buy a thoughtful gift. Such displays of empathy and affection often generate a positive response.

✔ **Take the initiative.** One effective way of dealing with your partner's negativity is to ask what's wrong and to share your observations. Another good approach is to communicate that you care by doing or saying something positive. Compliment your partner on his smile or his quick wit. Tell her how lucky you are to have such a beautiful and intelligent wife. Don't expect your spouse to respond immediately. If you're patient, you may begin to see positive changes. However, if your strategy doesn't seem to be working, try something different. Don't give up!

Some marital problems are symptoms of deeply entrenched personal issues or more serious marital problems than you may realize. If your spouse doesn't respond to any of your efforts, you will almost certainly need some outside professional help.

Recognizing the patterns in your marriage

My wife and I tried to breakfast together, but we had to stop or our marriage would have been wrecked.

— Winston Churchill, former Prime Minister of England

There are trends or patterns in every marriage that are often obvious to everyone but the married couples themselves. The key to the humor in many classic TV situation comedies is based on watching these patterns play out.

✔ In *The Honeymooners,* for example, the portly bus driver Ralph Cramden is a dreamer who is forever coming up with harebrained schemes to make a million dollars. His thin, attractive wife Alice is totally practical about the couple's very limited financial resources, and bitingly sarcastic in her response to Ralph's outrageous plans. Ralph usually addresses Alice's sarcasm by pointing a clenched fist to the sky and shouting, "One of these days, Alice. Pow, right in the kisser."

Ralph never comes close to actually hitting Alice, who is not the least bit afraid of her overbearing, but good-natured, husband. Still, she is never able to prevent Ralph from going ahead with his sure-to-fail schemes.

✔ *All in The Family* offers another set of prototypical marriage patterns. Archie Bunker, a self-righteous, belligerent political conservative thinks he knows all there is to know about the world. It soon becomes clear that Archie is far less perceptive than his kind-hearted wife Edith, whom he refers to as "the dingbat."

Every night when he comes home from his laborer's job, Edith asks Archie, "How was your day?" Archie's answer is always the same: "Lousy, as usual." At which point Edith asks, "Do you want to hear about my day, Archie?" "I certainly do not," Archie grunts. "I just want you to get me a beer and put my supper on the table!"

> Edith smiles gently. Then she invariably launches into a breathless, painfully detailed recounting of her day. Archie just looks up at the sky and groans, "Help me, Lord. She's going to tell me all about her day anyway."

Audiences have been laughing at the Bunkers and the Cramdens for decades. Part of what makes these couples so funny is the predictable or *patterned* nature of their interactions.

You may not realize it, but the patterns of all married couples are often as obvious as those depicted in the sitcoms. But, when you and your partner are the ones playing out these themes, it's hard to see yourself as others do.

When marriage partners are in the middle of a dispute, they are both too upset and emotional to step back and see the predictable ways that each of them are taking on predictable roles.

Patterns are neither bad nor good, in and of themselves. However, after they are locked into place, patterns can be hard to break. That's okay, as long as the interactions aren't hurting you, your partner, or your marriage. But often, breaking a particular negative pattern and establishing a more positive one is the key to having a stronger and happier relationship with your spouse.

Changing negative patterns through positive mirroring

Destructive patterns in a marriage are often caused by negative mirroring. When your spouse confronts you in an adversarial fashion, it's easy to feel that there's no other choice but to react in kind — or mirror that behavior. Before you know it, the two of you can find yourself caught in the middle of a destructive chain reaction.

The following sections can help you and your partner identify and change these patterns.

Don't respond to negativity with negativity

Do your best to respond with understanding and compassion. Let your partner know that you can see she's distressed. Ask what you can do to make the situation better. If your partner continues to act negatively, say something like: "I want you to know that I'm here for you. But when I feel attacked by your statements, it's hard for me to know how to help." If your partner still won't open up, offer a concrete suggestion to change the mood. Suggest going out for dinner or a quiet walk. Start a conversation about plans for an upcoming vacation or a special event your partner is looking forward to.

Visualize your marriage as a TV sitcom

Take a few minutes to write down the disagreements you have on a regular basis as if you were scripting dialogue for a TV show. What you're trying to uncover are the patterns underneath those disagreements, not what you're actually fighting about. For example, you may be upset at your spouse because he never cleans the bathroom after he takes a shower. Rather than focus on your different standards of cleanliness, concentrate on how the two of you play out the disagreement:

- Do you yell at him?

- If so, how does he respond to your yelling? Does he shout back — or does he brood?

- What do you then do in response to your spouse's reactive behavior?

- Are your strategies effective? Do they cause any change in his behavior?

- If your strategies don't work, do you continue doing more of the same?

Do something different to change the script

Couples in conflict often become competitive with each other in a negative way. One spouse acts nasty, so the other responds by acting even nastier. Next time you're tempted to engage in this kind of destructive communication, do something different to change the script.

If, for example, you're worried about family finances, don't express this in your usual way of telling your husband that his spending is out of control. Predictably, he will counterattack with something about one of your weaknesses, and the argument escalates. Instead, try expressing it differently. For example, say, "I'd feel a lot better if we can set aside a certain amount of money each week for our vacation next summer. Let's work out a budget so we can do that." This kind of strategic planning diffuses negative patterns before you and your partner have a chance to play them out.

Working Together to Build a Stronger Marriage

A good marriage needs the ongoing commitment and cooperation of both partners. When these ingredients are in place, most problems can be solved — whatever their source.

How is your marriage doing?

We have designed an exercise to help you identify opportunities for improvement in your marriage. Please don't worry if you find that your married life isn't all you'd like it to be. We've never met a couple who couldn't use improvement in some aspect of their relationship.

There is no one-size-fits-all way for partners to get along. Still, there are certain positive qualities most happy couples have in common. We have pinpointed ten signs of a good marriage, and we'd like you to use them to begin taking the pulse of your own relationship.

Rate each statement in the following list with a 1, 2, or 3. Answer 3 if you completely agree with the statement. Answer 2 if you agree more than you disagree with the statement. Answer 1 if you disagree more than you agree with the statement. When answering the questions, don't choose what you perceive to be a good or socially acceptable response. This exercise will be most helpful if you make the honest and candid choice. Answer every question from your own point of view.

After you take this test, you may want to give it to your spouse, and then compare the results. You may get important insights about the different ways that both of you view the same marriage.

1. **You and your partner genuinely like one another.**

2. **You and your partner are close, but respectful of each other's freedom and independence.**

3. **You and your partner are both flexible in what you expect from one another.**

4. **You and your partner respect each other's differences.**

5. **You and your partner share in making important decisions.**

6. **You and your partner trust each other.**

7. **You and your partner are both committed to maintaining a good sexual relationship.**

8. **You and your partner both place a high value on fun and in sharing common interests.**

9. **You and your partner both watch over one another and offer encouragement and comfort when needed.**

10. **You and your partner share common values regarding children.**

Now add up your score. A score of 20-30 shows that you and your partner are working together in creating a strong marriage. A score of 15-20 shows that you have a reasonably wide area of agreement, as well as some important issues to address. A score of 10-15 shows that there is a considerable amount of strife in your marriage, and may be an indication that you and your partner need professional help (see Chapter 16).

Troubleshooting marital problems

You may be attributing marital difficulties to the wrong cause. Middle-aged men, for example, commonly mistake their fears of aging for problems in their marriage. This lack of insight may cause a man to leave his wife for a younger woman, only to discover too late that he abandoned the most important relationship in his life for a short-term fling.

Other personal issues can distort your perception of what's going on in your marriage. We've seen people mistake career downturns, health crises, and temporary hormonal changes for defects in their partner or the relationship.

Any of these personal changes is bound to have an impact on your marriage. However, if you're able to pinpoint the main causes of distress, you're far more likely to take the proper corrective steps.

- ✔ If you seem to be experiencing some kind of personal crisis, don't automatically blame your spouse or the marriage. Instead, open an honest dialogue, in which both of you feel free to express your concerns and your frustrations.

- ✔ If your spouse seems to be going through a difficult period, consider putting his or her concerns first — at least for the time being. Instead of assessing blame, work at being a good listener and an active partner in helping him or her navigate the rough spots.

- ✔ If the problem is rooted in your patterns as a couple, work together to replace entrenched and destructive interactions with more flexible, positive behaviors.

If nothing that you try works, you may not have identified the "right" cause or hit on an effective solution. In either case, you may want to consider counseling or therapy. It is also possible that you have correctly identified the issue, but are unable to fix it without outside help.

Always be proactive in taking the lead to change any negative patterns or trends in your marriage, even if you don't know what's causing them. That is your best shot at making things better. The improvements may appear to be small at first, but small improvements may have a disproportionately large effect, and may end up making a big difference in you, in your partner, and in the overall quality of your relationship.

Chapter 4

Communicating with Your Partner

· ·

In This Chapter

▶ Understanding why husbands and wives are always communicating

▶ Recognizing the power of words and body language

▶ Developing powerful listening skills

▶ Applying effective negotiation techniques to marriage

▶ Keeping the conversation going

· ·

*G*ood communication is essential if you're going to have smooth transactions with other people. This is true, whether those people are co-workers, doctors, store clerks, or friends. But all of those dealings, even those with close friends, are relatively uncomplicated when compared to the ongoing back-and-forth that goes on between wives and husbands throughout the life of a marriage.

Good communication is at the heart of every working marriage. It's the only way for you and your partner to let each other know what you need and how you feel at any given point in time.

✔ Do you want your partner to stop (or start) acting in a particular way?

✔ Do you want to iron out certain differences between you?

Waiting around for your partner to read your mind won't do the trick. Neither will wishing and hoping that things will somehow change for the better.

There's only one way to make your marriage a place where your needs and expectations are met, and that way can be expressed in three simple words: Communicate! Communicate! Communicate!

In this chapter, we share with you the tools of effective communication — tools that can help you and your partner have a more satisfying relationship.

Recognizing That You're Always Communicating

Married couples who love each other tell each other a thousand things without talking.

— Chinese proverb

When couples complain that they're not communicating, we tell them that wives and husbands *can't not* communicate. When we make that statement, people sometimes respond by asking the following question: "Are we still communicating, even when neither of us is talking?" The answer is yes! Communication doesn't require either party to utter a single sound. In fact, you can sometimes communicate louder in silence than you ever could with words.

Imagine the following scenario: You are walking down the street, when a stranger knocks you down and steals your bag. You are terribly upset when you arrive home, and very much in need of your partner's attention. However, after you breathlessly finish telling your spouse about your awful experience, he says nothing. Then, he proceeds to bury his head in a newspaper.

Is your spouse communicating something through his wordless response? You bet he is, and there's probably nothing positive for you in that message.

Perhaps your partner is saying that he doesn't really care about what happened to you. Maybe he's too caught up in his own concerns, or he doesn't know how to respond to yours. Maybe he's just too upset to talk, because he feels powerless to do anything to help you. In any case, that kind of silent communication sends a message that is as loud as any shout.

Communication is about a lot more than talking. Many essential messages are transmitted through attitude, facial expressions, and body language — as well as through words that are left unsaid. Communication is also physical. Your spouse can convey a message of affection by gently touching your hand. However, if he squeezes your hand to the point of pain, that may be a very different kind of message.

To become an effective communicator, you have to pay close attention to what your partner is telling you through his moods, attitudes, gestures, movements, and actions. The flip side of this skill is recognizing the non-verbal messages you yourself are transmitting. You can sharpen your non-verbal communication skills by using the steps in the following sections.

Watch for changes in mood and attitude

Is your normally effervescent spouse suddenly down in the dumps? Is he distracted and forgetful in ways you haven't observed before?

These changes can be signs that there are things going on in your partner's life (or psyche) that he doesn't wish to discuss — at least not now. Still, you may want to say something like, "Honey, I've noticed that you haven't been your usual cheerful self lately." If she still won't address these changes with you, make a written or mental note of these shifts in behavior. Try to remain watchful of how they play out in the days and weeks to come.

It can be difficult to see yourself with the same objectivity you apply to others. But communication is always a two-way street, especially in marriage. That's why it's important to monitor your own tone of voice, attitudes, and other nonverbal behaviors with the same sharp eye you use to observe your spouse.

Tune into body language

Is your spouse making direct eye contact or avoiding your gaze? In general, a person who looks you directly in the eye is assumed to be forthright and truthful. On the other hand, a person who averts his eyes may not want you to know what he's thinking.

You can glean similar information by observing the way your partner's body reacts when you ask him a question. Is his body position relaxed and open, or tense and withdrawn?

In general, a person who maintains a relaxed, open bearing when you ask a direct question tends to be forthright and truthful. On the other hand, a person whose body suddenly becomes rigid may be concealing something.

Look for signs of nervousness or tension

If you notice that your spouse is anxious in the course of conversation, note this as a possible clue that some thought or feeling is not being verbally expressed. Uncharacteristic silence or talkativeness may be another sign.

The rules of interpreting body language and other non-verbal clues are well-known to salespeople and others who are skilled in the art of persuasion. A good sales agent, for example, may be able to look you directly in the eye while telling a baldfaced lie. He or she may also be practiced in maintaining a calm demeanor and conjuring up sincere-sounding laughter at will.

On the other hand, the non-verbal communications of some scrupulously honest people may give the mistaken impression that they're trying to deceive you. That's why it's wise not to draw any firm conclusion from any single clue. Instead, incorporate each non-verbal clue into the total picture of what your partner is communicating.

Double-check the meaning of gestures

Every gesture is a communication of some kind. But when each spouse assigns different meanings to the same gesture, it can cause friction in the relationship.

For example, a wife may call her husband at work twice a day because she wants to feel connected. However, the husband can interpret this gesture in a very different way. He may feel that his partner is checking up on him or trying to smother him.

Recently, we were at a party when a well-dressed man started talking about moving his factory to another state. "What kind of products do you make?" someone asked. "Oh, I manufacture cigarettes," the man answered. Both of us thought we were smiling politely, but we must have looked at this guy as if he were the devil incarnate, because he smiled and said, "I guess you aren't big fans of cigarette smoking." This man's interpretation of our body language was 100 percent correct, so no further probing was necessary.

The same principle applies to gestures exchanged by you and your spouse: When both of you agree about the meaning of a particular sign, no further explanation is required. However, when partners are out of synch in their interpretation of each other's nonverbal communications, it's important to find out what each one is thinking.

We were spending a quiet Saturday evening with some friends. At one point, the conversation turned to meddling in-laws. Suddenly, we noticed that Joanne and Al seemed to be having a problem.

Someone had told a mother-in-law joke, which caused Al to laugh heartily. Joanne, who had stepped out of the room to make a phone call, flashed a sour glance in her husband's direction. Al's laughter quickly ceased. A few minutes later, Joanne and Al excused themselves and went home.

We assumed that Joanne and Al's abrupt departure were triggered by some ongoing in-law dispute. However, this turned out not to be the case. In fact, Joanne later told us that she'd not even heard the mother-in-law joke that had so tickled Al's funny bone. When she walked into the room and saw Al laughing, Joanne did become angry, but for a completely different reason.

Joanne and Al had promised the teenager who was babysitting their young daughter that they'd be home by 11:30. It was already after 11, and Al was completely oblivious to the commitment they had made. The ride home would take at least 45 minutes, but Al was sitting around laughing, as though he had all the time in the world.

"It's interesting," Joanne confided. "When Al caught my troubled facial expression, he also assumed it had something to do with our in-law problems. Actually, we've been doing a lot better in that area. It's his forgetful attitude that has been bugging me lately."

You can easily misinterpret the meaning of a particular signal. Avoid such mistakes by taking the following steps:

✔ **If you're at all unsure, ask your partner to explain her nonverbal communication.**

Al assumed that Joanne was reacting to some previous in-law issues. Still, when they were alone, he said: "I'm sorry if you thought I was disrespecting your family. That is why you shot that look at me, isn't it?"

✔ **After you identify the emotion that provoked the gesture, work at addressing it.**

When Joanne told Al what was really bothering her, she was able to shift the discussion to the differences she and her husband have in honoring time commitments. (See Chapter 5 for a discussion on resolving differences in dealing with punctuality).

Like all couples, Joanne and Al still have any number of differences they need to work on. Still, their willingness to give each other meaningful feedback and to accept it in good faith are signs that they are committed to strengthening their marriage.

Understanding How You Talk to Each Other

Love involves a peculiar combination of understanding and misunderstanding.

— Diane Arbus, documentary photographer

Your ability to function as a couple depends largely on the effective exchange of information. And while no single form of communication is more important than another, there is no question that words are the most used currency of communication between married partners. A spouse's choice of words and tone of voice reveal much about how she feels about her partner — and her marriage.

Pay careful attention to how the married couples you know use words with one another. Consider how these interchanges compare to the verbal interactions between you and your partner as you reflect on of the following questions:

- **Do both partners feel comfortable talking to each other?** If one or both partners seems to be withholding information or walking on eggshells, this may be a sign of a passing problem. However, constant tension may indicate that one or both partners don't feel safe in expressing their thoughts and feelings.

- **Does the dialogue feel mutually satisfying to both spouses?** When one partner is pleased with the dialogue and the other is unhappy, there may be some temporary conflict going on. However, if this lack of mutuality becomes a pattern, that is a sign of a serious communication problem that can pose a threat to the stability of a marriage.

- **Does one spouse appear to be dominating the dialogue?** You don't have to count words to answer this question. People have different conversational styles that come out in how loud and fast they talk. The important thing is that both partners have a relatively equal opportunity to express themselves. In some relationships where one partner is dominant, the more passive partner may actually do more of the talking. However, the dominant partner will cut her off or say something demeaning in an attempt to shut her up.

Sharpening your listening skills

The first duty of love is to listen.

— Paul Tillich, theologian

Listening is sometimes described as the flip-side of talking. Actually, it's a lot more important — mainly because most people find it easier to talk than to listen. Even when people aren't talking out loud, they are often carrying on their own internal dialogue that makes it impossible to hear what others are saying.

It ultimately doesn't matter how effective one marriage partner is at expressing her feelings if the other partner doesn't hear her. But when husbands and wives truly begin listening to each other, they see an immediate improvement in the quality of their relationship.

Active listening is a technique that marriage partners can use to make sure they're being heard. After you've expressed a need or feeling to your mate, ask him to repeat back what you just said — until you're satisfied that you've been heard. It's not necessary for your partner to repeat your exact words — as long as he understands the substance of what you said.

For example, Sandra was upset because Bill came home late from a business meeting without calling, so she made the following statement.

"I need you to call me if you're going to be more than an hour late. Otherwise, I'll worry."

"There's nothing to worry about," Bill replied. "You know that these meetings sometimes run late."

"I don't think you heard me, Sandra responded. "Can you please tell me what you think I mean?"

"Okay, you're uptight unless you know exactly where I am at every minute of the day. It's kind of annoying."

"That's not what meant. I need you to call me if you're going to be more than an hour late so that I won't worry."

Sandra again asked Bill to explain what she had said — just so she'd know that he was hearing her.

"Okay," Bill answered. "You worry when I come home late, and you want me to call if I'm delayed for more than an hour."

"That's right," said Sandra. "Now that I know that you heard me, will you actually do it?"

Sandra then asked Bill if he wanted to express his views on the matter, so that she could be the active listener, but he declined. Perhaps he didn't have an opposing viewpoint to offer, or maybe he just wanted to end the conversation. However, Sandra has a right to expect an answer. Bill can say yes (and mean it), which would effectively resolve the issue. However, if he says no, or I don't know, they will have to talk about it more.

Few things provide as much emotional nourishment as the feeling you get when someone you love is truly listening to you. This kind of communication makes you feel valued and connected, and deepens the intimacy between you and your partner.

Chances are that you know far more bad listeners than good listeners. It's also quite possible that your listening skills are better than a lot of the people you come in contact with. Still, the important question is: Do you listen to your partner (and others in your life) as well as you can?

Please don't worry if you can't honestly answer "yes" to this question. It's easier than you may think to become a better listener. All you need is the desire to do so and a willingness to practice the skills in the following sections.

Make a conscious effort to be a better listener

Good listening can help you communicate better in every aspect of life, so why not try it in all your interactions? If you're a talkative person, start out by simply talking less. This one change will give others an opportunity to talk more — while giving you an opportunity to do more listening.

If you're someone who tends to get lost in your own thoughts, make it a point to focus more of your attention on the other person and less on yourself.

Don't be discouraged if you don't see a radical change overnight. You *will* become a better listener if you make a consistent effort to do so.

Write down the thoughts and feelings that stop you from listening

If you're a poor listener, you've probably been that way for many years. And while ingrained habits aren't easy to change, a very small improvement in your listening skills can make a big difference in how you communicate with your partner.

The next time you and your partner are having a conversation, make a mental note of what you were thinking about that interfered with your ability to hear her. Then, in a quiet moment when you're alone, replay the interaction and ask yourself:

✔ Why did you interrupt?

✔ Were you anxious or preoccupied with your own thoughts?

✔ Were you turned off by what she was saying?

After you identify the things that prevent you from listening, start working to reduce their impact. Slow down your mind — and your mouth — and shift your focus to opening up your ears — and your heart.

Enjoy the benefits of becoming a better listener

One of the advantages of becoming a better listener is that it tends to encourage others to put more effort into listening to you. Those benefits increase dramatically when marriage partners become more invested in hearing each other. As time goes on, you may notice the following improvements in your marriage.

✔ A feeling of being appreciated and loved

✔ The sense that you're truly connected to your partner

✔ Fewer and less-contentious arguments

✔ More frequent and satisfying sex

Unfortunately, active listening doesn't always work and may actually have the opposite effect. Some people are so self-centered, that they will mistake your willingness to hear them as an invitation to talk endlessly about themselves.

Recognize the impact of conversational pacing differences

Married couples are well suited when both partners usually feel the need for a quarrel at the same time.

— Jeann Rostand, biologist

Married couples sometimes have problems communicating because of clashes in *how* they talk. Sometimes, these style differences become so intense that spouses feel that it's impossible to speak to each other at all.

One partner talks in a slow and thoughtful manner. The other partner is a forceful speaker, with a rapid-fire delivery. There is no right or wrong conversational style — though you'd never know it from the kinds of gripes we hear from couples who clash over different styles of communication.

"He doesn't allow me enough room to express my thoughts and feelings," the slower-talking spouse complains. Meanwhile, the more effusive partner typically accuses his spouse of taking too long and never getting to the point.

Conversational pacing is largely an ingrained personality feature, so it can be difficult to forge a negotiated compromise between fast- and slow-talking partners. Still, spouses in an enduring marriage manage to savor and enjoy their differences in pacing, even as they work to effect subtle changes to smooth out the kinks in day-to-day living. The case of Frank and Sally illustrates how this can be accomplished.

Frank is such a fast talker, he can often finish your thought before you even have a chance to formulate it. When Sally relates a story, it can take any number of twists and turns before she finally gets to the point.

While they were dating, Sally found Frank's quick-witted intensity irresistible, while he found her quiet reticence a wonderful contrast to his style. But, after three years of marriage, these pacing differences became annoying — to say the least.

Our challenge was to help this couple acknowledge and accommodate to one another's pace before these differences interfered with their ability to solve problems. We encouraged Frank and Sally to do the following four-step exercise:

1. **Identify and verbalize your respective styles.**

    Frank grew up in New York, the product of a family where almost everybody spoke loud and rapidly. "Our lives were fast paced," he recalled, "and we didn't have a lot of patience for people who did things slowly. In fact, we sometimes called them dimwits. If you didn't jump in and talk fast around our dinner table, you'd never be heard."

Sally was from a rural area in Minnesota, a part of the world where people tend to take their time. She is just as intelligent as her husband. However, she is very soft-spoken and in no hurry to get to the punch line in a conversation. "I've always been this way," she admits, "but I can see that it's really getting on Frank's nerves."

2. Recognize the impact your pacing differences have on each other.

Frank was able to admit that his lack of patience was causing Sally to clam up, just as she began to understand that her more laid-back approach was a source of frustration to Frank. Under these circumstances, partners often become locked into a battle of styles — and that's what was happening to this couple.

Frank was inadvertently using his fast-paced approach to overwhelm Sally and shut her up. For her part, Sally had slowed down her pace even more to counter what she perceived to be an attack by her husband. As a result, this couple was finding it increasingly difficult to communicate.

3. Appreciate what is positive about your differences.

We reminded Sally of how much she used to love Frank's quick wit, and we encouraged Frank to recall that Sally's easy-going style was one of the things about her that he once found so appealing.

4. Work at modifying your behavior.

Frank and Sally will always have their respective fast and slow conversational styles, but that doesn't mean each partner can't make adjustments. Frank can make a conscious effort to slow down so that he and Sally can have a meaningful discussion. Sally can work at becoming more assertive in expressing thoughts and feelings, and letting Frank know if he is overwhelming her or shutting her down.

Husbands, Wives, and Their Communication Styles

When women are depressed, they either eat or go shopping. Men invade another country. It's a whole different way of thinking.

— Elaine Boosler, comedienne

Some of the differences in how married partners communicate are gender-based. In our culture, boys are raised to compete, while girls are often raised to be caregivers and nurturers. Researchers like Georgetown University's Deborah Tannen, author of *You Just Don't Understand*, have been charting the ways these differences in upbringing lead to differences in communication styles — differences that can impact a marriage.

The pursuer and the distancer

In a typical scenario, the wife is responsible for relationships and is always concerned with trying to find out how everybody is feeling. The husband tends to be far less concerned with relationship dynamics, and stays somewhat distant, while his wife pursues him. This can eventually lead to an impasse where the husband says: "Maybe you'd get further if you just stop bugging me." To which the wife answers, "Bugging you is the only way I can get your attention."

✔ Many girls are taught that talk is a way to maintain intimacy. Young girls often have best friends with whom they exchange secrets. When girls play in groups, they tend to make suggestions that further the common good. For the most part, they are not interested in giving orders to assert their power.

✔ Most boys, on the other hand, use talk as a way to assert their individual status. They are not especially concerned about what's best for the group. Boys often like games that have winners and losers. A boy's success in competitive games often determines his status within the group. And, it's not uncommon for the boys with higher status to push around those who are not as popular.

These lessons in communication that we learn as youngsters influence the way we relate to one another in marriage. A wife who has grown up believing in the power of verbal communication may expect her husband to do what she asks. All she has to do is tell him what that is. Meanwhile, a husband who has grown up believing that the real purpose of talking is to get the upper hand may interpret his wife's requests as an attempt to control him.

What often happens in these situations is that the husband will ignore his wife or put off responding to her requests as a way of asserting his independence. Meanwhile, the baffled wife thinks that the problem is that she didn't make her feelings clear enough. At that point, she may become more emphatic and start repeating herself. Soon, she sounds as if she's nagging — a strategy that usually winds up increasing the husband's resolve not to do what his wife wants.

If the communication pattern in your marriage is that of a nagging or pursuing spouse and a withdrawing or distancing spouse, we suggest you try the following two-pronged approach.

✔ **For the pursuing spouse:** Don't keep chasing your spouse to open up emotionally. Often, the more you pursue him, the more he withdraws. Remember, good communication is as much your spouse's responsibility as yours, even if you have more practice in talking about your feelings. To change the pattern, you sometimes have to wait for him to move toward you.

✔ **For the distancing spouse:** Don't interpret your partner's tendency to pursue as an attack. Your spouse is your collaborator — not your competitor. Think about the positive impact that better communication and more closeness with your spouse can have on every aspect of your life. Make a conscious effort to take the initiative to talk. Don't tune out or withdraw — emotionally or physically.

Understanding the Importance of Negotiation in Marriage

Compromise . . . is what makes nations great and marriages happy.

— Phyllis McGinley; poet, essayist, and children's author

If we've learned anything from our own marriage and working with married couples, it's that differences come with the turf. Research on marital communication suggests that even couples who rate their marriages as "good" resolve less than a third of their differences to the point that they are no longer issues of dispute. The other two-thirds of marital disagreements are never completely resolved to one or both partners' satisfaction.

So, the question is, if couples have so many differences, how do they manage to stay married — much less maintain a relationship that they consider to be "good?"

The answer is that the *way* couples discuss and negotiate their disputes is as important as whether or not those disputes actually get resolved. Some differences between married partners have to do with style issues like neatness and punctuality (both of which are discussed in Chapter 5). Other disagreements center around bigger questions, which include the following:

✔ How should we divide up our earnings and financial responsibilities?

✔ Should we live in a house or an apartment?

✔ Should we live in the city, the suburbs, or the country?

✔ Should we have children? If so, how many and when?

✔ How much time should we spend with our respective families of origin?

The list of potential controversies is almost endless — but the negotiating process that makes these issues tolerable to married partners is fundamentally the same.

The outcome of negotiations between marriage partners is often less important than the way differences are dealt with. Obviously, there are some issues that must be resolved in a satisfactory way for both partners. But whether or not it's essential to come up with a specific resolution, it's always important that each spouse feels understood and respected. When issues are discussed in an atmosphere where both partners feel free to speak their minds without fear of being put down, the lines of communication are strengthened — even if the particular controversy isn't resolved your way.

Applying the tools of win-win negotiation to marriage

A short pencil is better than a long memory.

— Rose Harrow Simring

Win-win negotiation is a well-accepted method in the business world for working out differences in a constructive and mutually beneficial manner. This process is effective in any situation where both parties have an ongoing relationship and, therefore, need to come up with solutions to disagreements that satisfy both parties.

Marriage is supposed to be the relationship where people have the greatest emotional investment, so it's especially important that every negotiation be win-win for both partners and that neither one walks away completely empty-handed.

It may be possible to badger or browbeat your husband or wife to get what you want in the short term. However, if one partner feels bullied or taken advantage of, the long-term health of the marriage will certainly suffer.

Karen and Mike have always had different social needs for family gatherings. Karen grew up in a large family that loved to get together on weekends and holidays. "Some of my warmest memories as a child were going to my grandmother's house on Sunday for a large family gathering," Karen recalled. "There were always lots of people around, laughing and making lots of noise. Even now, I love being in that kind of atmosphere because it conjures up such happy memories."

The family Mike grew up in was nothing like Karen's. His father was a brooding man, whose business problems took up most of his time. "My mother and father were both only children, and they had few friends," Mike recalled. "So, there were never any large family functions to attend. On holidays, like Thanksgiving, my mother would make a turkey for our small immediate family, but there were almost never any guests."

Shortly after Karen and Mike were married, their different expectations in this area came into focus. Karen's large extended family was constantly inviting the couple to join them for holiday feasts or summer vacations. Karen very much wanted to attend these events, but Mike found them too busy and boisterous for his taste.

"It became clear early on that this difference would require constant negotiation," Karen recalled. "And it was also obvious that neither of us was ever going to adopt the other's social preferences. But somehow, we had to find a way to work out our differences in this area.

"At one point, we had planned a two-week vacation at the shore. Coincidentally, most of my extended family was going to be there at the same time. They very much wanted us to stay with them at the same beach club and shore-front hotel where they had booked an entire floor. That sounded wonderful to me, but Mike objected strenuously.

"'It's my vacation,' he complained. 'I don't want to be forced to deal with all those people every day.'"

Karen and Mike were able to negotiate their differences by taking the following steps:

- ✔ **Separate personalities from issues.** Married partners sometimes fall into the trap of attacking each other instead of using collaborative negotiation to work out their differences. For example, Karen could have attacked Mike for being withdrawn and anti-social. Mike could have accused Karen of being more interested in her extended family than in her marriage.

  This kind of negative campaign may work in politics, because the only aim is to win. After the election, your opponent is no longer important. However, negative tactics almost always backfire in marriage because it stops you from having a constructive dialogue. When you talk about issues instead of personalities, it's easier to work together as partners trying to achieve a common goal.

- ✔ **Always communicate with "I" statements rather than "you" statements.** Saying "I feel" means that you are talking from your own feelings and expectations. Statements like "you always do this" or "your problem is," are bound to be received as accusations. Such pronouncements serve to make your partner defensive, and block further communication.

  By using "I" statements to express their needs and expectations, Karen and Mike were able to communicate their respective positions effectively.

  "I have so much fun being around all my relatives," said Karen. "I would feel that I missed something important if I couldn't spend time with them on this vacation."

"I genuinely like everyone in your family," Mike replied, "but I would much rather interact with them one or two at a time. Being around twenty or more people at one time is more than I can handle. I feel like there's too much noise — too many interactions going on at once."

✔ **Don't mind-read or analyze your partner.** People don't like to be told what they're thinking or feeling — much less the reasons why. Instead of acting like a dime-store psychologist, give your partner ample opportunity to express his own thoughts and feelings. Work at being a better listener, even if you think you already understand where your spouse is coming from.

✔ **Concentrate on finding mutually acceptable solutions.** For a marriage to go forward, partners need to develop a broad area of agreement as to the common goals of their relationship.

This means that neither partner can always get everything he or she wants when differences come up. However, a mutually acceptable solution will always take both spouses' needs and sensitivities into consideration. This kind of solution lets both partners walk away feeling that they've reached an agreement that's in the best interest of their marriage.

After a good deal of discussion, Karen and Mike reached the following agreement about their vacation: For one of the two weeks they were away, they would spend their days at the beach club where Karen's relatives were staying. This would address Karen's need to socialize with a large group of her relatives. To accommodate Mike's desire for more privacy, he and Karen would sleep at a hotel in a nearby coastal town, where they could have either a quiet breakfast or dinner alone each day.

There are usually several answers to a problem — keep trying different solutions until you come up with one that works.

✔ **Let go of the need to win or prove that you're right.**

The ultimate success of any negotiation between married partners hinges on working together to achieve a resolution that satisfies the needs of both spouses. It's going to be impossible to achieve that if you insist on attacking one another for your different needs and preferences.

Don't talk — or think — about differences in terms of who's right or wrong. This can be difficult to accomplish, because people tend to be attached to their own perspective. Still, avoid going for the moral high ground if you want to achieve an outcome that's satisfactory to both partners.

Don't look at your negotiation as a game where one partner has to lose for the other partner to win. What you want instead is an outcome where each partner feels that there has been a fair amount of give and take on both sides.

Your marriage is a collaboration — not a competition. Before you start fighting over your differences, work at identifying some areas of mutual agreement. Then start building on that common ground. Be creative in coming up with solutions that address the situation and are satisfying to both of you.

In the negotiation between Karen and Mike, there was no winner or loser. But that never was the goal. It's also unclear who gave in more, and that too was never a consideration. The steps in this particular negotiation illustrate how the process is supposed to work. They can be summarized as follows:

✔ **Both partners expressed their different feelings.** For Karen and Mike, their clashing preferences about socializing with large family groups had come up many times in the past. Still, both partners realized that it is an ongoing issue that requires constant discussion and renegotiation.

✔ **Both partners refrained from personal attacks and respected each other's wishes.** It is key that neither partner feels put down for his or her desires and preferences. Once that feeling of safety is established, both partners can start working toward finding the best way to handle the situation at hand — even if the underlying difference remains unresolved.

Neither Karen nor Mike have altered their feelings about large family gatherings. However, each took a positive step in understanding and respecting the other's feelings. While it's true that Karen and Mike both had to sacrifice part of what they wanted, they came away from the negotiation feeling good because they acted in a way that brought them closer together.

When Karen and Mike talk about their vacation, they don't feel any resentment about what each of them gave up in the negotiation process. Instead, they were both satisfied that they could find a win-win way to resolve their differences. The end result was that these partners felt better about each other — and their marriage. They also had lots of fun on their vacation.

Maintaining an ongoing dialogue — especially in matters of the heart

The most effective way to remember your wife's birthday is to forget it once.

— Anonymous

It's important to always keep the lines of communication open between you and your spouse — and not just when you're trying to negotiate differences. Feelings and needs can change from day to day or over a period of years. Partners need to relay information about these changes on a regular basis, and this may require you to renegotiate certain issues in your marriage.

One area that partners often have trouble discussing (and renegotiating) centers around the way love and affection are expressed. What happened to Sarah and Larry illustrates what can occur when changes in these feelings aren't openly communicated.

When Larry and Sarah married, they agreed not to give each other presents, even on birthdays or holidays like Christmas and Valentine's day. For the first few years, this arrangement seemed to work. As time went by, however, Sarah decided that she was no longer satisfied with not giving or receiving gifts. She did not want to confront Larry because she feared that he'd accuse her of going back on their agreement, but she was growing increasingly unhappy about it.

Sarah decided to try the indirect approach. She didn't want to come out and tell Larry that she now wanted to start exchanging gifts on special occasions. So, she began buying him small presents, hoping that he would respond in kind.

The strategy wasn't working. Larry didn't take the hint, even after Sarah started saying things like, "It would be so nice to get a box of candy this Valentine's Day." Finally, when Larry neglected to give her anything for her thirty-fifth birthday, Sarah broke down crying.

"How could you ignore my needs this way?" she sobbed. "I've tried just about everything to let you know that I wanted you to get me an occasional present — just to let me know you think our marriage is important to you. It's clear that you just don't care about me at all!"

Larry shot his wife a hurt and confused look. "I'm sorry you feel that way," he said. "But don't you remember? We made an agreement when we were first married not to exchange presents. I can't remember you ever telling me that you wanted to change that rule."

This may seem like an extreme example, but we've seen many couples run into this type of problem whenever one partner wants to modify the ground rules. One spouse agrees to certain terms as a way of avoiding conflict or because she is unsure of her feelings. Meanwhile, the other spouse is unable — or unwilling — to notice that his partner has grown unhappy with the existing arrangement. You can avoid the kind of problem that Sarah and Larry ran into if you aren't afraid of rocking the boat.

When expressing love and affection, both partners must acknowledge and authenticate one another's feelings — and recognize that some of those feelings and preferences can change at any time. Each person feels most comfortable giving and receiving love in a particular way. These preferences come into play in the way we exchange gifts, celebrate special occasions, and demonstrate affection — both physically and through words.

Be aware that your partner's needs may not be the same as yours. For example, spouses often have very different ideas about how birthdays and holidays are supposed to be handled. In our practice, we see a tremendous amount of anger expressed over feeling neglected on these special occasions. Husbands tend to be more forgetful than wives about such rituals. Some go so far as to minimize or make fun of what their partners think of as meaningful expressions of love on important days.

Your family of origin may not have been very big on gifts, or you may have decided that such rituals are superficial or childish. No matter. If your spouse expects a card or a present on birthdays and other occasions, it's both considerate and wise to honor that need.

Make a point to find out how your partner likes to be treated on certain special days — and how such rituals were handled in his or her family of origin. As much as possible, try to personalize all cards and gifts. Think about the rituals in your family of origin, and then work together to create new rituals that have personal meaning for both of you.

The way that you and your spouse communicate love and affection is often a function of comfort and personal style, rather than a measure of true feelings. When you and your partner accept this reality, you may have an easier time expressing your devotion. Some techniques that are helpful in this area include the following:

- **Make your partner queen or king for a day.** On certain special occasions, your partner should get to call all the shots — your treat. If he wants to check into a fancy hotel for the night without the kids, you make the arrangements. If she wants to have birthday dinner with her sister whom you can't stand, smile and take charge of the preparations.

- **Respect your partner's attitude about touching and physical contact.** Some people are very private and don't like public displays of affection. Others enjoy hugging and kissing out in the open. Here again, these preferences come down to what makes you feel good. But remember: There is another person to consider.

  If you're more demonstrative than your partner, find out what your mate is comfortable with. You may have to save your affections for private moments. Tell your partner that you may spontaneously show your feelings at times. Set up a private signal for you to tone it down if she thinks you've gone too far.

  If you're uncomfortable with public displays of affection, discuss this with your partner. Tell your spouse that you understand that she may sometimes act on her need to show affection in public. Talk about your feelings openly when the two of you are alone. Try to find humor in your differences.

- **Whatever else you do, don't ever stop maintaining open and caring communication with each other about what you're thinking and feeling!**

Chapter 5

Fighting the Fair Way

● ●

In This Chapter

▶ Understanding why fights are inevitable

▶ Recognizing how you and your partner fight

▶ Dealing with small annoyances that can cause big arguments

▶ Following the do's and don'ts of fair fighting

● ●

*P*artners in successful marriages find ways to live with their differences. They may repeat the same argument over and over again, but that somehow doesn't erode their love for one another. On the other hand, couples whose marriages are in trouble often can't get past their arguments. Their anger, which never seems to dissipate, constantly gnaws at their relationship until there's no love left between the partners.

The key difference between these two types of couples often rests with their ability (or inability) to have a fair fight. The arguments can be loud and intense, as long as they're fair. Couples who practice fair fighting aren't embarrassed to admit that conflicts are part of their marriage.

In this chapter we talk about fighting, and we give you the tools to start resolving your conflicts constructively — and fairly.

Understanding That Fights Will Happen

Love and religion are the two most volcanic emotions to which the human organism is liable.

— Havelock Ellis, psychologist

Wives and husbands who enter a marriage expecting not to argue soon find themselves sorely disappointed. Sure, we've heard some couples claim that they've never argued during the course of a long marriage. If that's true, it's a good bet they haven't been revealing their true feelings to each other.

Any two human beings who live together are going to battle, no matter how ideal the circumstances. You can almost predict that men and women will have conflicts based on gender differences, just for starters. Then there are potential clashes over any number of large and small issues, of which the following are just a few:

- ✔ Dividing financial responsibilities
- ✔ Raising children
- ✔ Maintaining good relations with family and friends
- ✔ Giving one another enough private space
- ✔ Arriving at places early or late
- ✔ Maintaining a neat or sloppy house
- ✔ Planning holidays and vacations

When you think about these (and all the other) potential disagreements between marriage partners, it's a wonder that couples don't fight twenty-four hours a day.

Because fighting is unavoidable, the best course is to accept this reality and plan to deal with it in a way that strengthens the marriage.

Apathy and indifference are often more telling signs of a troubled marriage than arguing. Lots of loving couples argue constantly — but none treat each other with indifference. An apathetic spouse who couldn't care less about her partner's attention may be going through an emotional divorce.

Looking for Signs of Unhealthy Fighting

Each one of an affectionate couple may . . . be willing to die for one another, yet unwilling to say the agreeable word at the right moment.

— George Meredith, novelist and poet

Answering the questions in this section can help you develop a clearer picture of how you and your partner fight. This knowledge also helps you avoid some of the common red flags that undermine constructive and fair arguing.

Does one spouse fear the other?

If one of you is afraid, you must pinpoint the source and reduce the fear, if possible. No one can speak her mind in an atmosphere of terror, so she exhibits only defensive behavior and not real communication. The fear may be loss of affection, or fear of angering your partner — even if no *physical* danger exists.

Fear or intimidation on the part of either partner may be a sign of serious imbalance in the relationship. On the other hand, the problem may be something that's relatively easy to fix. For example, your spouse may have a loud voice that frightens you. He may not intend to come across as threatening, and he'll agree to modulate his tone if you let him know the effect that his loud voice has on you.

Does one spouse become physically threatening?

Actual or threatened physical abuse is what we call a *poison communication* that shouldn't be tolerated in any relationship. We strongly suggest getting help in physically removing yourself from any situation where the threat of actual violence is present. When you're out of harm's way, don't return until you and your spouse have sought outside help (see Chapter 16).

If your spouse actually hits you, you need to take immediate steps to protect yourself. If you feel the situation is out of control or you're in danger of being hurt, immediately call the police.

Does one spouse destroy property?

Some people believe that it's okay for angry spouses to punch walls and throw objects around to express their anger. We're more skeptical. We think that such demonstrations need to be judged by the type of behavior and its effect on each spouse.

For example, when Tom gets really angry with Marilyn, he occasionally tears apart whatever book he happens to be reading at the time. Marilyn doesn't feel that this is a particularly violent act, because it doesn't frighten or intimidate her.

Sol, on the other hand, sometimes breaks dishes when he gets mad at Ruth. At first, Ruth was able to look at Sol's flare-ups as a relatively harmless way for him to release pent-up anger. But lately, Sol's displays have become more frequent — and he has started destroying the couple's most expensive china. This turn of events troubles Ruth.

"The value of the dishes doesn't bother me nearly as much as the feeling that he's starting to lose control," Ruth told us. "I'm frightened that he soon may start throwing things at me."

Destroying property can get dangerously close to physical intimidation. Therefore, we don't think it's an acceptable way to argue or to express anger. If the destructive behavior continues, the partner who expresses anger in this way should consider seeking professional help. If he refuses, or if the behavior continues to concern the other partner, she should physically get away from a potentially dangerous situation.

Does one spouse become verbally or emotionally abusive?

Some couples can use biting humor in non-threatening ways. However, it's far more common for one spouse to use insults and sarcasm as a means of intimidating the other.

Whenever you argue, the fundamental rule is to attack the issue under dispute — not the person you're disputing. The goal of a fair fight is always to find a resolution — not to hurt or wield power over the other person.

Research by psychologist Howard Markman shows that it can take as many as twenty acts of kindness to undo the negative impact of a single hurtful insult. And even that doesn't truly reflect the long-term damage verbal abuse can inflict on somebody who loves you.

✔ **If you do insult your partner, offer a sincere apology at once.** Make it clear that you understand the potential cost of your hurtful words, and promise that you will be more careful in the future. However, apologetic words are often not enough. You may have to make reparations and show through *actions* that you're sincerely sorry.

If you're on the receiving end of verbal or emotional abuse, make sure your spouse understands the damage that's been inflicted. If this is something that happens on a regular basis, tell your spouse that you're not going to accept the insults or demeaning comments.

✔ **Offer a pre-arranged signal.** A pre-arranged signal can tell your spouse: "I feel that I'm being verbally abused, and I want you to stop." That signal can be holding up your hand or some other sign that the two of you agree on. Hopefully, your spouse will abide by that signal. If not, it's up to you to remove yourself from the situation. That may mean going into another room, or getting into your car and going for a ride.

✔ **If your spouse is not usually verbally abusive, talk about what led up to the incident.** If he or she offers what appears to be a sincere apology, it may be best to accept it and move on. However, if he or she continues to scream at you, let your spouse know that this behavior is unacceptable — and a potential threat to your marriage.

Make no mistake — verbal abuse is an act of violence. While physical abuse is far more dangerous than verbal or emotional abuse, research shows that verbal abuse can often be more difficult to stop. The reason for this is that verbal abuse is more pervasive, less clear cut, and easier to deny. It also leaves no marks.

If you see an ongoing pattern of verbal or emotional abuse in your marriage, seek out a counselor or therapist who is experienced in dealing with these issues. For more information on finding the right kind of professional help, see Chapter 16.

Do you fight in front of your children?

As a rule, fighting or arguing should not take place in front of children. When a child hears his parents fighting, he is likely to become frightened or feel that he is the cause of the fight. He may also misinterpret what his mother and father are saying to each other, and take it much more literally than it was meant. It's not always easy to shield children from your arguments because disputes can erupt quite suddenly, when little ears are in range of the action.

One winter, when our daughter was nine, we were having a heated argument, and didn't realize she was listening. It was a cold and snowy day, but Kira went outside and wrote the following words on a snow bank — in great big letters, for all the world to see: MOM AND DAD, PLEASE STOP FIGHTING!

Children learn a great deal about marriage from observing their parents. If you can have a healthy disagreement, it's okay to let your children watch because it gives them an opportunity to see how a constructive argument unfolds. But when emotions run high, kids can be hurt by seeing their parents argue and bicker.

Does alcohol play a role in your fights?

Alcohol tends to exaggerate people's emotions, and it can quickly explode an otherwise relatively calm argument. Alcohol is often present in cases of spousal abuse. In fact, many women report that their husbands only become abusive when they are inebriated.

Some people are under the false impression that alcohol can serve as a truth serum. The fact is that alcohol is counterproductive when couples are trying to work out their differences. While a few drinks can sometimes loosen inhibitions and cause people to say things they may otherwise keep to themselves, most people are far less able to deal with those issues when they are under the influence. Plus, they tend to forget most of what was said when they wake up the next morning.

Drunk arguing is a lot like drunk driving. You go through the motions, without having much control over what you're doing. Even worse, you risk hurting yourself and your partner in the process.

Negotiating to Prevent Fights, When Possible

Marriage is not just spiritual communion, it is also remembering to take out the trash.

— Dr. Joyce Brothers, psychologist

It's not always easy to tell which issues are truly important to married partners. There are certain fundamental differences in major areas like child-rearing, in-laws, and money that are sufficiently big that we cover them in separate chapters. (Turn to Chapters 9, 13, and 14 respectively for more information on these topics).

Then there are differences that appear to be minor — but can wind up having an enormous influence in both the quality and quantity of marital arguments. We call these *toaster-setting-type issues,* or *thorns in the side*.

In the following sections, we talk about three thorns in the side that married couples most often complain about. We show you how to make sure that these molehills don't become mountains in your marriage.

Of course, the techniques we offer to deal with everyday differences can be used to work out many other kinds of disagreements that come up between the two of you.

Punctuality

You probably know at least one person who is a fanatic about punctuality. To that person, someone who's late is thoughtless and self-centered. Case closed! At the same time, there are other people who feel hemmed in by the need to always be on time. They consider punctuality a sign of uptightness — an annoying constraint that makes everything a chore.

In our practice, we see many couples whose lives are a constant struggle over this issue. We remember a particular case involving Alex (Mr. Late) and Jennifer (Ms. Early) that shows just how big a role punctuality can play in a marriage.

Alex is always behind schedule, while Jennifer is almost obsessively punctual. Whenever Alex is late, Jennifer seethes with anger. The longer Alex makes Jennifer wait, the more upset she becomes. By the time Alex shows up, Jennifer is usually ready to explode. She tries to hold her temper, but can't keep from lecturing Alex about his lack of consideration and the importance of being on time. Alex lost his patience for Jennifer's sermons a long time ago. He typically vents his frustration by making sarcastic wisecracks about his wife's intolerance and compulsiveness.

The arguments have become so bitter that Jennifer and Alex have stopped going anywhere together. Unfortunately, staying home all the time has only served to intensify their resentment. Here's how each of them describes the problem:

✔ Alex: She tries to make everything we do so tightly structured, my leisure time has become more of a chore than going to work.

✔ Jennifer: I feel so embarrassed walking into places late that I would just as soon not go out. But I've come to realize that spending all my time in the house ticked off at my husband isn't the answer.

Thorns in the side

"Most married couples, even though they love each other very much in theory, tend to view each other in practice as large teeming flaw colonies, the result being that they get on each other's nerves and regularly erupt into vicious emotional shouting matches over such issues as toaster settings."

— Dave Barry, humorist and author

After listening to Alex and Jennifer, we told them that punctuality is not a moral issue, though it can be an issue of respect and consideration for others. If you're going to a movie by yourself and don't mind arriving after the film starts, that's your call. But if there are other people waiting for you and dependent on your arrival, it's a different story. Sometimes promptness is critical, but in other situations, a looser, more relaxed approach is fine.

When you realize that punctuality has become a problem in your marriage, arrange to sit down with your partner and discuss how you should navigate various situations. Identify scenarios where both of you can compromise on your attitudes toward punctuality; find out when it's really important to be on time and when you can both take a more relaxed approach.

The following tips can help you get the most out of your negotiations about punctuality (and any other issue):

✓ State your differences openly.

✓ Admit that you're having a problem coming to terms.

✓ Admit your discomfort.

✓ Don't use sarcasm to manipulate your partner.

✓ Don't ridicule your partner's style.

✓ Don't try to embarrass or shame your partner into doing things your way.

Discussing specific situations forces you and your partner to find practical and mutually acceptable solutions to your differences regarding punctuality. For example, Alex and Jennifer agreed to the following terms:

Alex agreed to work at being more realistic about how long he needs to get ready. One technique he used was to add an additional twenty-five percent to the time he estimates it will take to dress when he and Jennifer go out. He promised to allow for extra time whenever they were going to an event to which they had tickets. Alex also agreed to be punctual in appointments involving the couple's two young children, or when other people might be hurt or inconvenienced. Jennifer agreed to be more flexible when they went to parties or other functions, if it really didn't matter when they arrived.

✓ Telling your partner that you'll be late and giving a realistic estimate of when you're going to arrive will often head off a confrontation. It's also far more respectful to the person who is waiting, because it gives the punctual partner the option of deciding what to do with that time.

✓ Separateness often serves as an effective safety valve in marriages where punctuality differences are sources of stress. If you can't come to a mutual understanding about when to arrive somewhere, sometimes it works out better to go at your own separate paces.

This approach worked for Jennifer and Alex. Both partners agreed that, whenever specific time issues couldn't be resolved, each would go separately. This means that even if Jennifer acknowledged that a particular gathering doesn't require being punctual, she may still want to arrive an hour earlier than Alex. In that case, she would simply go when she wished, and he would do the same.

Neatness

Some people can't tolerate a sloppy house, while others are perfectly comfortable living with dishes in the sink and clothes strewn all over the floor. This conflict between neat and sloppy styles is the focus of Neil Simon's *The Odd Couple,* a Broadway hit that inspired a movie and a popular television series.

The story centers on two divorced men who share a Manhattan apartment: Felix Unger is compulsively neat and Oscar Madison enjoys living like a slob. Their wrestling match of styles makes for great entertainment. But married partners who live with this Odd Couple scenario don't always find the battle so funny.

In our practice, we see many couples who struggle over this issue every day. We once worked with a couple we'll call Felice (Ms. Neat) and Oscar (Mr. Sloppy), who eventually managed to work out this style difference. Here is how each of the partners explained the situation in separate initial interviews.

✔ Felice (Ms. Neat): "I guess you could say I'm a neatness nut. It drives my husband crazy that I spend hours cleaning our house the day before our cleaning person comes. I can't make him understand that you have to get rid of clutter before someone can actually clean up. If it were up to my husband, the house would always be a mess. I find it hard to live that way, and I'm embarrassed to invite guests over. He thinks it's all a big joke."

✔ Oscar (Mr. Sloppy): "I know Felice gets upset when I leave a newspaper on the couch or dishes in the sink. I eventually clean these things up most of the time, but she can't stand looking at the smallest mess for even a few minutes. Having a perfectly neat house just isn't that important to me, but I know it's a real sore point for my wife. When she sees the clutter on my desk, Felice always reminds me that a cluttered desk means a cluttered mind. But she gets angry when I ask her how that same logic applies to people with an empty desk."

Arguments over neatness can be serious; however, such style differences can be worked out if partners aren't at the extremes. Felice's neatness and Oscar's sloppiness were not at levels that we consider pathological. Still, the arguments had become sufficiently troubling for this couple to create a power struggle.

We explained to Felice and Oscar that neatness and sloppiness are relative concepts. When two people live together, one is bound to be neater than the other. The more tidy partner takes on the role of the neat nut, which relegates the other partner to the role of designated slob. We could see that this observation struck a chord in Felice.

"That's an interesting point," she began. "When I was growing up, my mother always accused me of being a terrible slob. Even now, my house is never neat enough to meet her standards. We helped Felice recognize that no particular style is necessarily better than another.

Oscar also related to the idea that neatness and sloppiness are relative. He recalled a college roommate who was "a much bigger slob than I. It drove me crazy, and I switched roommates after a term." It took some time, but Oscar began to see the problem through his wife's eyes.

We suggested to Felice and Oscar that the key issue revolved around consideration and respect — not right and wrong. We encouraged them to discuss specific situations, not broad generalizations in finding workable solutions to their differences regarding neatness and sloppiness.

We showed Felice and Oscar how to structure a game plan that worked for both of them. Its terms included the following:

- **Define areas of the house where each person's neatness style prevails.** This gave Oscar the freedom to keep his home-office as sloppy as he wished. Meanwhile, Felice selected a room as her private library, which she could maintain in as orderly a state as she desired.

- **Negotiate compromises for areas that must be shared.** Felice agreed not to throw out Oscar's newspapers from the living room without first asking him. Oscar agreed to discard his newspapers as soon as he was through reading them. Felice agreed that dishes did not always have to be washed immediately; Oscar promised not to leave unwashed dishes in the sink overnight.

- **Divide specific cleaning and house maintenance chores.** For example, Oscar agreed to do the majority of the shopping in exchange for Felice doing the bulk of the vacuuming.

- **Agree to be flexible when it really counts for the other person.** Oscar agreed that he would defer to Felice's preference for neatness whenever company was expected. Felice agreed to be more flexible when Oscar had to meet a deadline for work.

Planning

Planners need to have everything prearranged, or else they're uncomfortable. The non-planner has a far more spontaneous approach to life. "When you work out every detail in advance," the non-planner reasons, "you kill all the fun and adventure."

When a planner and a nonplanner marry, the planner is constantly tense about the perils of leaving things to chance. Meanwhile, the partner who hates to plan can't understand why her mate can't ever just hang loose.

Don and Kathy were married for less than a year, when they decided to take a summer vacation in Italy. Don, a planner, started mapping out an itinerary. He called several airlines to find out what bargains were available and contacted a travel agent to make hotel reservations. After he had laid out some tentative plans, Don told Kathy what they were.

"What on earth are you doing?" Kathy asked. It's only April, and we're not leaving until mid-August. There are last minute seats available on most flights, and I've never been shut out of a hotel room when I've traveled in the past. Why can't you trust that things will work out?"

Kathy's words threw Don for a loop. "I like to plan ahead," he answered. "For me, that's a big part of the fun. Not only that, but what happens if you can't make arrangements at the last second? Our entire vacation could be ruined."

Many couples find themselves constantly at loggerheads over planning. Fortunately, this is a difference that lends itself to compromise.

Ultimately, planning styles are comfort-zone issues. The key is to find a way to compromise and to uncover those areas where your needs overlap. As you pinpoint some mutual comfort zones, work on expanding those areas instead of allowing yourselves to get stuck on "my way versus your way."

When you and your partner clash over planning or not planning something, ask yourselves the following two questions:

- ✔ What's the worst that can happen if you do plan?
- ✔ What's the worst that can happen if you don't plan?

Then compare the consequences of each alternative. This can help you come to a decision.

For example, think again about Don and Kathy's disagreement over vacation plans. Assume that the potential consequences of not making travel and hotel arrangements in advance will result in an added cost of $2,000. That amount of money would be excessive for many couples. But what if the cost of leaving things loose would only be another $50 or $100? The nonplanner could make a good case for taking a more spontaneous approach.

Some factors (aside from money) that you may consider in making planning — and other kinds of decisions — include:

- ✔ Which partner feels more strongly about the issue?
- ✔ Who would have to make the bigger sacrifice in terms of comfort level?
- ✔ Who gave in last time you disagreed about planning?

Some couples have success dealing with this style difference by following a simple strategy: Do it his way this time, her way the next time. That way, both partners feel satisfied (at least part of the time). For example, Don and Kathy may agree to do this vacation one partner's way and the next vacation the other partner's way. But this kind of accommodation won't work if Don loses sleep whenever things aren't nailed down ahead of time. Obviously, for this compromise approach to work, each partner must agree to allow the other partner's style to prevail, at least temporarily.

With couples like Don and Kathy, one of the terms of compromise may require the nonplanner on a vacation to take responsibility for the consequences of hanging loose. That could mean that the nonplanner agrees to call every hotel in town until a room is secured. That spouse should not expect much assistance or sympathy from the spouse who wanted to make reservations in advance.

Having a Healthy Fight

Marriage is the only war in which you sleep with the enemy.

— Anonymous

Given that fights are inevitable in marriage, couples must know how to fight in a way that's healthy. When you and your spouse arrive at the point when you know an argument can't be avoided, follow the steps outlined in this section to make sure the battle is conducted fairly.

Defer to the partner who feels most strongly

In any argument, one person often feels more strongly about the issues in dispute than the other. In general, it's a good idea to figure out whose feelings are more intense, and to try to let that person have his or her way.

Some arguments are never resolved in a manner that's equally satisfying to both partners. This can be especially problematic when the two of you are fighting about something where no middle ground is possible.

John and Loretta had been arguing about whether or not to install a swimming pool in the backyard of their suburban home. Loretta loves to swim and had always longed to have her own pool. Swimming was something John could either take or leave, but he had other reasons for not wanting a pool in the backyard.

"Installing and maintaining a pool would cost tens of thousands of dollars," John told us. "But money never has been the issue. I wouldn't want a pool if someone gave it to me for free. As far as I'm concerned, having a pool is an extra burden that I would rather not deal with."

"Okay, Loretta replied. "But you know how much I like to swim. If we had a pool, I'd use it every single day — and maybe two or three times on certain days."

"I know," John chimed in, "but think of all the ramifications. Our house would become a magnet for guests — all of whom would be coming to use the pool. This would put me in the position of having to play host to an endless series of pool parties. Not only that, our entire social life would revolve around the pool, which means we wouldn't have time to spend our weekends doing lots of other things we both enjoy. Then there's the matter of safety. Our two young daughters and their friends would probably never want to get out of that pool. I'd have to worry about their safety — and I'd find that incredibly disruptive."

"I've told you again and again that I'm willing to take responsibility for our kids and their friends," Loretta answered. "You wouldn't have to worry about that at all."

John paused for a moment before responding. "I believe you're being sincere, but think about it. There would be times when you had something else to do, and then the kids' safety would become my responsibility."

In John and Loretta's case, there were only two possible resolutions:

- ✔ They would get a pool.
- ✔ They would not get a pool.

After a good deal of two-way discussion, Loretta concluded that John's feelings on the matter of the pool were stronger than hers. This wife felt that her husband understood and respected her viewpoint — just as she respected and understood his viewpoint. In the end, the fact that they both felt understood was more important than winning the argument. Loretta still wanted the pool, but decided that it would be better for the marriage if she did not force it on John.

Assume good will

In a marriage where both partners assume good will, the partner who yields on a particular issue has reason to believe that her spouse will defer to her on other major issues when her needs are more intense than his. Partners who've been married for a relatively short time may need to make this assumption as a matter of faith. However, those who've been together longer should be able to draw on instances when their spouse deferred to their stronger needs.

Loretta remembered that, when they were first married, John wanted to live in the city, while she much preferred the suburbs. They had wrestled over this difference for months. Eventually, John recognized that Loretta's needs were stronger than his. They ultimately wound up buying a house in a suburbs.

John never acted as if he expected to be compensated later on for giving in. And he never threw that lifestyle choice up to Loretta when they argued — even though she could tell that he'd still prefer living in the city.

The sense that both partners were more concerned with the overall health of the marriage than with getting their way helped Loretta yield to John on the matter of the swimming pool.

Maintain a balance, but don't keep score

Partners who are good (and fair) referees can usually tell if things are getting too one-sided. Maintaining a balance is a lot different than keeping score — an undertaking that's both useless and non-productive. After all, how can anybody tell how many points to assign for each victory or loss? Still, that doesn't mean you may not have to remind your partner (however gently) that it's his turn to give in.

Loretta may not have gotten her backyard pool, but that didn't lessen her love for swimming. When she suggested that the family join a local pool club, John was less than enthusiastic. "That means I'm going to have to spend my afternoons hanging around some strange pool with a bunch of people I don't even know."

Loretta then reminded John that, since she'd yielded to his strong desire not to install a backyard pool, she expected him to accommodate her need to swim. If that meant John would sometimes be expected to accompany Loretta and the children to the local pool club, he'd just have to live with it.

After a period of discussion, John said: "Okay, it's only fair that I participate in this with you." Both partners felt okay with this compromise, which was made for the sake of balance — and not on a tit-for-tat basis.

In a marriage, there are no referees to arbitrate a couple's disputes and differences. Through practice and commitment to building a stronger relationship, you've got to find a way to do it for yourselves.

Following the Rules of Fair Fighting

Be of love a little more gentle (than of anything else).

— e.e. cummings

For a fight to be fair, one participant must never violate the rights of the other. In a perfect world, married partners wouldn't use unfair tactics, but emotions run high in intimate relationships. Marriage is the closest and most intense emotional relationship most of us will ever have. Because of this intensity, married partners frequently resort to hurtful tactics when they fight — without realizing that they may be putting the future of their marriage at risk.

The fair-fighting tips in the following sections give you the guidelines that marriage partners need to have constructive arguments. The better you become at implementing these skills, the better your chances of sustaining an enduring marriage.

Be clear about what you (and your partner) want

Everyone is subject to feelings of anger and frustration at times, but this may not have anything to do with your partner — or your marriage. Before you enter into an argument, be aware of what you want the outcome to be.

The same principle applies to your partner. If he or she appears to be fighting just for the sake of venting emotions, ask your spouse what's really on his or her mind, so that the two of you can work together to address the problem.

Limit the scope of the argument to the issue at hand

When you're arguing, be careful not to *garbage-bag,* which means bringing up every other gripe you've been harboring in addition to the issue you're arguing about. Stick to just one issue at a time.

Seek a resolution that both of you can live with

In a good marriage, neither partner should emerge from an argument feeling like he or she has been forced to cave in. Sometimes, the resolution may favor one partner over the other. At other times, there may not even be a clear resolution. Still, partners who are committed to the long-term health of their marriage understand that if either spouse suffers an ongoing inequity, the bonds of the relationship will be weakened.

Go to bed angry, if necessary

There is an old saying that it's bad for arguing couples to go to bed angry. We often find the opposite to be true. In many cases, it's better to go to bed with an argument unresolved than it is to stay up all night trying to work things out. At bedtime, the two of you may be tense and exhausted from the trials of the day. In that atmosphere, fights can continue to escalate.

Look for exceptions

It's natural for partners who are battling to forget what's good in their relationship. They frequently make comments like: "You're always insensitive," or "You never take the time to show that you care." In fact, when you think about it, you can usually find one or more exceptions.

Get a good night's sleep and argue in the morning

Going to bed angry was something we had to deal with earlier in our marriage.

Steve: You may recall that there was a time when you absolutely refused to let me go to sleep angry. You had to know why I was mad — or at least get me to make up with you.

Sue: That's right. I'd pursue you and chase you to come to some kind of resolution. The next thing I knew it was three in the morning, and we were both totally burned out.

Steve: Yeah. I would put the pillow over my head, hoping and praying you'd go away.

Sue: And then, I'd pull the pillow off of your head. And it would go on like that for hours.

Steve: Do you remember what finally happened?

Sue: At one point, I realized that I was better off carrying around that anger for a few days. Eventually, you'd always come around and tell me what was bothering you. I actually started to enjoy allowing myself to be angry more than I did chasing you all the time. I liked waiting for you to approach me.

TRUE STORY

Dinner canceled due to argument

A number of years ago, we used to have dinner periodically at the New York apartment of two very close friends. This married couple never failed to prepare a deliciously elaborate meal. Afterwards, the four of us would sit around and have a wonderful conversation — about music, politics, relationships, or whatever.

But on this one particular Saturday evening, something was different. When we arrived, we were greeted by a sign on the door that read: "Very sorry, dinner is canceled. We are in the middle of an argument."

We were a bit surprised by the tack our friends had taken. But as we talked about it over dinner

at a nearby coffee shop, we decided that we liked what they had done. Instead of going through the motions of an evening feeling tense and frustrated about unexpressed feelings, this couple had decided that it was more important to have their argument.

We aren't suggesting that you make it a practice to cancel your dinner dates for the sake of a fight. Nevertheless, we'd like to see more couples place as high a value on airing their disputes as these married partners did.

When you and your partner are in a particularly intense or hurtful cycle of fighting, it can help to recall a time when things were going well. As you do that, ask yourself the following questions:

- ✔ What were we doing differently that made it easier get along?
- ✔ Was there some difference in those conditions that you can reproduce?

When married couples become embroiled in constant fights, there's a tendency to feel as if everything is wrong with the marriage. In most cases, you have positive aspects to build on — if you and your partner will only stop bickering long enough to look for them.

See the glass as half full, not as half empty

Each person possesses a great deal of power in shaping positive outcomes in our relationships. Part of that power rests in making an effort to focus on what you have, not on what's missing.

Research has shown that optimism is a skill almost anyone can learn. The key lies in making the following principles part of your mindset:

- ✔ Be aware that pessimistic thoughts lead to pessimistic behaviors.
- ✔ Work on emphasizing what's good in your relationship; don't dwell on what's bad.
- ✔ Accept the fact that most negative situations (including marital problems) can be altered for the better — if you're willing to be proactive in making that happen.
- ✔ Be the one to start the ball rolling.

You can wait around for your partner to change, but why do that when it's within your own power to start turning things around? Making small changes in the way you interact with your partner will empower you to effect bigger improvements in your relationship.

Remember to be kind

It is always a good idea to include kindness and thoughtfulness in your dealings — especially with your spouse. Even when you're embroiled in an argument, a kind word, a compliment, or a gentle touch can go a long way in showing you care — and that you're optimistic that things will get better.

How to say — and when to believe — the words "I'm sorry"

If I die, I forgive you. If I recover, we shall see.

— Spanish proverb

An insincere apology like, "I'm sorry, okay?" can make a bad situation worse because there appears to be no attempt to address the offensive act. However, a sincere, thoughtful apology can help heal the wound — and even have a positive long-term impact on the relationship.

The offended partner should be given as much time as necessary to articulate her position and feelings. Meanwhile, the partner who is apologizing needs to demonstrate that he understands why his words or actions were hurtful. In the process, he should not attempt to make excuses for his unacceptable behavior.

The aggrieved partner can choose whether or not to accept the offending spouse's apology. If necessary, she can tell her partner she needs more time to figure out what he will need to do to make things right.

Keep in mind, however, that if you flatly refuse to accept your partner's apology, it won't leave much room for either of you to go forward with the relationship.

Apologize when you need to

Some arguments are more contentious than others, and require time for healing. If, for example, one partner has verbally abused the other, even his most sincere apology may not gain instant acceptance. He may have to do more or wait longer for those wounds to heal.

Avoiding the Don'ts of Fair Fighting

Fair fighting is just as much about what you don't do as it is about what you do. To avoid letting a healthy fight turn sour, watch out for the fighting pitfalls described in the following sections.

Don't look for total victory or unconditional surrender

As an argument unfolds, one partner may feel that he or she has the upper hand. If this was an athletic competition, you could corner your opponent and go in for the kill. But marriage isn't supposed to be a contest. Therefore, the whole idea of winning needs to be recast.

When you sense that you have the upper hand in an argument, the best thing to do is take a step back and help your partner understand that you're committed to the principle that neither of you can win if one of you walks away feeling like a loser.

The two of you are partners and collaborators. Therefore, your ultimate fight is not for a victory — but for a stronger and happier marriage.

Don't intentionally prolong the argument

Many arguments can't be concluded in one session — and some will never get totally resolved. If your partner appears to have had enough, it's usually best to drop the issue, at least for the present.

If your battle is over some long-standing dispute (which is the case with many marital arguments!), you don't have to worry. Chances are you'll get back to it soon enough.

Don't nag or withdraw

When people feel they're getting nowhere in the same old argument, they sometimes resort to nagging. The main reason a person nags is because he or she can't get the spouse either to do something — or stop doing it. When the first round of nagging doesn't work, the natural reaction (although not a very logical one) is to nag even more intensely. This strategy is doomed to failure because the partner being nagged inevitably tunes out and withdraws from the situation.

Expressing frustration by tuning out or emotionally withdrawing from the argument doesn't work either, because the issues at hand have not been addressed. What you're left with is an impasse that is unsatisfying to both spouses.

When you find that any strategy has become counterproductive, the wisest course is to try a different one. The case of Lynn and Mark shows how couples can make this switch.

Lynn and Mark were embroiled in an ongoing battle over how to discipline their five-year-old daughter, Nancy. Lynn was angry that Mark seemed unable to say no to the little girl. Lynn was always cast as the bad guy and the naysayer. Even then, Nancy would go crying to her father, who would then say: "Let me try to talk Mom into it."

Lynn told Mark that she felt he was undermining her, but this had no effect. As a result, Lynn found herself constantly nagging her husband to be stricter with their child. "Why do you always give into her?" she would shriek. "How is she ever going to learn responsibility?"

Mark would nod his head, as if he was agreeing, but his behavior hadn't changed one iota. It seemed to Lynn that he had stopped listening and was agreeing just to shut her up. We suggested that Mark and Lynn take the following steps to work out their problem, steps that can help partners stop the cycle of nagging and withdrawing.

Face the fact that the current strategies are not productive. When things are working, there's no motivation to change. However, when your patterns of arguing are getting you nowhere, it's time to consider trying something else.

Lynn and Mark had been fighting the same battle since Nancy was a toddler. It had become apparent that their little dance of nagging and tuning out were not helping them resolve the problem. Even worse, their constant bickering — which sometimes took place in front of the child — was making them feel less affectionate toward each other.

Lynn and Mark agreed to sit down and talk about how they felt.

- ✔ Lynn: "I am hurt and upset because I can't seem to get across how strongly I feel about the way that we act with Nancy. I want to talk with you about these differences so that we can find a better way to deal with them."

- ✔ Mark: "I feel that she's going to be a little kid for a very short time. I want her to be able to enjoy those years without a lot of restrictions."

- ✔ Lynn: "So do I. But at the same time, I think it's important for Nancy to have limits."

Agree on a common goal and a strategy for achieving that goal. Arguments can begin to dissipate after spouses acknowledge that they have the same objective, even if they have different ideas about the best way to achieve that objective.

Lynn and Mark both loved their daughter. Both genuinely wanted to be good parents. They both realized how important it is for parents to be consistent in their dealings with a young child. After Lynn and Mark understood that their goals were the same, they were able to agree on the following game plan:

- ✔ Lynn would decide about matters concerning bedtime and responsibilities around the house; Mark would agree to support her decisions.

- ✔ Mark would have more of a say in deciding about weekend activities, and Lynn would respect that.

- ✔ If one parent disagreed with the other's decision, they would discuss the matter when the child wasn't in hearing distance.

- ✔ Lynn and Mark would periodically talk about how well this new approach was working, and try something else if it wasn't.

After a married couple puts an end to the pattern of nagging and withdrawing, they are much more likely to begin a constructive dialogue to address their differences. A couple like Mark and Lynn may never agree on the best way to raise their daughter, but at least they are no longer working at cross purposes.

Don't bring out the heavy artillery

Married partners generally know a great deal about each other's vulnerabilities and sore spots. One of the worst things you can do in the course of an argument is to attack your mate where he or she feels most unprotected. Likewise, it's a bad idea to bring up past sins or old fights that you've presumably resolved.

Threats of divorce can be especially devastating to the health of a marriage. You can always walk out or institute divorce proceedings if things get bad enough, but making these threats in the heat of an argument is always counterproductive.

Both of you took your marriage vows "for better or worse." If your marriage is solid, even bad arguments are likely to get better — if you and your spouse abide by the do's and don'ts of fair fighting.

Marital arguing: You just can't get away from it

A 65-year-old man came home one evening to find his wife of forty years packing.

"What do you think you're doing?" he growled.

"I can't stand all this bickering and fighting anymore," she cried. "I'm leaving."

The husband stood there watching as his wife began walking toward the door with her packed suitcase. Suddenly, he ran up to the bedroom and grabbed another suitcase from the closet.

"Wait a minute," the husband cried. "I can't stand it anymore either. I'm coming with you!"

Most married couples can't get away from their arguing — nor should they necessarily want to.

Part III
Making Marriage Sexy

The 5th Wave

By Rich Tennant

"When I asked you to put on some mood music, 'On Wisconsin' wasn't the mood I was going for."

In this part . . .

Good sex is key to a successful marriage. However, after a number of years, many couples complain that their sex life is tailing off. Having sex with your spouse is new for just so long, so you may have difficulty sustaining the excitement that you shared during the early stages of your relationship. Plus your daily responsibilities take up so much energy that sex sometimes gets pushed to the back burner.

In Chapter 6, we show you how to keep the sexual chemistry between the two of you alive. We give you techniques that help keep your children, work, and other distractions from ruining your intimate life. We then explore the destructive myths that often serve as barriers to good sex. In Chapter 7, we show you how to identify and deal with problems that cause sex to stall. We also explore the role of Viagra in treating sexual dysfunction, and help you recognize when sex therapy can be useful.

Chapter 6

Developing a Great Sex Life

Married couples often complain about a lack of "good sex" — or about having no sex at all. Wives and husbands often become upset when they find that they're having less and less intimate contact with each passing year of marriage. They recall a time when sex was passionate and frequent. But then, as they've settled into married life, everything else starts taking priority.

Career and financial demands are time-consuming, exhausting, and sense-dulling. The addition of children drains whatever bits of energy are left over, and take away the privacy of living as a couple. Good sex is harder than ever to come by, and sometimes seems in danger of disappearing altogether. Even more troubling is the feeling of becoming distant as a couple and having a lot less fun together — both in and out of bed.

In this chapter, we help you understand the expected changes in chemistry that married couples face, and show you how to make the most of them. We explore the special communication skills that can help you and your spouse improve your lovemaking. Finally, we deflate some of the myths that prevent wives and husbands from having great sex.

Understanding Changes in Sexual Chemistry

Lord make me chaste — but not yet.

— Saint Augustine

When two people are drawn together by a strong sexual attraction, a powerful force is unleashed: You wonder what making love with each other will be like, and the anticipation is delicious. When the time arrives, that sense of excitement and wonder can override the need for all other forms of communication.

As your relationship develops, sex may still be good — though perhaps a bit less intense than those first few weeks or months together. But, as you settle into married life, the passion and frequency of sex often begins to ebb. After as little as one or two years, those steamy first encounters may start to seem like a distant memory. However, you and your partner can explore new, more fulfilling sexual horizons, if you do the following:

- **Forget comparing your early sexual encounters to sex later in the marriage.** When two people really don't know each other, sex has an edge of excitement that can't possibly last. During the early stages of a relationship, lovers block out each other's flaws and quirks in order to heighten their romantic fantasies. But after they come down from this high, they begin seeing each other as ordinary human beings. One night, they suddenly discover that good sex is no longer automatic.

  This is a critical turning point in many marriages, because suddenly, sex requires more thought and effort. If a wife and husband recognize this transition as an opportunity for growth, they have a chance to take their sexual relationship to places they never imagined. But if they're not willing to talk about their needs or to negotiate ways to please each other, their sexual relationship will falter — and the marriage will suffer.

  Research shows that sexual desire and frequency of sex gradually level off in the majority of marriages. If you and your partner aren't having sex as often as you once did, that's normal. It doesn't mean that your marriage is heading downhill, and the two of you may be satisfied with having less sex. Don't worry if you're not living up to some kind of Hollywood standard of seductiveness or virility.

  A decrease in sexual frequency becomes a problem when one partner would like it more often than the other. The partner who wants more sex may feel suspicious or rejected, while the spouse who wants less may feel pressured or guilty. Too many excuses can kill your sex life. There's nothing wrong with telling your partner that you don't feel like making love — when you really don't. But, if that happens too often, both partners have to take a look at what's behind those excuses.

- **Take full advantage of the benefits married sex offers.** Marriage provides a level of closeness and comfort that more than compensates for the heat that both of you felt during those early sexual encounters. As you can become more intimate and increasingly secure with each other, you can become less inhibited and less anxious about expressing your deepest fantasies and sexual desires.

✓ **Stretch yourself.** A trick to maintaining good marital sex is to find a favorable balance between comfort and risk. One reason you still recall those early sexual experiences is that they gave you a sense of adventure and excitement that transported you outside the safe and comfortable limits of your everyday life. You can bring those elements of risk and uncertainty back into your sex life if you're willing to stretch yourself by trying something different.

Your marriage should be a safe place for experimenting sexually with your partner. The further you move out of your comfort zone — and the more often you do this — the more exciting your sex life will be. However, it's essential to find a risk/comfort level that you both feel good about.

Communicating Your Sexual Desires

Sex is hardly ever just about sex.

— Shirley Maclaine, actress

Sex has all sorts of meanings. Aside from being the way humans perpetuate the species, it's a physical release, a way of sharing love and commitment, and an opportunity to be creative. Sex is also a means of working through our fears and inhibitions — as well as a place where healing and growth take place.

From the viewpoint of pure physical release, masturbation is as satisfying as sexual intercourse. (The orgasms that result from masturbation are actually stronger.) However, sex needs a union of two people to achieve its greatest potential. When two individuals are drawn together by a strong physical attraction, sex between them is an urgent expression of blind desire. As these two people progress in their married life, sex is no longer automatic and cannot be taken for granted. To sustain an exciting and fulfilling sex life, they will have to develop effective communication skills.

In Chapter 4, we fully explore the principles of good communication in marriage, which also apply to your sex life. These skills include the following:

✓ Express your feelings using "I" statements.

✓ Listen to what your partner has to say.

✓ Negotiate solutions that address both your needs.

Communicating your sexual desires can be an especially delicate matter. People often feel vulnerable or embarrassed in this area. You may worry that, if you express your true needs and wants, you'll be rejected or hurt your partner's feelings.

Be sensitive when experimenting

If you're going to introduce a new wrinkle into your sex life, be sure to consider the meaning it may have to your partner.

Fifty-one-year-old Peggy and 56-year-old James came into therapy because, as Peggy put it, "Our sex life has died." She said that they hadn't had sex in about six months. James sheepishly admitted that was the time he started bringing home erotic videos and sex toys, and told Peggy that he wanted to incorporate them into their lovemaking. Peggy had just started going through menopause, and felt especially anxious about growing older and less attractive. She took James' suggestion as a personal affront — a sign that he no longer found her sexy.

"I was always able to excite James before," Peggy confided. "Suddenly, he wanted to bring all these props into our bedroom. I started wondering, 'What's wrong with me? How come I'm not enough for him anymore?'"

James was equally baffled. "I love Peggy as much as ever," he told us. "The videos and things are just to add a little variety."

We helped Peggy understand that James wanting to incorporate erotic material into their sex life wasn't a sign that his love for was her waning, or that he suddenly found her any less attractive.

We also helped James appreciate what his wife was going through. Peggy was an exceptionally beautiful woman, who had a great deal invested in her looks. She was still very attractive, but Peggy was worried about getting older. She was in the midst of a struggle to come to terms with the physical and emotional midlife changes we explore in Chapter 10. Suddenly, James walks in with a bunch of pornographic videos that feature sexy young models. We helped James understand that his approach wasn't especially tactful or sensitive to Peggy's needs at that time.

Embrace novelty as an effective way to maintain sexual excitement in a long-term relationship. The use of erotic materials and fantasy can be a real turn-on — if both partners are comfortable with how they are introduced and used in the context of lovemaking. When Peggy understood that James' desire for novelty wasn't a sign that he was losing interest in her, she was able to start accepting the use of erotic tapes in their lovemaking sessions.

You may not be able to stop yourself from feeling afraid of saying what you want, but you can minimize these fears by doing the following:

✔ **Talk first; worry later.** You have a much better chance of getting past your inhibitions if you talk about your needs and desires with your partner, instead of trying to sort them out on your own. You may have to force yourself to take this riskier approach. But the more you open up, the easier talking becomes.

Talk directly to your partner about all important matters, especially something as vital as sex. Even if you and your spouse know each other well, you may be clueless about what your spouse is thinking and feeling. You can use two ways to find out these vital pieces of information:

- **Talking:** Be as clear as you can about what you want your partner to do. For example, tell him or her where you want to be touched, how hard or softly you want to be touched, and how fast or slowly you want your partner to proceed.

  Always express yourself using positive, first-person statements. For example, instead of saying, "You're much too rough," say "I get so excited when you kiss me softly." When you use positive, first-person statements, you let your partner know what you want, in a non-threatening way.

- **Showing:** You can show your partner how you want to be touched in a variety of ways. For example, after you've asked him to kiss you gently on the back of your neck, go ahead and kiss him exactly as you want to be kissed.

  You can also show your partner what you want by demonstrating the rhythms and types of stimulation you enjoy on yourself, and encouraging him to add those moves to his sexual bag of erotic tricks.

Verbal responses during sex are a kind of bridge between telling and showing. Most women and men are turned on by their partner talking about how good they feel — and enhancing that message with sighs and other sounds of pleasure.

✔ **Don't expect the two of you to always be in synch.** It's great when you both want to have sex at the same time, and both feel the same level of desire. That may happen occasionally, but you're being unrealistic when you expect it on a regular basis.

Each of you has a separate mechanism that activates your sex drive. Gender differences and other biological differences come into play, along with variations in mood and energy level at any given time. Good communication can help you iron out these incompatibilities. If you honestly let each other know how you're feeling, and if you're willing to accept each other's differences, you can work at finding a meeting ground where both of you can come away satisfied.

✔ **Negotiate and compromise to find a balance that works for both of you.** Meeting in the middle can be a tall order — especially if your sexual needs and desires are on the opposite ends of the spectrum. However, as long as no one is angry or bitter, most married couples can negotiate a solution that makes both partners happy.

Sex doesn't always have to be a 50/50 proposition. If your spouse is in the mood and you're not, why not find some way to please him or her? There are many ways to do it besides sexual intercourse. Most people derive as much satisfaction from giving their partner pleasure as they do from receiving it. Plus, your spouse is more likely to return the favor some night when you're in the mood and he or she isn't.

Breaking Down Three Major Roadblocks to Good Sex

There will be sex after death. We just won't be able to feel it.

— Lily Tomlin, actress

Married couples have unsatisfying sex for any number of reasons. One of the partners may be depressed or suffering from a physical dysfunction or the side effects of a medication. However, many of the problems that interfere with the sex lives of married couples stem from the choices they make, or are reactions to the strains of daily living. The following sections discuss three of the most common barriers to good sex.

Children

Comedians joke about the sex life of parents with small children. "What sex life?" they ask. Despite the wisecracks, physical intimacy can remain exciting and satisfying, even with babies or young kids at home. However, it does require planning and effort to adjust to the various phases of parenting.

Having a child

The addition of baby to the family can put a temporary halt to your sex life. Sex may be physically impossible for a woman in the last weeks of her pregnancy and the first weeks after childbirth. Newborns also need lots of care, and new mothers are prone to devote all their attention to the baby. Fathers end up becoming jealous, though they're often embarrassed to admit that they feel competitive with their own baby for their wife's attention. So, they sulk or get angry. As frustrated as they feel, sex is usually the last thing those new parents talk about.

Some new fathers have also confided that they have trouble making love with their wives after watching the birth of their baby — but these feelings usually fade after a few months. Many couples find it convenient to have the baby sleep with them for the first few months (a practice that some experts now believe is dangerous), and this can also put a temporary crimp in a couple's sex life.

You may experience a wide range of unfamiliar feelings after a baby enters your home — and these can take a toll on your marriage and your sex life. However, you can help regain some balance by doing the following:

- **Talk to each other about your mixed feelings — and the impact they have on your desire for sex.** This kind of give and take helps you understand what your partner is going through, and will diffuse much of the tension between you.

- **Share the responsibilities for childcare.** Aside from breast feeding, fathers can do everything that mothers can do for their babies.

   Most men enjoy participating in caring for a baby — and the shared responsibility often brings couples closer together. However, many men need to be invited by their wives. Research shows that both partners are happier when husbands share in childrearing and housework.

Raising a child

Raising young children presents a different set of challenges. Toddlers and preschoolers can be more emotionally demanding than babies — despite their growing physical independence. They can also hurt your sex life in a number of ways. Children of this age are aware of what's going on, so you have to be more quiet and discrete when you have sex. You may also find that much of your life centers around the kids. That's fine, as long as you make time for the two of you to be alone.

The following are some ways you can accomplish that:

- **Find something to do each day that doesn't include the kids.** Some couples like to take walks. Others enjoy hanging out and talking about their day. If you can't find someone to watch your kids while you're alone, schedule something they can do that doesn't require your attention.

   The point of spending time alone together isn't to give you time to sneak in a quickie. It's to give you a chance to simply be together and remember that you're still a couple. Then, when you finally do make love, you won't feel like complete strangers.

- **Get away for an evening or night together at least once a month.** This is an important step for maintaining a good sex life. As you become a family of three, four, or more, you may begin to lose touch with your spouse. A night spent alone in a nearby hotel or at a bed and breakfast can reinvigorate your spirits — and your sex life.

   Many couples have difficulty spending a night away from home without the kids. However, with careful planning, you can usually find a way to be alone. Perhaps you can leave the kids with a relative or a friend. Or, maybe you can hire someone reliable to spend the night at your place. If once a month is too much, make it every six or eight weeks — just get away as often as you possibly can.

Stress and marital tensions

The sexual organs are the true seat of the will, of which the opposite pole is the brain.

— Arthur Schopenhauer, philosopher

Anger and tension between spouses is probably the single, most important barrier to good sex. Anger is often not overtly verbalized, but is communicated through a lack of desire or indifference to lovemaking. Fear of becoming too close or dependent on your spouse can also inhibit desire. If one spouse feels a lack of interest in being sexually intimate, both partners need to look at the meaning behind these feelings. (See Chapter 4 for advice on communicating with your partner. Take a look at Chapter 16 for assistance in getting outside help.)

Modern life is stressful, even when the two of you are getting along. Household responsibilities, financial pressures, and problems at work can wreck your sex life.

If you think your partner is stressed-out, try talking to him or her, and trying to find out what the problem is. Say, "I get the feeling that you're very tense. If you tell me what's wrong, maybe I can help." Listen with empathy and offer support. Don't push for an answer — and don't aggressively pursue having sex, at least not intercourse.

Touching always works to relieve stress. Try giving him a backrub or a spontaneous massage — or ask if she'd find a bubble bath relaxing. These very basic soothing techniques are big sexual turn-ons.

Workaholism

While a person does not give up on sex, sex does not give up on the person.

— Gabriel Marquez, author

People need to work hard in order to keep pace in a culture obsessed with success and money. And you have to spend lots of money to run a household, even if you don't have kids. But today, a growing number of people are living to work instead of working to live — and that has had a devastating effect on marital sex.

Marriage theorist Betty Carter finds that many dual-career couples have stopped having sex completely. They are so career-oriented and overextended in their lives that sex has virtually dropped off their priority list.

In her book, *Resiliency*, psychotherapist Dee Barlow observes that, "[Sex] and workaholism are mutually exclusive. Success and power provide a buzz that, for some couples, becomes a substitute for sexual excitement. Pretty soon, a downward spiral begins: The less frequently spouses make love, the less sexual they feel toward each other, the less they want to make love."

The concept of an upward or downward spiral is key to understanding the progression of sex in marriage. A couple can build on a few good nights of excellent lovemaking. But when partners fall into a pattern of rarely having sex — things usually go downhill. Sometimes the only way to avoid this kind of downward cycle in your marriage is by actually scheduling sex. When overwork is the primary reason for not having sex, the most effective treatment is to pencil special times for lovemaking in your schedule.

People usually don't have to be reminded to do other pleasurable things — particularly if they are based on normal biological drives — like eating and drinking. However, not having sex has become a similar to another recent epidemic — not sleeping. Married people often complain that they're too busy to sleep. "How am I supposed to sleep?" they ask. "I work sixty-five hours a week. Plus, there's all those things I have to do around the house. I'm getting three hours of sleep a night, and that's actually more time than I can afford."

Any system that you constantly neglect will eventually shut down. For example, it's okay to pull an occasional all-nighter to meet a deadline. But, if you are always sleep-deprived, your sleep mechanism will no longer function normally. The same goes for sex. If you allow sex to completely fade out of your marriage, that mechanism begins to shut down too.

Understanding Why People Don't Know What to Expect from Sex

Whoever called it necking was a poor judge of anatomy.

— Groucho Marx, actor and comedian

Most people are exposed to a wide variety of sexual images from the time they're very young.

- First, you may get an impression of your parents' sex life from their overall relationship. Then, throw in whatever they choose to tell you about sex. When kids first find out about "the birds and the bees," they're sometimes shocked by the realization that their parents actually did *it* too!

- Kids also realize that people do *it* on television — a place where advertisers and programmers manipulate sexual images to press viewers' hot buttons. The goal: gaining a larger audience share and selling products. Painting a true picture of sex is the last thing the entertainment industry wants to do.

✔ Things get even more complicated when the child attends religious services. There, yet another version of sex is delivered — a version that's bound to be at odds with most of the other things that child has seen and heard.

✔ With all the talk in school and on TV about childhood sexual abuse, children may get confused about whom they can trust. Unfortunately, sexual abuse is much more common than we used to believe, and children often know friends or classmates who have been victimized.

✔ The first real testing ground for this complex mixture of fact, fiction, and moral dogma takes place among peers. Young people bounce around these conflicting sexual images and expectations, and sometimes take them for a test drive.

All of these sexual images are part of the baggage that many people carry into marriage. Often, it needs to be unpacked and repacked (or thrown out) before a couple can even begin to understand what true sexual fulfillment is all about. Through a certain amount of work and rethinking, most men and women can sort out the myths and inconsistencies on their own or with each other. Some couples need professional help to reframe their confused images of sex.

Stop comparing your sex life to what you see in films or on television. People who do that are guaranteed to fall short and feel inadequate. Real sex almost never lives up to the way it's depicted in the movies — not even the sex you have on your honeymoon or on that first night of ecstasy. Real sex can be luscious, but its joys are far more subtle and enduring than manufactured Hollywood fantasies.

Deflating Five Common Sex Myths

Women complain about sex more often than men. Their gripes fall into two major categories: 1) Not enough 2) Too much.

— Ann Landers, advice columnist

Many myths about sex are repeated so often that people accept them without question. Some of these beliefs are harmless. Others can affect one or both partners' abilities to have good sex — and wind up taking the joy out of a marriage.

We want to correct those misconceptions — and replace them with the truths that can help you reap the joy and satisfaction that good marital sex has to offer.

The real deal on marital sex and lovemaking

Here's an unusual description of marital sex that we recently came across in *The Guide To Getting It On!* by Paul Joannides. We think it's right on the money:

"There are a lot of wonderful dimensions to sex besides just huffing and puffing while the bedsprings squeak. Sharing sex with a partner allows you to discover where the different emotions are stored in each other's bodies, where the hopes and dreams are hidden, where the laughter and pain reside, and what it takes to free the fun, passion, and hidden kink. To achieve that level of sharing, you have to take the time to know someone, to feel what they are feeling, to see the world through their eyes, and to let a partner discover who you are in ways that may leave you feeling wonderful.

"Granted, there will be plenty of times when all you want from sex is a quick jolt of sensation, but if that's all you ever expect from sex, then you may be coming up a bit short."

Men are more interested in sex than are women

One of the most pervasive myths is that men use love to get sex, while women use sex to get love. The truth is that women are as much into the physical enjoyment of sex as are men. However, certain physical and psychological differences exist between women and men that make sexual intercourse a different experience for each of them.

"A woman lets a man enter her — she lets him in," observes Ona Robinson, a New York-based psychotherapist who specializes in women's issues. "That is much more profound than what a man experiences — because the process takes place inside her. Also, a woman's sexual organs are hidden, while a man's are exposed. That means that a woman cannot see directly the parts of her body from which she is deriving pleasure. This also implies a greater need for trust."

Men are more easily aroused than women, so women need to take longer before they're ready for intercourse. Women readily get turned on by attractive men, but they are socialized to hide feelings of easy arousal. For men, the ability to get a quick erection is a sign of masculinity, and something to brag about.

Married people don't (or shouldn't) masturbate

It took a while for the news to come out of the closet, but we now know that masturbation is practiced by most husbands and a large number of wives. According to one study, the more highly educated a woman is, the more likely she is to masturbate.

Most men arouse themselves through fantasies — sometimes supplemented by explicit pictures or videos. In general, men don't require props and toys, though they may use a bit of Vaseline or baby oil as a lubricant.

Women also pleasure themselves with their hands, but they are more prone to use vibrators and other props to enhance the response. Psychologist Lonnie Barbach, who has done studies on female masturbation, talks about women who have orgasms during physical activities like rope-climbing or rubbing up against chairs.

We encourage husbands and wives to masturbate in any way that gives them pleasure, because it's totally safe and always available. Masturbation has many side benefits, including the following:

- A great way to explore your body
- An effective way to get aroused
- A clear method of showing your partner what you want him or her to do
- A good form of release when you're partner's not around or doesn't want to have sex
- A supplement to sexual intercourse, either before or after intercourse itself

Sex therapist Lonnie Barbach suggests that women enhance their enjoyment of intercourse by manually stimulating the clitoris and the outside of the vulva or labia during sex, or asking their partner to do it. (*Sex For Dummies* by Ruth Westheimer [IDG Books Worldwide, Inc.] is an excellent resource for this topic and for many other areas that we discuss in this chapter and in Chapter 7.)

Foreplay is a separate part of the sexual experience

This is one of the more controversial myths, partly because men need a lot less time to get ready for sex than do women. If you look at sex as simply the literal act of intercourse, you completely miss the point. As Paul Joannides so aptly puts it in *The Guide To Getting It On!:*

"There's usually more to a good sexual experience than the simple hydraulics of sticking hard into wet. For some people, what separates the good sexual memories from the bad are intangibles like fun, friendship, love, and caring."

Think of lovemaking like a complete meal. When you go to a good restaurant, don't you consider the appetizer, the salad, and the desert important parts of the total experience? Have you ever had a meal consisting of two appetizers, or just soup and dessert? The steak may be the main course, but it's only one part of the meal — and not necessarily the best part.

Sex isn't simply a matter of doing *it*. Everything you do to lead up to that moment, as well as the things you do afterwards, are equally valuable parts of the total experience. On certain nights, the two of you may only want to cuddle and kiss — without having intercourse. On other nights, you may experiment with several positions during intercourse, and bypass kissing and cuddling altogether. Whatever the two of you do that gives you pleasure and draws you closer are important components of lovemaking.

There's a difference between clitoral and vaginal orgasms

Research shows that there's only one kind of orgasm: It involves stimulation of the clitoris (or some other sensitive part of the woman's body, such as her breasts or her thighs), with the response taking place in the entire vagina. The clitoris (or the breast) is the stimulus loop and the vaginal orgasm is the response loop — but the whole process takes place in one circuit.

You can blame Sigmund Freud for starting this myth of clitoral versus vaginal orgasms. It has continued to detour and confuse generations of women who worried that they weren't having the "right kind of orgasm."

It's important for women (and their partners) to be aware of what contributes to their climax. These can be very subtle conditions, including colors, smells, types of touches — as well as different physical and emotional states. Contrary to popular belief, though, penis size doesn't matter. A man sometimes fears that his wife won't achieve orgasm because his penis isn't large enough. In fact, penis size has no relation to a man's ability to pleasure a woman — even while having intercourse. With most couples, it's the position and the degree of contact that counts, as well as everything that leads up to the intercourse experience. In any case, studies show that most women prefer an average-sized penis to one that is very large.

Travels through the orgasmic crescent

In her book, *Are We Having Fun Yet? The Intelligent Woman's Guide to Sex,* psychologist Lisa Douglass reports that women achieve maximum pleasure when all three parts of the so-called orgasmic crescent are stimulated. The orgasmic crescent is a curved area that extends from the tip of the clitoris across the urethral opening (the *U-spot*), and then inside the vagina to the *G-spot* — a small erotic area in the front wall of the vagina.

To locate your G-Spot, push up about two inches into your vagina with your finger until you feel an area that begins to swell. The G-spot can be stimulated through masturbation or through any intercourse position that delivers direct pressure from the penis.

Many women are skeptical about the whole concept of the G-Spot, and doubt that it even exists. However, even women who have trouble finding the G-spot report that just probing around for it gives a sensation that contributes to fantastic orgasms, so it's worth a try. Don't be alarmed if you feel some fluid in the vagina; that's the result of what's been called *female ejaculation,* and it's perfectly normal.

If you're a woman, talk to your husband about how he can help you achieve an orgasm, so that he can understand what's involved in bringing you to climax. Most men mean well, but they are woefully ignorant of female anatomy, and they really don't know what to do. Your husband may see it as his job to give you an orgasm — men are often more result-oriented than women. Unfortunately, this kind of determination usually ends up backfiring. You may start out not even caring whether you have an orgasm. However, as you sense anxiety on the part of your husband, you may become too worried and distracted to enjoy yourself.

Using their fingers and their mouths is a great way for husbands to help their wives achieve orgasm. It takes the emphasis off sustaining an erection. Plus, it's a sexual activity that many men enjoy.

It's not uncommon for wives to fake an orgasm, so that husbands won't feel like they've failed. Consequently, the night ends with both partners feeling disappointed and frustrated.

Sex fades as a couple ages

The truth is, healthy women and men who are free from debilitating physical and mental illness can have sex well into old age. Unfortunately, Western culture is so obsessed with youth, that the myth that older people don't want or need sex gets carried out in cruel ways. For example, nursing homes have rules prohibiting sexual contact between competent older men and women.

It's as if these institutions were dealing with teenagers in boarding schools, where there's a risk of getting pregnant. The grownup children who place their folks in nursing homes don't want to think about their parents doing *it.* The administrators figure they will have an easier time keeping order if the residents aren't allowed to have sex.

While some older men and women find their sexual desire waning, many people in their 60s, 70s, 80s, and beyond are anything but asexual. They may have more difficulty getting aroused or need more time to reach orgasm. However, this can actually be an advantage because it leads to longer love-making sessions.

When older people do have sexual problems, usually the cause is not aging itself, but age-related illness. For example, older people have more diabetes and more hypertension and more depression. Both the illness and the medications to treat the illnesses interfere with sexual desire and performance.

There's a big difference between losing your youthful sex appeal and losing your sex drive. Over 75 percent of menopausal women experience as much — or more — sexual satisfaction than they did when they were younger. See Chapter 11 for more information.

If you continue working at keeping good sex alive in your relationship, the joy can continue unabated. As the years go by, there are bound to be changes in the ways you get pleasure from each other. But, for the most part, these changes are part of the process that makes it possible for wives and husbands in long-term, monogamous relationships to have great sex indefinitely.

Chapter 7

When Sex Falters

* *

In This Chapter

▶ Recognizing relationship problems that show up in sex

▶ Increasing sexual compatibility between you and your partner

▶ Making the most of fantasies and sexual enhancements

▶ Identifying and dealing with sexual problems

▶ Understanding the role of Viagra and other medications

* *

*W*hen sexual intimacy between you and your spouse stalls, you may be experiencing differences about the type and frequency of sex each partner wants (see Chapter 6 for more information), or you may have serious marital conflicts that have nothing directly to do with sex (see Chapter 3). It's also possible that one of the partners is having a physical or emotional problem with sexual functioning.

In this chapter, we explore the different reasons why sex between married partners can falter. We offer techniques to help couples turn around an unhappy sex life, and start enjoying each other again. We also help you understand when it's time to seek the advice of a couples or sex therapist.

Recognizing Potential Blocks to Sexual Pleasure

> *After forty years, my wife and I finally reached total sexual compatibility. We both had a headache.*
>
> — Milton Berle, comedian

When problems come up in a marriage, the first thing to do is to pinpoint their exact cause. This section offers remedies for different sexual problems — depending on the source and the nature of the underlying issue.

If your interest — or your spouse's interest — in making love has decreased noticeably, you may start by asking yourself the following questions:

✔ **Does either partner have a medical problem?** Men and women often beat themselves up because of diminished sexual desire or ability to perform. Many of these problems are related to stress and other emotional issues, especially undiagnosed depression. However, a significant percentage of sexual difficulties is partially or fully based on chronic medical illnesses and the medications that are used to treat them. (Often the medications do more harm to you: sex life than the illnesses themselves.) Some of the most common physical conditions include the following:

- Diabetes

- Arthritis

- Hypertension

- Cardiovascular disease

- Breathing problems

- Obesity

- Endocrine disease, especially thyroid problems

- Prostate disease

- Gynecologic problems, including hysterectomy

- Neurologic disorders like Parkinson's

- Infertility and its treatment

- Disfiguring surgeries (for example, mastectomy)

- Cancer and the effects of chemotherapy and radiation

Women are more likely than men to have their sexual health problems misdiagnosed. Studies show that women's sexual dysfunctions aren't nearly as well understood as men's — even though they are just as common, if not more so.

✔ **Does either partner have a problem with clinical depression or anxiety?** Even if your doctor gives you a clean bill of health, you may be suffering from an emotional problem he or she is unable to diagnose.

The line between normal changes in mood and mental illness isn't always easy to distinguish. However, if you or your spouse has noticed significant changes in your energy level, motivation, or sleeping or eating habits, consult with a psychiatrist or another mental health professional. He or she can rule out or diagnose clinical depression or some other emotional condition that can affect your sexual desire or performance. Turn to Chapter 16 for more information on the treatment of clinical depression.

✔ **Has either partner been under an unusual amount of pressure?**
Financial, family, or career-related stress can drain your sexual energy, and throw all your systems into turmoil. Your boss may be the one who's giving you grief — not your spouse. Still, stressed out spouses tend to blame their partners, and even avoid them. Sex with your partner can help relieve some of those tensions, not make them worse. However, you'll need to reach out and talk to him or her about what's bothering you.

✔ **Has either partner started on a new medication?** Prescription drugs are one of the major causes of sexual dysfunction in both men and women. Millions of people have medicine-related sexual dysfunction, but often don't connect the medication to their problems. Over one hundred drugs can cause sexual dysfunction in a significant number of patients. These include most blood pressure medications, anti-depressants like Prozac or Zoloft, diabetes medications, and even stomach remedies like Tagamet, which can now be obtained without a prescription.

Patients often feel embarrassed to discuss their sex life, even with their physicians, and doctors often shy away from asking sex-related questions. Make the effort to talk to your doctor about all the prescription medications you're taking, and find out if any of them includes sexual dysfunction as a possible side effect. If so, ask your doctor to lower the dosage or give you an alternate medicine that won't hinder sex.

✔ **Is either partner drinking too much or using drugs?** William Shakespeare was right when he observed that alcohol increases the desire, but decreases the performance. By loosening inhibitions, small amounts of liquor can enhance sexual desire. However, alcohol is a central nervous system depressant, so moderate to large amounts of alcohol will ultimately decrease your ability to perform.

If you want to use alcohol to relax or put you in the mood for sex, limit your consumption to no more than one or two drinks. If you have a history of problem drinking, the use of any alcohol will destroy sexual performance.

Most illegal and prescription drugs diminish sex. Narcotics, such as heroin and pain medication, tend to shut down your sex drive altogether. Even drugs like cocaine and amphetamines, which have a reputation for boosting sexual desire, ultimately decrease your ability to perform sexually.

Understanding the Causes and Treatments of Sexual Dysfunction

Sex is like a language. Some of us can converse just enough to get along, like travelers in a foreign land. . . . Some of us . . . are poets.

— David Schnarch, psychologist and sex therapist

The scientific study of sexual dysfunction was pioneered by William Masters and Virginia Johnson, who published the book, *Human Sexual Response* in 1966. Before their landmark work, sexual problems were seen in purely emotional or psychological terms. Freud and his followers believed that men and women had difficulty performing sexually because of emotional problems that were carried over from childhood. On the other hand, therapists who dealt with married couples viewed virtually all sexual dysfunctions as symptoms of problems in the relationship.

No one doubts that developmental and relationship problems can cause sex to falter. However, Masters and Johnson demonstrated that even couples who have a good marriage, in which both individuals have no significant psychological hang-ups, can still have all kinds of sexual problems. On the other hand, a couple in which one or both partners have significant emotional problems or are in a painful relationship, is often able to maintain a functional and pleasurable sex life.

Masters and Johnson put men and women in a room and filmed them having sex. They measured such unsexy biological functions as their subjects' heart rate and blood pressure, as well as sexual functions like how long each woman's vagina took to become lubricated, how long before each man's penis became hard, and the speed and quantity of the ejaculate as it left each man's penis.

Masters and Johnson broke down the sexual response cycle into specific phases, and found that people generally have sexual problems directly related to one or more of these phases. Their model was then modified by sex therapist Helen Singer Kaplan, who added a psychological dimension and came up with a triphasic system — desire, arousal, and orgasm — for categorizing sexual problems. This system is currently used by doctors and other therapists to design treatment plans for people with sexual dysfuctions. The following sections discuss these three phases.

Problems with sexual desire

People who experience so-called sexual desire disorders generally don't have a physical problem. In most of these cases, one or both partners come into therapy voicing one of the following complaints:

- ✔ She (or he) doesn't turn me on.
- ✔ I don't seem to excite him (or her) any longer.
- ✔ We rarely have sex anymore.

In some cases of sexual desire disorder, underlying problems exist in the relationship — or one of the partners is having a personal crisis. The following are some of the questions we ask when people complain about a lack of desire:

✔ **Is the partner who seems uninterested having an affair?** If so, infidelity is probably the real culprit, as opposed to a true sexual dysfunction. Unless the unfaithful partner acknowledges the infidelity, the therapeutic process will come to a dead halt. (See Chapter 15 for a complete discussion on what to do if your partner is having an affair.)

✔ **Is the partner who lacks desire secretly homosexual?** If the dysfunctional partner is really not interested in members of the opposite sex, the problem will be next-to-impossible to resolve. Some people with latent homosexual desires don't admit these feelings even to themselves, and wind up leading asexual lives.

✔ **Is there unexpressed anger or serious conflict in the relationship?** Relationship problems may be expressed by a lack of desire. Before sexual issues can be addressed, a couple must first deal with the underlying tension and anger. In Chapter 5, we explore the techniques that you need to do that.

✔ **Is there a marked discrepancy in sexual desire?** In many marriages, one partner wants to have sex a lot more often than the other. These differences about how often to have sex are often misinterpreted as rejection.

Assuming the relationship is fundamentally solid and that the partners genuinely care for each other, but you or your spouse still has a lack of desire, we suggest trying the following techniques:

✔ **Be sensuous with each other.** Instead of pressuring yourself and your partner to have sexual intercourse, start to rediscover each other on both a physical and emotional level. Show affection by gently touching or kissing your partner at unexpected moments. Give each other backrubs and massages — and let one another know the kinds of touches you enjoy most. This kind of contact feels good, and you never know where it may lead.

Research shows that hugs and other sensuous touches help increase endorphin levels. The higher these levels, the more pleasure your body will embrace.

✔ **Fantasize about someone else.** If the thought of having sex with your partner isn't all that enticing, maybe picturing yourself with someone else will do the trick. A sexy TV star, a steamy porn film that you've seen, or thinking about an ex-lover may be enough to get you started. We suggest using any or all of these images to increase your desire.

Fantasizing is not cheating on your husband or wife. You have a right to let your imagination go in any direction it wants — and so does your partner. In fact, some couples enjoy sharing their fantasies with each other.

✔ **Hold hands or make out like you used to do, even if you don't feel much lust.** Often, behavior leads to excitement, not the other way around. Besides, it's fun, and we promise that you won't get arrested.

Problems with sexual arousal

If it were weren't for pickpockets, I'd have no sex life at all.

— Rodney Dangerfield, actor and comedian

People with sexual arousal disorders have plenty of desire. The problem is physical functioning.

For men

The most common form of sexual arousal disorder for men is called *erectile disorder* or *impotence*. The guy wants sex, but he either can't get an erection or he can't keep the erection long enough to have an orgasm. The two main reasons for erectile disorder stem from age-related medical problems and performance anxiety.

✔ Almost half of men's erection problems have physical causes, ranging from diabetes to prostate conditions to years of cigarette smoking that have resulted in constricted blood vessels. Have a complete physical checkup so that your doctor can treat any underlying medical conditions that may be contributing to your symptoms.

✔ Research shows that healthy men can have good erections well into old age — although with age, erections don't come as rapidly or as firmly as they once did. Older men and their partners who take a relaxed approach to this evolutionary process sometimes discover that this "problem" can be an advantage, because it leads to longer lovemaking sessions. For this to happen, both partners must gradually adjust their pacing, and enjoy spending more time in bed.

✔ Men may develop performance anxiety after they fail to have an erection a few times during sex. These incidents lead to a vicious cycle in which the man gets so uptight about failing again that it becomes a self-fulfilling prophecy. The harder he tries, the softer he becomes.

There are a number of effective techniques for dealing with erectile dysfunction. These include the following:

✔ **Take the emphasis off sexual intercourse.** Concentrate, instead, on enjoying the process. Many men have trouble realizing that sex isn't a performance. The goal is supposed to be enjoyment.

A better way to look at foreplay

Steve: When married couples begin to lose interest in each other, that's the time to become more creative with foreplay.

Sue: Good idea, but, when you think about it, there's really no such things as foreplay. Anything you do in lovemaking is part of the experience.

Steve: As long as it leads to intercourse!

Sue: Now there's a typical male point of view. It really doesn't matter whether or not you have intercourse. It's whatever gives you pleasure.

Steve: Just kidding.

If a man has a performance-related problem getting or keeping an erection, the less focus he places on it, and the more likely it is to happen by itself. A man can be a good lover, even if he doesn't get an erection or have sexual intercourse. He can please his partner by using his hand, his mouth, or a vibrator to bring her to orgasm. Many women actually prefer a hand or tongue to a penis. In any case, if a couple can find a way to have a pleasurable experience that doesn't pressure the man to have an erection, everybody wins. The wife is sexually satisfied, and the husband doesn't end up feeling like a failure.

✔ **Use sensate focus exercises.** This is the most important tool that many sex therapists use. *Sensate focus* is a non-demanding, non-pressured situation in which the couple uses sexual and erotic mutual stimulation. Both partners take turns making each other feel good. Pleasure is the goal, rather than achievement of erection or orgasm. Becoming familiar with each other's bodies — not getting turned on — is the purpose of the sensate focus exercise. Intercourse is off limits. Quite frequently, though, erections come by themselves when you least expect them, and masturbation is okay when the exercise is over.

✔ **Consider using Viagra.** All sorts of remedies and devices have been developed to deal with male erectile dysfunction: penile implants, vacuum pumps, and countless prescription drugs and herbal remedies. Some of these methods have had limited success. But in 1998, Viagra was approved for use in treating male erectile dysfunction — and the results have been dramatic.

Viagra works, no matter what the cause of a man's erectile disorder, as long as the desire is there. Viagra will help a man get hard if he's diabetic, if he's had prostate surgery, if he's aging, or if his problem is performance-based. Viagra increases blood flow into the penis and keeps it there, and that's what gives a man an erection.

We've treated a number of men who've told us that their marriages were saved by Viagra. "I always loved my wife," one said, "but I felt so inadequate because I couldn't get it up. Now that I can perform, I feel better about myself, my wife feels better about me, and our marriage is back on track."

Viagra isn't for everybody; nor is it a panacea. Viagra is not advised for men with certain kinds of heart problems. Also, it's not an aphrodisiac — although lots of men (and women) try to obtain it for this purpose. Viagra does only one thing — it enables men to get and sustain an erection.

For women

The difference between pornography and erotica is lighting.

— Gloria Leonard, adult entertainment artist

A woman's problems with sexual arousal often aren't as obvious as a man's. However, the physical process is similar. A woman needs a sufficient blood flow to her vagina to lubricate, just as a man requires sufficient blood flow for his penis to get hard.

Much of the research on women's arousal problems has focused on age-related issues. When a woman reaches menopause, it takes longer for her to lubricate. Her vagina is also likely to be dryer because of the decrease in estrogen.

The physical components of aging play an important role in arousal problems for women. However, there is often an emotional component, too. For example, sex therapist Lonnie Barbach finds that women who never enjoyed sex very much in the first place sometimes use menopause as an excuse to abandon sexual activity altogether.

Fortunately, women of any age who want to be aroused can do so by using the following techniques:

- ✔ **Give yourself a head start.** Masturbation either before or during sex with your partner is helpful in several ways. It gives you pleasure, and gives him clues about how he can arouse and pleasure you. In addition, studies show that women who masturbate regularly achieve better vaginal lubrication.

- ✔ **Create a sensual environment.** The mind is your most important sex organ, so you need to surround yourself with cues that remind you of good lovemaking. Is there a certain song that you find sexy? A type of scented candle that puts you in the mood? A piece of clothing that feels delicious against your body? Try to think of things that turn you on. Don't hesitate to use any combination of mood enhancements that works for you.

Investigate whether Viagra can help. Although the research is not complete, evidence now shows that Viagra helps some women who have arousal problems. It's worth talking to your doctor about it.

✔ **Negotiate differences in pacing with your partner.** Men can often be aroused much faster than women. Research shows that a man can get hard and have an orgasm in five to ten minutes. However, it takes more time than that for most women to even begin to get aroused. In fact, some studies suggest that many women need at least thirty minutes to become fully lubricated.

There's room in a marriage for different speeds and styles of lovemaking:

- **The quickie:** Men often prefer the *quickie* (which lasts less than 5 or 10 minutes), because they don't need as much time as women to get fully involved in the lovemaking experience. This type of sex is comparable to a fast-food meal.

- **Everyday sex:** This type of sex takes roughly half an hour, and (hopefully) accommodates both partner's needs. This is comparable to a nice, but standard dinner that you prepare at home.

- **Gourmet sex:** John Gray, author of *Men are from Mars; Women are from Venus* coined the term "gourmet sex." In this scenario, the couple takes a lot of time to make leisurely, romantic love — which is often more well-suited to the woman's physiology and temperament. This type of lovemaking is comparable to a long, delicious dinner at a fine restaurant.

You and your partner will have to negotiate differences about what kind of sex to have and when. This process is much like the one you use to work out other conflicts, which we explore in Chapter 4.

As her husband, you can do the following:

✔ **Encourage your wife to relax and let her know that she doesn't have to rush.** Tell her that you don't expect her to have an orgasm for your sake. As long as she's feeling pleasure, that's great.

✔ **Don't just head for the vagina.** Explore the rest of her body — all of it — with your hands and your mouth.

✔ **Suggest you'd like to give her oral sex.** Some women are afraid to ask because they're fear it will be a turn-off for their husbands. Most men love it.

Problems reaching orgasm

People with orgasmic disorders have lots of interest and desire for sex. They have no trouble getting aroused, having an erection, or becoming lubricated. The problem is an orgasm which comes too soon, too late, or not at all.

For men

Sex is like bridge: If you don't have a good partner, you better have a good hand.

— Charles Pierce, entertainer

When men have trouble achieving orgasm, the condition is called *delayed ejaculation* or *retarded ejaculation*. This is sometimes caused by a physical problem or a medication side effect. Psychological causes include fear of losing control, fear of becoming too excited, or withholding because of anger toward the partner. The most common group of medications that inhibit orgasm are the newer antidepressants, such as Prozac, Zoloft, and Paxil.

The following techniques can help men who have trouble reaching orgasm:

- ✔ **Focus on the experience — not the orgasm.** This is the basic rule for all men and women who have difficulty with orgasm — pay attention to the sensation, not the outcome.

- ✔ **Alternate masturbation with intercourse.** This can be a helpful exercise for men with delayed orgasm — especially if you reach orgasm more easily by masturbating.

- ✔ **Don't push too hard or too fast.** Men who have problems achieving orgasm often become anxious and start thrusting harder and faster. This tends to have the opposite effect and slows down orgasm even more, because the penis becomes numb after a while.

Premature ejaculation is an even more common male orgasm problem, particularly with young men. Here, the man reaches climax the minute his partner touches his penis, or as he attempts to enter her vagina. This condition is embarrassing and unsatisfying to the man, because his anxiety has gotten too far out in front of his desire. It's also unsatisfying to the woman, who may not even have begun to be aroused.

June Reinisch, director emeritus of the Kinsey Institute and author of *The Kinsey Institute New Report on Sex* believes that the problem is a remnant of ejaculation contests that are common among teenage boys. In masturbation contests, the boy who "comes" first is declared the winner, like in any other race. That may explain why some men don't consider their premature ejaculation to be a problem, because fast to them is better.

Good sexual timing meets the needs of both partners. If a husband ejaculates before he wants to or before his wife is ready, she can use the following techniques to help him slow down:

- ✔ **Encourage your husband to relax.** If he reaches orgasm too quickly for your pleasure, reassure him that being together is more important to you than his performance and remind him that there are other ways to pleasure you.

✔ **Suggest that your husband use his hand or mouth to bring you to climax.** Under the circumstances, taking the emphasis off his penis can prove to be a smart move.

✔ **Use the *squeeze technique*.** This is a time-tested way of helping men overcome premature ejaculation. Just before your spouse is about to ejaculate, gently squeeze his penis to slow down the ejaculation. Men can also try doing this themselves.

✔ **Use the *start-stop method*.** June Reinisch describes this three-phase treatment as follows:

1. **During the first phase, the husband or wife strokes his penis until he's about to ejaculate.**

   At that point, stop stroking and wait for the level of arousal to subside. As soon as he becomes less erect, resume stroking. The man becomes familiar with his *point of no return,* the premonitory sensation that there's no turning back from an orgasm. He then learns to stop himself before he reaches that point. After three repetitions, he's allowed to ejaculate.

2. **In the second phase, intercourse is simulated.**

   During this "pretend" intercourse, the man stops and starts, while masturbating with the aid of Vaseline or a similar lubricant.

3. **Intercourse with the man on top.**

   Now that the man has become aware of his point of no return, he can stop thrusting and let things subside as soon as he feels he has come too close. He should begin again several times before he allows himself to ejaculate.

4. **In this forth and final phase, the woman becomes actively involved in the process.**

   She gets on top of her partner and directs the start-stop sequence with her vagina, instead of her hand. After several sessions, many men are better able to control their ejaculations.

✔ **Ask your doctor or psychiatrist to consider Prozac.** One normally troublesome side effect of Prozac is slowing ejaculation, but this can work to a man's advantage if he comes too fast. However, Prozac is not appropriate for everybody, and it has a number of side effects, including preventing some men from having orgasms altogether.

If you're a man, don't try to hold back your orgasm by intentionally distracting yourself. You've probably heard a myth that you can prevent premature ejaculation by running off football plays in your head or using some other mental trick. Wrong! Distractions usually don't help a man last longer.

For women

Sex is God's joke on human beings.

— Bette Davis, actress

As with men, women's difficulties with orgasm can result from chronic illness, medical treatments, alcohol, or drugs. Many women are given antidepressant agents by their doctors, who often fail to warn them that delayed orgasm is a common side effect of Prozac and similar medications. Psychological causes for problems reaching orgasm include childhood sexual abuse, deep-seated inhibitions, shyness, anger, and anxiety.

A woman's ability to have an orgasm has little to do with sexual intercourse. Research shows that two-thirds of women can't achieve orgasm through intercourse alone. Contrary to some popular myths, this is not a sign of sexual dysfunction. A women is orgasmic — whether she climaxes through some kind of contact with her spouse, through self-pleasuring with a hand, or with objects that include anything from vibrators to bananas and zucchinis. As long as a woman can climax, she doesn't have an orgasm problem.

The following techniques can help any woman enhance her orgasms — as well as her enjoyment of sex:

✔ **Experiment with a variety of positions.** While sex can be a magical and mystical experience, mechanics is a key to good sex. If two healthy, functional people who are in love with each other have intercourse in a position that's not right for their particular anatomical configurations, they're not going to be satisfied.

Some intercourse positions give much more clitoral stimulation to a woman than others. So, if having an orgasm during intercourse is important, experiment or consult a sex manual that contains pictures and explanations of the various positions. You and your partner can have fun experimenting until you find the one (two, three, or more) that work best for you.

Many women get more stimulated when their partner uses his hand or mouth rather than his penis. This is partly because it's easier to achieve direct stimulation of the clitoris using those techniques.

✔ **Explore your body.** Aside from being a highly pleasurable activity, masturbation is a key to helping many women climax. A woman can stimulate herself by masturbating, both when she's alone or when she's with her partner.

Masturbating in front of your mate is both healthy and fun. Most men like watching a woman pleasuring herself. Plus, they get attuned to how you enjoy being touched, and are likely to imitate what they see you do.

Mastering the Kegel technique

You can find many instructive guides to doing Kegels, but here's a brief description to get you started squeezing and relaxing the muscles.

1. **Start by holding each squeeze for around three seconds.**

2. **Try a faster sequence.**

3. **Alternate between faster and slower squeezes.**

You may have to do up to 150 Kegels a day for a month to achieve a noticeable improvement. However, as the muscles get stronger, you'll be able to sustain tension in the pelvis — or to alternate between tension and release. The stronger this muscle, the greater the potential for a more orgasmic pleasure.

✔ **Use a vibrator.** The stimulation that a woman receives from a vibrator feels very different from manual rubbing or sexual intercourse. Choosing the right vibrator and using it well can add greatly to her enjoyment.

✔ **Strengthen your pelvic muscles.** A number of exercises can heighten a woman's arousal and increase awareness and pleasure in her vaginal sensations. One of the best are called *Kegels* — a series of exercises that have helped many women achieve satisfying orgasms.

Kegel exercises are a kind of pelvic pushup designed to strengthen the *pubococcygeus* (or PC) muscles that surround the vagina. Contracting and squeezing these muscles enhances the stimulation and lubrication that are necessary to achieve orgasm. If you're uncertain about where your PC muscles are, try stopping the flow when you urinate. Once you do that, you've found them! See the "Mastering the Kegel technique" sidebar for more helpful hints.

Finding the Right Kind of Professional Help

Anyone who goes to a psychiatrist ought to have his head examined.

— Sam Goldwyn, film producer

You can work many sexual difficulties out on your own, and with the help of your partner. However, if the techniques in this or other self-help books don't result in an improvement, that's the time to seek professional help.

First, have a thorough medical examination. Then, seek out a therapist or physician who has experience in diagnosing and treating sexual disorders. Not all therapists are qualified to treat all sexual complaints. If the problem is based on depression or some other emotional condition, you may need a psychiatrist to prescribe the appropriate medication. If the difficulty is rooted in the relationship, a marriage therapist or counselor who specializes in couples' issues should be able to help.

If there is a specific sexual dysfunction, you'll need to see a doctor who can prescribe a medication like Viagra, or a sex therapist (preferably one who is ASSECT certified) who is specifically trained to treat sexual disorders. A good sex therapist should be trained as a marriage therapist as well, and can help the couple determine where their issues are. Most are very willing to refer to psychologists for testing or psychiatrists for medication evaluation. (Also, see Chapter 16 for information on choosing the right therapist.)

We can't help thinking that if more married couples approached sex with a sense of wonder and playfulness, their sex lives would be a lot more satisfying. If they could only forget about ego and performance, they may discover how pleasurable sex can really be. If that ever happened, psychiatrists and therapists would have a lot more free time — and that would be just fine with us!

Part IV
Examining the Marriage Life Cycle

The 5th Wave   By Rich Tennant

@RICHTENNANT

McGRATH
MOVING AND STORAGE
Since 1929

CARLTON
TOOL AND DIE CO.
SINCE 1953

MAGUIRE
FAMILY
SINCE 1972

In this part . . .

Human life has a cycle that includes childhood, adolescence, early adulthood, midlife, and old age. Marriage follows a somewhat parallel life cycle. It starts when a couple first marries, goes through the early, formative years, takes a significant turn when one or more children enter your life, and winds its way through a midlife period that can last for more than 30 years. A great deal happens in each of these phases, and our journey through them reflects the importance of each one.

In Chapter 8, we explore the early years of marriage, and help you adjust to the coming together of two personal histories and two different sets of expectations under one roof. We show you how to negotiate this critical phase, and how to develop positive patterns that will serve you well on your travels through the rest of the marriage cycle.

In Chapter 9, we help you prepare for the emotional and financial impact of children, as well as the effect this change will have on your marriage. We explore the challenges that come with the growing family, and give you the tools to deal with them skillfully. We also discuss infertility, adoption, and the decision to remain child-free.

Chapters 10 and 11 deal with midlife. Because this is such a lengthy and potentially rich period, we explore midlife from both the husband's and wife's perspective, as well as from the point of view of the marriage. We tell you what to expect during the various phases of midlife, and show how to turn potential crisis points into rewarding life phases.

In Chapter 12, we address the issues that women and men face when they find themselves living in a second marriage or a stepfamily. We explore the special considerations that couples need to think about in order to handle these more complicated situations effectively. We also explore ways to deal with the complex finances and loyalty issues that remarriage often entails, and show parents how to develop a cohesive stepfamily unit.

Chapter 8

The First Years of Marriage

In This Chapter

▶ The new most important person in your life

▶ Dealing with your family — and your in-laws

▶ Understanding the shifting role of friends

▶ Coming to terms with changes in sexual chemistry

▶ Adjusting to each other's rhythms and quirks

The first years of marriage are a time for feeling your way through an unfamiliar world. New couples sometimes expect married life to be a lot like unmarried life — just with another person added to the equation. However, when two personal histories and two different sets of expectations come together under one roof, conflicts are inevitable.

There's his need for family contact versus your need for family contact; his taste in friends versus your taste in friends; his night-person tendencies versus your morning-person tendencies. The list of potential clashes couples can experience during the first years of marriage is almost endless.

In this chapter, we show you how to get through this critical first stage of the marriage cycle. We also share tips for developing patterns that will set the stage for the rest of the marriage cycle.

The New Most Important Person in Your Life

A little girl at the wedding afterwards asked her mother why the bride changed her mind. "What do you mean?" responded her mother. "Well, she went down the aisle with one man, and came back with another."

— Anonymous

You may never have thought of it this way, but, as soon as you get married, your new husband or wife automatically becomes your closest relative. That's a major change, because most unmarried people think of their family of origin as home base.

We're not saying that you aren't as connected to your parents and siblings. Indeed, solid extended-family structures tend to stabilize a marriage. However, all newly married partners need to spend time figuring out how to balance what may feel like competing allegiances.

Conflicts involving you or your mate's family of origin can be tough to negotiate, because so many potential loyalty issues come into play. If your spouse dislikes your family, or vice versa, there's sure to be trouble. However, loyalty conflicts are bound to surface — even if all the parties like each other.

During the early stages of a marriage, you may still feel more attached to your parents or siblings than to your spouse. That will have to be redefined and renegotiated if you and your spouse are going to create a viable marriage.

Negotiating family loyalties

The family is the first and essential cell of human society.

— Pope John XXIII

It takes some time for newly married partners to begin thinking of themselves as a distinct family unit — as opposed to two people who are spending lots of time together. Whatever else our families of origin may be, they are our primary models for how a household is supposed to work. When you get married, your family's patterns often become pitted against those of your spouse. Suddenly, you find yourselves dealing with three families: your family of origin, your spouse's family of origin, and the new family that you and your mate are trying to build.

One bone of contention we often see in newly married couples centers around the way holidays and family get-togethers are handled. This may seem like a minor matter, but it can be a highly emotional issue in the first year of marriage.

Ever since she was little, Leah's parents always prepared an elaborate Sunday dinner for their large, close family. Although they'd never talked about it, Leah assumed that after she and Kyle were married, she'd continue going to Sunday dinner at her folks' house — accompanied by her husband. However, Kyle had a different set of expectations, based on a very different family history.

Kyle's father died when he was nine; his mother had remarried and was now living in a distant city. Kyle had one sister, whom he hardly ever spoke to. Sunday was Kyle's one day off from work, and he wanted to spend it alone with Leah. Kyle was willing to go to dinner at Leah's parents' house once in a while, but he didn't feel comfortable being obligated to do it every week.

"I understand that you've always gone to your parents for Sunday dinner," Kyle said. "But now, you're my wife — and certain things have to change."

"What's the big deal about spending Sundays with my family?" Leah shouted. "It's something I've been doing all my life, and there's no good reason why I can't continue."

Leah's anger hardly masked the hurt she was experiencing. She felt that Kyle was being insensitive about her need to stay close to her family. Kyle felt that Leah was being disloyal by choosing her parents over him.

Of course, you don't want to cut your parents out of your life. However, your first priority is to establish a strong partnership with your mate — even if that means temporarily putting more distance between you and your family than you're used to. After you are more secure as a couple, you can start devoting more attention to your original family. We recommend the following steps:

- ✔ **Sit down and openly discuss the various feelings and expectations that have surfaced — especially those that were never broached before you were married.** The first step in resolving loyalty conflicts is to identify the emotions that are fueling your disagreements. That's why we asked Leah and Kyle to talk about their feelings, without accusing each other of disloyalty or lack of consideration.

  Leah genuinely wanted to go "home" (i.e. to her family's house) for Sunday dinners. We explained that these were understandable feelings, but "home" was now the one-bedroom apartment she shared with her husband.

  Kyle also felt the need to take a stand, because he thought there were important underlying issues. "Leah's parents are nice people, but I feel that they want things to stay as they were when Leah was single. I'm afraid that if we keep doing everything Leah's parents ask, they'll continue to see her as their little girl instead of a grown woman — my wife!"

- ✔ **Recognize that sorting out family loyalties takes patience and practice.** When people get married, they almost always have to redefine relationships with their own families. Then, of course, there's a parallel set of issues with your in-laws.

  It takes time to find a comfortable style of relating to someone else's family that you've suddenly become part of. In most lasting marriages, spouses eventually figure out a comfortable way to become daughters-in-law or sons-in-law. They often grow to love their brothers-in-law and sisters-in-law. However, it's part of a life-long process of give and take between you, your spouse, and your families.

Newly married spouses who have had close bonds with their own family sometimes keep a distance from their new in-laws, for fear of appearing disloyal to their parents. Phil recalls that, even before he and his wife were married, his future in-laws wanted him to call them Mom and Dad. Phil felt awkward about this, because he had a close relationship with his own parents. Even after Phil's folks passed away, he preferred calling his in-laws by their first names.

Phil remembers receiving a birthday card from his in-laws that read: "Happy Birthday from the Cliffords." He took this as an expression that they resented his coolness toward them. "Actually, I've always liked my in-laws," Phil told us. "But I can never think of them as my parents."

In time, Phil's in-laws accepted his calling them by their first names, and they had a reasonably warm relationship. "In a certain way," said Phil, "I think they respected me for being honest about my feelings."

Husbands and wives often end up developing loving relationships with their spouse's family. In some cases, these new relationships can meet needs that were unfulfilled with one's own parents.

Ariel, for example, describes her own father as having always been cold and distant. In contrast, her father-in-law is "one of the warmest, most loving people I've ever known." Max, an attorney, recalls that he and his late father had an "okay" relationship, even though they had very little in common. On the other hand, he considers his father-in-law, who is also an attorney, a mentor and good friend.

The truth about in-laws

In some countries, in-laws are warmly accepted as a "second families," where the mother-in-law is called "my second mother." However, in many cultures, relationships with in-laws have long been given a negative cast. You've heard songs and poems written about brotherly love and motherly love, but, we've never heard anyone say, "I love him like a brother-in-law," nor can we quote a single sonnet to a mother-in-law. On the other hand, there is no end to the disparaging remarks and jokes on the topic:

✔ *I just came home from a pleasure trip. I took your mother to the airport.*

✔ *A pharmacist told a customer: "You need a legal prescription in order to buy arsenic. A picture of your mother-in-law just isn't enough."*

✔ *I just received good news and bad news. My mother-in-law just drove over a cliff in my new Cadillac.*

Have you ever thought about where all this negativity comes from? We all have unresolved negative feelings toward our own parents, but this resentment is far more easily directed toward our in-laws. After all, they're your spouse's family — not yours!

Setting boundaries with both your families

Each member of your respective families needs time to find a comfortable way to interact with your spouse — and with you as a couple.

Parents can find it especially difficult to view you as a half of a married couple first — and their child second. You can ease this process by setting clear, but flexible, boundaries.

The limits that you establish with your parents and in-laws are issues that will have to be continually negotiated and renegotiated throughout your marriage. However, they are particularly important during the early stages — while a couple is beginning to define itself as a unit.

We suggest that you use the following steps to begin creating boundaries with your families:

✔ **Put relationships with your family of origin into a new perspective.** It's impossible to maintain the same connection with your family that you had before you were married. Even small changes in family relationships can be threatening if they have physical or emotional consequences. For example, a widowed parent may be fearful about "losing" her only son. An infirm parent may fear that her daughter will no longer help her with shopping and other chores after she is married. These fears are understandable — as long as both parties accept the changes and challenges that marriage brings.

Two types of parental relationships should raise a red flag to newly married couples:

• One or both partners are overly dependent on their original families. The husband who has to call home twice a day. The wife who has to check with her mother before making the smallest decision. These are signs that the couple isn't functioning autonomously enough.

• One or both partners are using the marriage as a way to escape from their families of origin. People who say they hate their families and want nothing to do with them think they can completely separate from their parents by getting married and starting a family of their own. This kind of person tends to become overly dependent on the new spouse to meet all of his needs, and usually winds up putting too much pressure on that spouse — and the relationship. Many couples learn the hard way that family of origin problems can't be avoided or solved by getting married.

✔ **Be clear — but sensitive — in setting the tone with your families.** You can't measure an exact amount of closeness married couples need to maintain with their families. However, you don't ever have to be insensitive or uncaring in the way you negotiate these dealings. Put yourself in your parents' (or in-laws') shoes. Wouldn't you feel at least a little anxious about being left out of your child's life after he or she gets married?

You can minimize anxieties and hurt feelings by clearly stating that it's not your intention to exclude your families from your lives. Small gestures like sending cards and thoughtful gifts on birthdays and holidays can help. So can talking to them about mutual interests and concerns and exchanging personal stories. At the same time, help your families be clear about the balance between privacy and closeness that you want.

✓ **Come to a mutual decision with your mate about the kind of relationships you want with your families.** It's only natural for you and your spouse to have disagreements about such a highly charged issue. However, these decisions need to be worked out privately — and not aired in front of your families.

If you want to see your family once a week and your spouse doesn't always want to join you, decide if this is something you can at times do on your own. If you or your spouse feels that your parents are too free in offering their unsolicited advice, tell them that you appreciate their concern. Then add that the only way the two of you can find your way as a couple is to make your own decisions.

✓ **Realistically assess where you are as a couple.** The more experience you have — both as an independent person and as a couple — the easier time you'll have establishing boundaries.

We almost always recommend that individuals live on their own (i.e. away from their family) for a period of time before getting married. This gives them an opportunity to develop a more independent sense of self.

If you've never lived on your own, you may have a hard time establishing new boundaries with your family of origin, and giving your marriage the privacy it needs. We sometimes give couples who are trying to negotiate this transition the following advice: Build a temporary cocoon around your marriage. If, for example, your parents expect you to come to dinner at their house every Sunday and you want to change that pattern, tell them that you and your spouse have reserved that time for the two of you to spend alone. If you wish, you can offer to come less frequently or at an alternate time.

At first, your families may feel rejected. They may even accuse you of being cold or unsociable. However, it's up to you to help them understand that your most important concern is nurturing your new family unit while maintaining a connection to your family of origin.

The younger and less established you are as a couple, the more difficulty you may have avoiding intrusion from well-meaning family members. But all newly married couples have to deal with loyalty issues — even those who have married for the second or third time.

In remarriages, loyalty issues often revolve around children from a previous marriage. Things can get complicated when your current spouse (who also may have children from a previous marriage) is competing for your loyalty with the children of your former spouse. But here, too, you and your partner must make a special place for each other. For a complete discussion on remarriage and stepfamilies, see Chapter 12.

Don't use your spouse as a tool to deal with your parents, particularly in unpleasant matters. For example, what looks like a fight between a daughter-in-law and a mother-in-law may actually be a problem between a son and his mother.

Whatever your age and experience, commit to making your time together sacred — and help your families understand that you need to do that.

Understanding the Shifting Role of Friends

After you get married, friends start to take on a new role in your life. As with family, issues of loyalty often come into play. In part, this is because some newlyweds assume that a spouse is supposed to be his or her best (if not only) friend. Marriages do benefit when the partners share many of the same values and goals. At the same time, it's unrealistic to expect your mate to be your one-and-only friend. The following are some of the reasons why friends are important to the health of both spouses — and the marriage:

- **Friends give married partners the opportunity to become more well-rounded, both as individuals and as a couple.** Partners who are each able to maintain their own friends are able to pursue interests and concerns that the other partner may not share. As both mates grow as individuals, they're able to bring more to the marriage.

- **Women and men have different ways of relating.** Therefore, they often find it easier to communicate with friends of the same gender. Women tend to look to one or two close friends for emotional support. Men often prefer friendships that revolve around business or competitive sports.

- **Many spouses are attracted to each other because of their differences, not what they have in common.** These differences often lead to a powerful sexual attraction. For such couples, friends play a particularly important role in filling the need for support and other kinds of companionship.

During the early stages of marriage, recasting the role of friends can be a difficult adjustment for the spouses — and their friends. The following tips can help you deal with some of the friend-related issues that couples encounter during the first years of marriage.

✔ **If your spouse has a general problem with your having friends, it's up to you to help him or her recognize the importance of maintaining separate friendships and separate interests.** When you encourage this kind of freedom, you acknowledge that each of you is an individual with her or his own needs, and that your growth as individuals ultimately makes your relationship stronger.

✔ **If you sense that an unmarried friend feels threatened by your marriage, assure that person that your friendship is still important.** Openly discuss the differences in your situations. Make it clear that you'd like your friendship to transcend these and future changes — even though you may not have as much time to get together. As much as possible, try to encourage cordial (if not warm) relations between your spouse and your single friend.

If you have a problem with a particular friend or group of friends, ask yourself the following questions:

✔ **Is there something problematic in the nature of the friendship?** Some friendships can pose a danger to the health of your marriage. If, for example, your husband or wife regularly goes out drinking or gambling with a particular friend, you need to assess if those behaviors are a relatively harmless way of letting off steam or a sign of deeper trouble.

If you feel troubled about the activities your spouse and his friends are engaged in, criticize the activity, not the friends:

   • Do say: I worry when you go out drinking.

   • Don't say: I can't stand those guys you go out with on Wednesdays. They're a bunch of drunks.

Assuming that you have no specific objection to what your spouse and his friends are doing, it's not necessary that you like his friends — just as it's not necessary for him to like yours. In Chapter 2, we describe the benefits of making room for separateness in your togetherness. That means giving one another room to do things with people you may not necessarily seek out on your own.

If your spouse's relationship with one or more friends continues to bother you (or if your friendships continue to bother your spouse), try to get to the root of the problem by asking yourself the following questions, and using them as the basis for an open discussion:

   • **Is the problem based on a real or perceived personality clash?** Some people seem to rub each other the wrong way. However, even if you and your partner's close friend never become completely comfortable with each other, you can still accept your spouse's relationship with that person — as long as you conclude that there's nothing in that friendship that's threatening to you, to your mate, or to your marriage.

- **Does the problem stem from feelings of competitiveness?** During the early stages of a marriage, husbands and wives often feel that they must wage a battle of control to assure themselves that they are their partner's number-one priority. In that case, almost any friend can be perceived as a threat — especially one who appears to be important to the partner.

It may be possible to pressure your spouse to abandon a close friendship. However, this strategy is more likely to weaken your long-term relationship than to strengthen it.

Negotiating opposite-sex friendships

Some spouses have trouble accepting that any opposite-sex relationship can ever be platonic. They may even admit that these feelings are irrational, but that doesn't make them feel any less jealous. If the friend is a former lover, those jealous feelings can become explosive.

You can handle conflicts about opposite-sex friendships in one of the following ways:

- ✔ **Encourage your spouse to participate in the friendship.** This approach works best when you sense that the two people are likely to get along.

For the five years before Ethan and Kelly married, Ethan had maintained a close friendship with his former girlfriend, Joanne.

"Joanne and I went out for about a year," Ethan recalled. "But eventually, we realized that we were meant to be friends — not lovers. Kelly was very jealous at first. Shortly after we were married, Joanne invited us to a party she was hosting. Kelly barely said hello and acted extremely tense all evening.

"I understood that the friendship with Joanne would eventually end if Kelly insisted on forcing the issue," Ethan told us. "But I hoped the situation could be worked out in a more satisfactory way. I was sure that these were two women who had the potential to like each other, so I suggested that we double-date with Joanne and the guy she was seeing at the time.

"That evening went well. So, a few weeks later, we invited Joanne over to our house for dinner. In time, the two women became good friends. They found they had a great deal in common — including the ability to laugh at some of my quirks."

✔ **See your opposite-sex friend without your spouse.** This approach can work only if your partner doesn't feel threatened by the friendship. This was the case with Allison and her husband Fred. "When we first got married, I was upset that Fred wanted to maintain his long-standing friendship with Marge. They'd been close since college, but were never romantically involved. After they graduated, Fred and Marge attended the same medical school, and both of them became internists. Since we've been married, Fred has arranged dinners and other evenings with Marge. I like her well enough, but I prefer that Fred see her without me. Mostly all they talk about is medicine anyway."

In most marriages, weekday meetings with your friend are less intrusive than weekends; just as lunches with your friend are likely to be more acceptable to your spouse than dinners.

Any friendship that provokes conflicts between you and your partner will cause problems. This goes double for friends of the opposite sex.

✔ **Consider the possibility of ending the relationship.** If you believe your partner is justified in opposing your friendship with a particular man or woman, you may want to think about ending it.

If, for example, the friend was an ex-lover, but never really a friend prior to the marriage, your spouse may have reason to feel threatened. In that case, it may be best for you, your spouse, and the marriage if you stop seeing that person. However, it's your decision to make — not your spouse's.

If your partner displays an ongoing pattern of possessiveness or excessive jealousy, no matter how innocent your friendships are, this can lead to serious problems that pose a threat to the marriage.

Just because you're married, you don't automatically surrender your right to choose your friends — including those of the opposite sex. Although few relationships with members of the opposite sex are likely to be completely gender neutral, partners in a healthy marriage don't usually have much trouble granting each other a reasonable measure of trust and freedom.

Developing friendships with other couples

As a wife and husband continue to solidify themselves as a unit, it's important to develop friendships with other couples. Many marriage theorists view a married couple's ability to develop and maintain friendships with other twosomes as a healthy sign. We agree that couple friendships often help bring newly married wives and husbands closer together. Nevertheless, two-on-two relationships can sometimes be difficult for even happily married couples to negotiate.

Marci and Peter had problems developing couple-friendships during their first year of marriage. If Marci got along with the other wife, Peter found the husband intolerable. The few occasions where there was good cross-gender chemistry, the husbands or the wives didn't like each other. Marci and Peter had single friends they enjoyed, both separately and as a couple, but it was hard for them to find couples they both enjoyed.

If you and your spouse are finding it difficult to meet other compatible couples, you may want to try the following tips that we suggested to Marci and Peter:

- **Pinpoint the issues that could be interfering with your ability to develop friendships with other couples.** Are one or both of you being too critical? Do you expect to have an instant chemistry?

  It often takes more time to make a four-way friendship work, so expect to have a feeling-out period before all of you are comfortable.

- **Sit down with your spouse and think about activities you enjoy doing together.** Seek out places where you're likely to meet other couples who enjoy the same activities.

  Marci and Peter listed tennis, science fiction, and Japanese cooking as their most important shared interests. They decided that a good first step would be to join a tennis club that was popular among couples who lived in the area. They scheduled times on Wednesday evenings and Saturday mornings. After about a month, Marci and Peter began playing doubles with another couple, and going out for coffee afterwards. Everybody seemed to get along.

- **If you meet a couple that seems compatible, take the initiative in pursuing the relationship.**

  Marci and Peter decided to invite their new tennis friends to their apartment for Sunday brunch. "I don't know if this is going to work out to be a long-term friendship," Marci told us. "Still, even if it doesn't, at least we're making an effort."

Don't put undue pressure on yourself — or your spouse. One reason couples' friendships last is because the interaction is fun for all concerned. If things don't work out, it's not the end of the world, and you'll have lots more opportunities to meet other couples.

Coming to Terms with Changes in Sexual Chemistry

I know nothing about sex, because I was always married.

— Zsa Zsa Gabor, actress

As newlyweds begin to settle into the routine of daily living, they almost always find that the intense passion that first brought them together is beginning to fade. It may be hard to believe, but you may actually discover practical benefits to being a little less turned on by each other.

Think about what life would be like if you and your spouse spent as much time making love as you did during those first heady days and nights of passion. Neither of you would want to go to work. Everyday chores like laundry and housecleaning would never get done You'd soon be without gas and electricity because nobody would pay the bills. We realize that many people would gladly make those sacrifices — if only that first rush of passion could last forever. Sorry, that's just not going to happen.

A lessening of passion during the first year or two of marriage is about as predictable as autumn following summer. After a couple settles into marriage, the initial passion that lovers feel is bound to change for the following reasons:

✔ **The "newness" of making love can't last forever.** No matter how attracted you and your mate are to each other, the fresh excitement of being together is bound to level off with time. Eventually, you grow accustomed to the way your lover looks and feels.

✔ **There are no longer obstacles to overcome.** Before two people make love, there's usually a period of courting or seduction. During that time, neither of you is certain if and when you're going to wind up in bed. There's often a sense of adventure — even naughtiness — that accompanies the first flush of passion between lovers.

After you're married, you don't feel any more taboos. You have few impediments to making love whenever you want. What you have instead are comfort and predictable routines that have important benefits of their own.

Newly married spouses who are not prepared for these predictable changes in chemistry sometimes attempt to recapture their lost passion by looking for sex outside of the marriage. This strategy is bound to fail. Cheating in the first years of marriage indicates a serious problem in the relationship, and may signal difficulty with closeness and commitment.

Even though the chemistry will never be exactly as it was during those first weeks and months of intense lovemaking, the overall quality of your sex life can actually be better. As partners grow more comfortable with each other, they often become freer in sharing their deepest erotic fantasies and discovering new ways to excite and please each other. For a detailed discussion of how to get the most out of married sex, see Chapter 6.

Research shows that the most satisfying and meaningful lovemaking takes place between intimate partners who feel totally safe and secure with one another. By continuing to look for satisfaction inside (rather than outside of) your marriage, you can achieve the deepest and most fulfilling level of lovemaking.

Adjusting to Each Other's Rhythms and Quirks

The course of true love never did run smooth.

— William Shakespeare, playwright

Each person has rhythms and quirks. Before you get married, you don't have much reason to spend much time thinking about them. But afterward, you discover that your partner has his or her own peculiarities — some of which are on a direct collision course with yours. The following are just some of the rhythms and quirks that can lead to marital conflict:

- Morning person versus night person
- Light sleeper versus heavy sleeper
- Snores versus can't stand snoring
- Prefers eating home versus prefers eating out
- Decisive versus indecisive
- Gregarious versus reserved
- Physically active versus sedentary
- Impulsive versus thoughtful
- Loves TV versus hates TV
- Smoker versus non-smoker
- Leaves toilet seat up versus always closes toilet seat

Eighty percent (or more) of your habits are unlikely to cause trouble. It's the other twenty percent (or less) that turn out to be problematic.

Are you and your partner in synch?

When jazz musicians are in synch, each can anticipate what the others are going to do — and accommodate their parts accordingly. But even the most compatible musicians need time to adjust and readjust to all their collaborators' tendencies. Newlyweds are a lot like jazz musicians in that way, trying to get in synch with one another's moves. In both cases, the players operate within a structure that's only partially predictable. Compatible players can usually improvise many of the unexpected twists and turns. However, some passages are bound to require work before partners can develop a true synchronicity.

Disputes over rhythms and quirks usually don't come out until after two people get married and feel comfortable enough to let their hair down. Some of these idiosyncrasies are based on inborn biorhythms. Others are based on habits and expectations that people learn from their families of origin.

Because your spouse comes from an entirely different family culture than you, he or she brings a completely different set of habits and expectations into the relationship. During the first year or two of marriage, all of your idiosyncrasies will start coming out. It's up to you and your partner to find ways of adjusting to them.

We suggest using the following techniques to work out your differences in rhythms and quirks:

- ✔ **If your spouse tells you that she's annoyed by something you're doing, always acknowledge that the complaint is sincere, even if you don't agree with it or it can't be proven.**

- ✔ **State your complaints using "I" statements.** It's important that you talk about your problem from the point of view of your discomfort, rather than in terms of what's wrong with your partner. For example, if your partner snores, you're likely to make more progress if you start out by saying, "I'm sensitive to noise when I'm trying to sleep," instead of: "You snore so loudly, it sounds like there's an elephant in the room."

- ✔ **Don't frame your complaints as moral or ethical issues.** Most problems adjusting to rhythms and quirks are not about who's right and who's wrong. For example, instead of trying to prove that it's healthier to be a morning person than a night person, try to come up with possible ways to compromise that will make you both more comfortable.

✔ **Choose your battles carefully.** Habits that are based on deeply ingrained personality traits can be especially hard to change. In some cases, the discord you create by trying to change your partner isn't worth the potential benefits.

✔ **Think of your marriage as a journey.** The expression "don't sweat the small stuff" applies to many of the conflicts married couples have over various quirks. It may be hard to believe, but some of the things that drive you crazy today are going to seem microscopic a few years down the road.

Committed couples who trust and respect each other take a long view of their relationship. They realize that marriage can't solve all the problems both partners bring to it. Instead of striving for perfection, they work at finding ways to change those things that need to be changed, and accept the fact that there are some (hopefully less important) quirks and clashes that will always be there.

We've got rhythms and quirks

During the course of our own marriage, we've had to adapt to many of each other's quirks. The process of adjustment is still ongoing after all these years.

Steve: Could it be that we still haven't worked out all the kinks that came up during our first year of marriage?

Sue: I still like the bedroom to be pitch black when I wake up in the morning, while you like it completely bright. That's why I asked for a darkening shade and you want nothing on the windows.

Steve: So we compromised on blinds.

Sue: I think that's worked for both of us, although I still get up as soon as the sun comes up.

Steve: For years, you complained that I snored, but I never thought it was a problem.

Sue: You used to say things like: "Oh, it's not that bad." In fact, you had no way of knowing how bad it really was.

Steve: It was easy for me to claim that I didn't snore because I never heard myself. Then one evening, we were at a party, and I fell asleep on the couch. My friend took a portable tape recorder, and taped me snoring. When I woke up, he gave me the recorded proof. I could hardly believe it, but there it was.

Once I admitted that my snoring was a problem, we tried to come up with a solution. I even considered going for surgery, but you didn't think that that was a good idea. Eventually, you found a noise machine that sounds like a babbling brook and forest whispers. That solved the problem. I continue to snore happily away, and you're pretty much oblivious to it.

Pinpointing Early Marriage Danger Zones

Recognition is always the most important first step in making positive changes. That's why we want you (assuming you're in the first year or two of marriage) to take a few minutes to assess how you're doing at this early stage in the cycle.

Complete this exercise in private. If you feel comfortable doing so, ask your partner to complete it as well; then compare results. This will help you begin a constructive dialogue about the differences in the ways you perceive the state of your relationship.

1. Has marriage met your expectations up to this point?

　　a. Everything I had hoped for.

　　b. Satisfactory.

　　c. Disappointing.

　　d. A disaster.

2. How are you getting along with your own family?

　　a. Great.

　　b. We're working out our differences.

　　c. Strained since the wedding.

　　d. It's never been good.

3. How are you getting along with your in-laws?

　　a. We're getting closer and closer.

　　b. About the same as before the wedding.

　　c. We're working out our differences.

　　d. It's getting worse.

4. How have your friendships changed since the wedding?

　　a. Most of them are thriving.

　　b. About the same.

　　c. Our friends seem to be avoiding us.

　　d. We have no time for friends.

5. The disagreements between you and your partner:

　　a. Generally end up getting resolved.

　　b. Sometimes end up in a standoff.

　　c. Seem to be getting worse.

　　d. We never have disagreements.

6. **Compared to shared activities before you got married:**

   a. We do many more things together now.

   b. We spend about the same amount of time together.

   c. We're doing less.

   d. We never seem to see one another.

7. **How would you assess your personal growth since you've been married?**

   a. My marriage has helped me grow more than I expected.

   b. I feel that I'd be in the same place if I remained single.

   c. I've been concentrating so much on the relationship that I haven't had much time for myself.

   d. The marriage is stifling my personal growth.

8. **How is your sexual relationship since the wedding?**

   a. Great.

   b. Getting better.

   c. Stagnant.

   d. One or both of us seems to be losing interest.

9. **Do you feel that the household chores are distributed fairly?**

   a. We're negotiating things well.

   b. It's reasonably fair.

   c. One of us feels it's fair, but the other doesn't.

   d. We're both resentful.

10. **How well are you negotiating money issues?**

    a. We have similar attitudes about the way money should be handled.

    b. There are some disagreements, but we're usually able to work them out.

    c. One of us feels controlled or dominated by the other.

    d. We don't discuss it.

Scoring: 4 points for each "a" response; 3 points for each "b"; 2 points for each "c"; 1 point for each "d."

In general, an "a" or "b" response indicates that the issue raised by the question does not present a problem at this point. A "c" response indicates a potential area of difficulty. A "d" response indicates a significant problem in your marriage.

Now add up the numbers. A score of 30 points or more means you're doing well. A score of 20 to 29 suggests that you may be experiencing some problems, which you can probably fix with the help of this book. A score of less than 20, or a wide disparity between your score and your partner's, suggests that you may need professional counseling. (See Chapter 16 for assistance with getting outside help.)

Chapter 9

The Growing Family

. . . .

In This Chapter

▶ Understanding the impact that children have on your marriage

▶ Preparing yourselves for children — financially and emotionally

▶ Coordinating career and family responsibilities

▶ Deciding how many children you want

▶ Having a happy, child-free marriage

. . . .

After a husband and wife survive the early trials of marriage, they often go through a relatively carefree period in their relationship. During the first few years of the marriage cycle, couples tend to be comfortable with one another — but not yet overwhelmed with responsibilities. And if both partners are working, the financial demands are usually manageable. This is a time when it's relatively easy for partners to experiment with their lifestyles, change careers, or continue their education.

When a child comes into the picture, however, everything changes. Suddenly, you have to do some hard thinking about budgets, escalating expenses, and the massive emotional changes that happen when your family expands from two to three.

In this chapter, we talk about the thinking (or *lack* of thinking) that compels most couples to have children. We explore the challenges that come with the growing family, and show you how to surmount them in ways that strengthen your marriage.

Deciding Whether You're Ready for Children

First comes love, then comes marriage, then comes a baby in a baby carriage.

— Child's limerick

When couples seek our advice about whether they're ready to have a child, we congratulate them for being thoughtful enough to ask that question before making such an important decision. Most young couples have a child before they understand the effect that it will have on their lives.

It takes time for two individuals to feel secure in their relationship and begin functioning as a team. After you and your partner have created a foundation as a couple, you're far better prepared for the enormous changes that will come about when you have a child.

Don't make the mistake of thinking that a child can fix a troubled marriage. If you have serious underlying problems in your relationship, adding a new person to that explosive mix will only make the situation worse.

In general, it's a good idea to be married for at least two to three years before you start thinking seriously about having a baby. Having a child too soon can put enormous stress on a relationship that has not yet solidified. Research shows that couples in the following situations are at especially high risk of divorce:

- ✔ **When pregnancy occurs before the couple is married.** This circumstance is usually the result of an "accident," so it's unlikely that the couple has given much forethought to how the addition of a child can change their lives.

  Raising a child takes a good deal of emotional, financial, and lifestyle planning. A young couple needs time to hammer out decisions in these critical areas.

- ✔ **When one or both partners are under 21 years old.** Unlike virtually every other species on the planet, humans are unique because their physical readiness to bear children precedes their emotional readiness by many years. Teen pregnancy is all too common, yet we come across very few people under the age of twenty-one who are ready for parenthood.

- ✔ **When pregnancy occurs during the first year of marriage.** Partners who've been married for less than one year are often just starting to sort out the unfamiliar demands and shared responsibilities of married life. We've seen very few just-married couples who are emotionally or financially prepared to assume responsibility for a baby so early in the game.

Choosing when to have a child

In recent years, a growing number of couples are waiting until they've been married ten or more years before trying to have children. Some want to become more set in their careers before assuming the additional financial responsibilities. Others want to wait until they feel more settled, both within themselves and their marriage. However, the majority of married couples have their first baby after they've been married between three and five years.

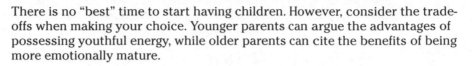

There is no "best" time to start having children. However, consider the trade-offs when making your choice. Younger parents can argue the advantages of possessing youthful energy, while older parents can cite the benefits of being more emotionally mature.

"I've done the things I want to do," Max, a forty-five-year old who recently became a first-time dad, explained. "I feel far more ready to give to a child now than I did in my twenties or thirties."

Sarah, Max's thirty-seven-year-old wife, shares her husband's enthusiasm about being an older parent.

"When I was in my twenties, I felt as if I lacked the maturity to be a good mother," she confided. "At the same time, I was fully aware that my biological clock was ticking. I'm happy with my choice, but I was very fortunate that my pregnancy went off without a hitch."

Fertility problems and high-risk pregnancies are far more common for women whose first pregnancy occurs after age 35.

In the best of all possible worlds, parents would be able to combine the life experience and wisdom of a 50-year-old with the exuberance and stamina of a 25-year-old. In reality, you have to be aware of the inherent tradeoffs in whatever choice you make.

Age is a factor that should never be ignored in deciding whether or not you're ready to have a child. Couples who have children when they're too young may not be ready to provide the necessary financial and emotional stability. Couples (and especially women) who wait too long are more likely to have problems conceiving.

What if you and your spouse can't agree about having children?

The question of whether a couple wants to have children should be explored before marriage. Unfortunately, many couples never have a serious talk about this matter. Or, one partner doesn't believe the other when that person says that he or she doesn't want to make the necessary sacrifices to raise a family.

In many relationships, this is an issue that can be negotiated — as long as the partner who wants to delay having a child isn't stalling in an effort to get the other partner to change his or her mind or give up trying.

It's not uncommon for two people to get married and be undecided on whether (or when) they want to have kids. However, for a marriage to work, both partners need to share a similar vision of the relationship. If one partner's vision doesn't include children and the other can't visualize a childless marriage, it's essential to find a way for both partners to come to a decision that will leave neither feeling railroaded or bullied.

If one partner truly doesn't want to have children and the other does, there can be no compromise. This issue is a deal breaker because one spouse or the other will ultimately have to prevail.

If the spouse who wants children is forced to endure a childless marriage, he or she is bound to feel short-changed and dissatisfied. On the other hand, a person who genuinely doesn't want kids should always be taken seriously. After a child is born, you can't go back. If one partner feels parenthood was forced on him or her, it can lead to the end of the marriage, and profound feelings of guilt and loss for all concerned.

If you and your spouse are experiencing serious disagreements about having children, we strongly recommend that you consult with a professional who can help you resolve your differences.

Getting Ready for the Financial Hit

There's some truth to that old saying, "Two can live as cheaply as one." But we've never heard anyone say that three can live as cheaply as two. Unless you're financially independent, the addition of a child is likely to have some important financial consequences.

In order to make an informed decision about whether you and your partner are financially prepared to have a child, we suggest that you sit down with him or her and attempt to answer the following questions:

- ✔ **Is your current home as suitable for three people as it is for two?** One of the first major child-related expenses many couples face is the need for bigger living quarters. That one-bedroom apartment may be comfortable now, but it's sure to seem a lot smaller once a baby is added. So, before you decide to put the crib in your bedroom, ask yourself how you're going to get up for work after a sleepless night of rocking a crying infant to sleep.

  Make a list of changes or additions that you need. Then set a timetable for making those changes.

- ✔ **Do you currently live in a neighborhood that provides a safe, stimulating environment for young children?** An apartment in an urban area close to work may fit your current lifestyle, but it may not suit the changing needs of your growing family. For example, you may want to live in an area that's close to parks and playgrounds, so that your child has an opportunity to play outdoors and interact with other kids.

Observe whether a significant number of families with young children live on your block and in the surrounding area. Talk to parents who reside in the neighborhood. Ask them if they feel the area is conducive to raising children. Check with a regional newspaper to see how the schools are rated. Don't rely on what a real estate agent tells you.

✔ **If you decide that you need to move, can you agree on a home and neighborhood that suits your growing family?**

In making that decision, consider the impact that such a move may have on other lifestyle issues, such as increased travel time to work, and proximity to family, friends, and leisure activities.

Even if you don't have to move to a larger dwelling, you have many other expenses to consider: clothes, diapers, baby furniture, medical care — and that's just for starters. If both partners are working full-time, one of you may have to take a leave or work part-time. That can put a sizable dent in your joint income at a time when expenses are skyrocketing.

If both of you plan to work, you must also consider the cost of childcare. This expense can easily run as much as $10,000 per year or more. The following guidelines can help you calculate whether or not it makes economic sense for both of you to work full-time.

✔ **Sit down with pencil and paper and add up the following expenses you incur just by going to work:**

- Cost of childcare
- Commuting
- Clothes and cleaning
- Eating out
- House cleaning
- Taxes

Adding up the costs of having a child

According to the U.S. Department of Agriculture, the average middle-income, two-parent family will spend over $153,000 to raise one child between birth and age 18. That child will eat almost $55,000 worth of food and go through over $22,000 worth of clothes. By the time a baby born in 2000 goes to college, parents can expect to pay upwards of $150,000 for tuition, fees, room and board at a good, public, four-year university. Private colleges will cost substantially more.

When you deduct the total from your weekly after-tax income, you may be surprised to find that it actually pays for one of you to stay home with the child.

Even if it makes financial sense for one partner to stay home, he or she may still want to work. If the other spouse doesn't support that decision, you may have ongoing conflicts.

✔ **Calculate the difference in taxes and health benefits between one and two full-time incomes.** Some two-income couples find that there's a significant tax advantage in having one partner stay home with the child. For one thing, you may be in a lower tax bracket. For another, you can still take most of the same tax deductions when only one of you works.

Health insurance is often provided to the entire family of a working spouse. So, determine which one of your policies offer superior benefits, and factor that into your decision.

Don't forget to plan for your growing family's long-range financial future. The decision to have a child implies certain responsibilities that you may not have considered. All of a sudden, you have to think about things like saving for college, purchasing life insurance, and making a will. You don't have to do all these things right away, but financial experts strongly recommend that you have an emergency fund of at least six months salary in case one of you loses your job or decides to stop working.

✔ **Create a budget based on the projected lower income.** Are you ready to simplify your lifestyle to accommodate your reduced income? Some people have difficulty giving up any of their discretionary income, while others find the tradeoffs in extra time with their children more than worth the sacrifice.

To get a feel for what it would be like to live on a reduced income, figure out how much money you'd have if one of you stopped working. Then, do an experiment. Pretend that you're earning less money and see what it's like to live on that reduced income. Reward yourself by putting the money you're not spending into stocks or a special savings account.

No matter how hard you try to plan ahead, there's no way to know how you're going to feel once the child arrives. So, even if both of you decide to continue working after the baby is born, you may find that one of you wants to care for the child for a period of time. On the other hand, you may have planned to take a year off from work, and then change your mind after a month or two of staying home.

Understanding the Emotional Impact

The greatest gift parents can give their children is to love one another.

— Anonymous

A baby may be life's greatest blessing, but it can also test the emotional strength of a marriage in ways that you may have never anticipated.

WARNING!

The change from a two-person family to a three-person family is one of the most difficult transitions you and your partner will have to endure.

You will face many challenges when the baby arrives. A lack of sleep is one of the more mundane tests that you have to endure on a daily basis. On the other hand, you've signed on for a lifetime of responsibility — and the impact of that commitment may take years to sink in. Meanwhile, the relationship that you once had with your spouse will be undergoing changes that can either strengthen or destroy your marriage.

When a child is brought into a marriage, the woman usually becomes the primary caretaker — especially for the first few years of the child's life. A mother's close relationship with her baby can cause the husband to feel jealous and resentful.

TRUE STORY

Some years ago, we asked a friend whose only son had just turned two how he felt about being a father.

"It's been great," he answered. "But I don't want to have any more children." When we asked why, the friend replied, "My wife was so involved with the baby, she pretty much ignored me for well over a year. I don't want to play second fiddle again." We understood exactly what this friend was talking about, because we experienced similar feelings after our first child was born.

Bringing up baby

Steve: I felt resentful when Eric was born, because he seemed to command all your time. That was bad enough, but he also laid claim to your affection and energy. I had trouble accepting that there was another person in the world that you loved as much as me — if not more!

Sue: My resentment came from a different place. Before Eric, we shared everything. Both of us were working, and our marriage was a completely equal partnership. Then, the baby came along, and suddenly, most of the burden fell on me. Eric didn't sleep much, so I was up all of the time, and I felt completely exhausted. I was also trying to hold a full-time job, which proved to be almost impossible. You were working 12- to 14-hour days, and I was all alone, trying to organize childcare — which we both assumed was my job.

Steve: Things were also very stressful from my point of view. I was working much harder than I ever wanted to in order to pay the bills. I would come home dead tired, expecting you to greet the conquering hero. Instead, you'd be fast asleep — dead to the world. Before the baby, we had spent lots of time together, but afterward, you were hardly ever available. I didn't think we'd ever sleep together again.

Sue: Looking back, it was all over so quickly, but it seemed then like forever.

Because a newborn child requires so much attention, a woman can become more concerned with being a mother than a wife. This is normal, just as it's normal for the father to experience competitive feelings with his own child for his wife's attention.

The following measures can help you deal with these unfamiliar changes:

✔ **Make special time to talk to each other about the emotional shifts that you're encountering.** This helps you understand what your partner is going through and diffuse much of the tension between you.

 • **For husbands:** Recognize that your wife is experiencing all sorts of profound psychological and hormonal changes that train much of her attention on the baby and away from you. Think of it as a natural expression of the maternal instinct.

 • **For wives:** Talk to your husband about how he can become more involved in caring for the baby. There's no reason he can't share in chores like feeding (if you're not breast feeding), bathing, or changing the baby's diapers. Your partner is likely to feel less resentful about your lack of attention as he becomes more involved in caring for the child. He will also develop a better understanding of what you're going through.

A marriage can be hurt if either partner becomes overly possessive, or allows resentment and competitive feelings to fester.

✔ **Treat the changes in your spouse's behavior as a temporary condition.** A baby's need for its mother's exclusive attention is a passing phase. As children develop, they soon require less intensive care from their parents, and spouses can more easily re-focus attention on each other.

If you can recognize these changes in priorities as part of the larger mosaic of your lifetime commitment to one another, you may have an easier time keeping your feelings in perspective and appreciating the joy of having children.

You and your partner are likely to have problems adjusting from a two to a three-person family, but that doesn't mean that you don't have a good marriage — or one that's in danger of falling apart. Committed partners can use the addition of a child as an opportunity to work out some of the unspoken expectations of their marriage and re-order their priorities.

Balancing Career and Family

Love and work are the cornerstones of our humanness.

— Sigmund Freud, neurologist

Here's to the working mom

According to a study by the Whirlpool Foundation, almost half of working mothers contribute more than half of household income — and that number is increasing each year. Twenty-first century men are making more of a contribution to caring for children. Nevertheless, working women still do most of this unpaid second job after they get home.

The Whirlpool researchers found that working mothers spend 32 hours a week doing household chores and an additional 28 hours a week caring for children — only slightly less than stay-at-home moms.

This and other studies clearly show that working mothers care just as much about their kids as their stay-at-home counterparts. Nevertheless, over 70 percent of working women told researchers that they regret not being able to spend more time with their children.

Until fairly recently, the roles of husbands and wives were well defined. In the traditional scheme of things, the man was the *conqueror* who went out into the world and earned money. Meanwhile the woman was the *nurturer* who cared for the kids and maintained the house.

By the end of the 1950s, women had made their way in the workplace in so-called "caretaking" professions, such as teaching and nursing. In subsequent years, women have become a growing force in virtually all professions and businesses. Over two-thirds of mothers with school-age children now have full-time jobs, yet they continue to remain their children's primary emotional caregiver.

In the 1970s, a best-selling book titled *You Can Have It All* sent a message that appealed to women who'd grown up in an era when many of them were told that "a woman's place is in the home." Women have long since proved that they can do virtually anything they want. However, in the process, many discovered that any woman (or man) who tries to "have it all" will eventually collapse from exhaustion.

You can only accomplish so much in a day. So, instead of trying to "have it all," accept the fact that life involves a series of choices and tradeoffs — and set your priorities accordingly.

Time versus money is a key tradeoff when you're trying to strike a balance between career and family. Every extra hour you devote to work amounts to one less hour that you can spend with your spouse and kids.

The following steps can help you negotiate this tradeoff:

- ✔ If possible, try to leave work a little earlier. If both you and your partner work, find a way to stagger your schedules so that one can be home and available to the children.

- ✔ Consider moving closer to work, so that commuting time can be turned into more hours available to spend with your family.

- ✔ Try budgeting more carefully to ease the financial pressures that require you to work such long hours. Then, cut down on your work hours.

- ✔ Consider downsizing. This is a strategy that goes against the grain of a culture that has conditioned us to keep acquiring bigger cars, bigger houses, and greater affluence. However, we know several families who have decided to drive less-expensive cars and live in less-expensive homes so that they can work less and spend more time together.

- ✔ Look for ways to work smarter rather than harder at your job. Becoming just a little more efficient can result in more time left for your family.

- ✔ As much as possible, try to devote weekends to spending time together as a family. Rather than filling those days with planned activities, leave some time for talking and just hanging out.

Resolving the Childcare Dilemma

I hate work. That's why I got married.

— Peg Bundy in *Married with Children*

Working mothers often feel a tremendous amount of ambivalence and guilt about going back to work following the birth of a child. "Isn't it wrong for me to leave my baby?" some anxious mothers ask. "Will my child be damaged if I put him in daycare?" other moms worry.

Despite all of the conflicting views on this highly charged subject, we have found that there is no one right answer for every mother and every family. However, many studies show that there's no difference in the emotional well-being of children whose mothers work outside the home. Research also indicates that high-quality infant care has no adverse effect on either the child's emotional development or the parent-child relationship. The most important factor seems to be that babies have a warm and consistent relationship with their caregivers.

You also have to think about your own needs. Your child will probably be well cared for if you choose to go back to your job. However, both men and women need to think about how much care of their child they want to delegate to someone else. It's a personal decision that each parent makes, based on his or her own needs as well as on an understanding of the needs of the child. A sense of balance is essential, because too much work on the part of either parent can end up depriving him or her of the incredibly rich experience of early childrearing.

Considering alternate work styles

If you want to work and still have more time to spend with your family, you can approach this issue a number of ways, including the following:

✔ **Part-time work:** If your boss is willing to employ you on, say, a half-time basis, this can be a viable alternative — assuming you can afford the cut in salary and the likely loss of benefits.

Part-time childcare tends to be more expensive than full-time care. For example, one learning center in our area charges $175 for a full week, but $60 on a daily basis.

✔ **Flextime:** A growing number of companies have found that it pays to accommodate their employees' desire to devote more time to their children. One large communications company allows some workers to leave early so that they can take their children to school or accompany them to after-school classes.

Flextime arrangements don't reduce the total number of hours you're required to work. However, a flexible schedule can help you adjust your week in ways that make it possible to spend more time with your family. This work option is especially helpful if your spouse and his or her employer can negotiate a flextime schedule that complements yours.

✔ **Shortened work weeks:** A growing number of companies have made it possible for employees to work four ten-hour days instead of five eight-hour days. Typically, the extra day off is a Monday or Friday.

✔ **Telecommuting:** As computers and electronic communications become more widespread and sophisticated, it has become feasible (even desirable) for companies to allow some of their employees to work at home and submit their projects via e-mail.

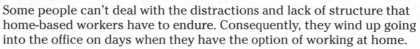

Some people can't deal with the distractions and lack of structure that home-based workers have to endure. Consequently, they wind up going into the office on days when they have the option of working at home.

Thanks anyway, I'd rather be at the office!

In her book, *The Time Bind,* sociologist Arlie Russell Hochschild presented research demonstrating that many wives and husbands would much rather work than spend time with their families — to the point that they postpone or decline paid vacations. The main reason for this is that people find work to be so much more enjoyable and interesting than life at home that they actually "come to work to relax."

At work, people have buddies, celebrate birthdays, and carry on flirtations. Hochschild concluded that the superficial buzz of office life is a source of intense pleasure for many individuals. For these women and men, work is an escape from a home life that seems far more complex and difficult to control. Hochschild concludes that this is why "many working [parents] are both prisoners and architects of the time bind in which they find themselves."

Dividing parental responsibilities

Who knows of the possibilities of love when men and women share not only children, home, and garden, not only the fulfillment of their biological roles, but the responsibilities and passions of the work that creates the human future and the full human knowledge of who they are?

— Betty Friedan, feminist author

The addition of a child means a lot of extra work for both of you, and you must ensure that this work is divided in a fair manner.

The following steps can help you and your spouse hammer out an equitable way to divide family responsibilities:

✔ **Give yourself an attitude adjustment.** It's important that both of you acknowledge one another's contribution to the family's well-being. Husbands who are married to full-time homemakers sometimes have difficulty acknowledging how hard homemakers work. This is a sign of an imbalance in a relationship.

If your spouse expects you to assume responsibility for all the childcare, remind him or her that marriage is a 50-50 partnership and that you expect your spouse to assume a significant role in this (and all other) aspects of family life. If you are both working full-time, your spouse needs to understand that childcare amounts to a second (unpaid!) full-time job. It's wrong to think of childcare as "woman's work" — even if that's the way it was done in your spouse's family of origin.

✔ **Strike an equitable split of family responsibilities.** We hear many husbands talk a good game of shared responsibility, but far fewer who are ready and willing to follow through. Many husbands (and wives) have trouble overcoming the belief that the spouse who earns the most money has more value than the one who does the most housework — even if they recognize that it's no longer in vogue to say so.

Full-time homemakers do much more than just take care of the children. They assume the primary responsibility for creating and maintaining the family home. All things considered, that non-paying work is no less important than the working spouse's paying job — even if it has been traditionally less valued by our culture.

Any husband who doubts the value of his wife's efforts as a full-time homemaker should be aware that divorce courts usually assess the monetary value of housework in a marriage as equal to that of the husband's full-time career, even if he earns hundreds of thousands of dollars.

An equitable split of responsibilities doesn't mean that every duty and chore is split 50/50, or that both spouses are doing half the work at all times. Some couples find it helpful to write down a list of their respective duties for a given week. But ultimately, there's no meaningful way to assign points for what each partner contributes. The key question is: Do both partners have equal influence in how family responsibilities are divided?

✔ **Sit down on a regular basis, and talk to each other about what goes on in your day.** This exercise helps you gain mutual respect for what each of you does with your time. When you make an effort to understand what's involved in one another's way of life, you develop a deeper appreciation for what the other person brings to the relationship.

✔ **Stay flexible.** Partners who function as a team recognize that there's a certain amount of work to be done to keep their family afloat. Both are ready to do whatever is necessary to accomplish that goal — even if it means giving more than they receive at any given time. This kind of approach requires both partners to be ready and willing to forgo their expectations about who does what for the good of the relationship.

In a flexible, team-oriented relationship, the working spouse does not feel demeaned if he or she is asked to make the bed or do laundry. By the same token, the stay-at-home spouse is willing to look for income-generating work, should that become necessary.

The more flexibility that you and your partner can build into your relationship, the easier you can adapt to unexpected circumstances and renegotiate new arrangements.

Deciding to Have a Second Child

Just when I think I'm out, they pull me back in!

— Michael Corleone in *Godfather III*

Not that long ago, the majority of parents didn't anguish about whether or when to have a second child. In most cases, that event automatically followed the birth of the first child by two to three years.

There is no right or wrong number of children for every couple, just as there is no best spacing between children. Every choice you make has different financial, emotional, and lifestyle consequences. The key is figuring out which choices suit your family.

Before you make your decision, we suggest that you consider the following questions:

- **Why do you want another child?** Sit down with your partner, and discuss the tradeoffs involved in having a second child. If you conclude that this is the right decision for you, ask yourself if the time is right.

  All children require work, but some are more difficult than others. Your first child may have been an "easy" baby — one that slept through the night, was good-tempered, and had no special physical or emotional problems. Have you thought about how your life would change if your next child were not so easy?

  He or she may be colicky, hyperactive, or chronically unable to fall asleep. In a more poignant scenario, the second baby may be born with a physical or mental disability. At that point, the child's special needs can become the central focus of the family's entire existence, and all family members have to make sacrifices.

- **Are you caving into family pressures?** Your own parents often reinforce negative stereotypes about "only children" because they're anxious for you to conform to what they think of as normal.

  Some couples are made to feel that they're not a "real family" until they have at least two children. Others fear that their first child will be harmed by growing up without a sibling. These are not sound reasons for having a second child.

- **Have you considered the impact a second child can have on your finances and career goals?** The decision to have another baby often signals the need for a bigger car, a larger home, and increased childcare expenses. The financial consideration is particularly important for women who put their careers on hold to stay home with the first child.

How we spaced the children

We waited the standard two-and-a-half years to have our second child. And, truth be told, we didn't think much about family spacing or what would best suit our family. Most people were having two children — and we pretty much followed the trend. While we have no regrets, a little more planning on our part would have been helpful.

Steve: Eric had gotten past the terrible twos, and there was finally a shot of getting back some of our freedom. But instead of taking advantage of it, we had another child.

Sue: Then, for two years after Kira was born, I was home again — taking care of two small kids. Having two children requires ten times more work than one, and I wasn't prepared for it.

Steve: It was at that point that we really had to confront the issue of sharing responsibilities. And those responsibilities were much greater than when there was only one baby in the house.

Sue: As time passed, we were very happy that we had expanded our family. Still, it would have been better if we'd been able to anticipate some of the consequences of this choice, or had delayed having a child for a few years. I don't know where the idea came from that the kids should be spaced 2 or 3 years apart. I think a little more time between Eric and Kira would have been better for us. It would have given us more time with each child. But then again, some families love the chaos of a whole bunch of little kids running around.

Steve: People buy into the notion that there's something wrong with having only one child. We are told that only children are too self-centered and don't know how to share.

Sue: I think those stereotypes are ridiculous. Our third child, Owen, was born 12 years after Kira. He's essentially an only child — and he's just great. I never have any regrets about waiting that long to have him.

Assume that your child is now three and ready for an all-day preschool. This would finally give you the opportunity to get your career back on track. But if you have another child, going back to work may mean paying the cost of two spots in a childcare facility.

Many women find themselves in a vicious cycle. It often makes good economic sense to stay home with both children, but that means delaying professional goals for several more years.

Whatever you decide, you will have to make tradeoffs among money, career advancement, and family planning.

✔ **Are you prepared for a child-oriented family?** With one child, you can still maintain an adult-oriented household. One child is relatively portable, and you can still travel and do many of the things you did when you were childless. However, two children always require major lifestyle alterations.

In considering whether or not you want a second child, don't ignore the chaos. Two children will almost always fight and squabble and make lots of noise. If you're not comfortable with that kind of commotion, you may decide to stop with one.

Some couples see lots of kids in the house as a hassle. Others find this kind of family life exciting. The ultimate decision about how large a family to have needs to be based on you and your partner's collective vision of what kind of a lifestyle you want. That vision should be based on honest dialog, not on some idealized version of a family that you see on TV.

Marriage without Kids

As long as there is one child on this planet, we are all parents.

— Joan Brady, author

Part of the mythology about marriage is the assumption that every couple should have children. In fact, most married partners do wind up having at least one child, whether by birth or by adoption. However, there are some couples who make a deliberate choice not to have children. Although, society frowns upon the child-free choice as abnormal and somehow wrong, we disagree.

The decision not to have children is a valid lifestyle choice. Couples who select the child-free option need not apologize to those who would criticize this very personal decision.

Child-free couples often have more time and financial freedom to pursue their careers and other interests. In many cases, they are able to have a greater impact on the community than if they were preoccupied with caring for their own children.

We have a friend who is a pediatrician married to a high school teacher. They both decided at the start of their marriage not to have their own kids. Over the years, they have both dedicated themselves to working with children in the inner city. Their efforts have had major positive effects on the lives of thousands of young people. "We don't need to raise our own children," our doctor friend told us. "There are plenty of kids out there to keep us busy."

However, the majority of childless couples didn't originally plan on a child-free lifestyle. Their choice is often the result of a losing battle with infertility. Over the past twenty years, advanced technologies such as in vitro fertilization have given new hope to infertile couples. However, each of these procedures costs thousands of dollars, and the success rate is no better than 20 to 30 percent. By the time a couple endures several of these high-tech procedures, they often find themselves tapped out financially and emotionally — and still without a baby.

Adoption offers another recourse for childless couples, but this is also not an easy or inexpensive proposition. In the United States, the cost averages around $15,000 for a domestic adoption and $25,000 for one overseas. Adoptive parents often go through a gut-wrenching process of broken promises and disappointments before they finally come home with a child, but many are thrilled with the ultimate result. Still, not everybody wants to adopt. Some couples can't accept another person's biological child. Others are unable or unwilling to deal with the financial and emotional strains.

Diane and Lou had gone through five unsuccessful high-tech fertility procedures over three years. They were both in their early forties and completely exhausted by the ordeal of what had become an emotional roller coaster. This professional couple had the financial means to pursue an adoption — but they had gone as far as they could emotionally.

"I know that adoption can be a very trying process," Diane told us. "I don't think either of us could stand the strain — not after all the disappointment we've already gone through."

We give couples like Diane and Lou the following advice to help them deal with the challenge of facing the finality of having no children:

- **Allow some time to grieve for your loss.** Whenever you lose something — even if it's a dream of a child you never had — you need to go through a process of grieving. You need time to alter your life-long vision of what your family is going to look like, and this is likely to generate a great deal of sadness.

  People sometimes try to dull their pain by turning to alcohol or drugs. This is a particularly destructive step because the high you feel is actually an artificial block that prevents you from dealing with your grief in more constructive ways.

  You can take a number of positive steps to deal with the sorrow that follows the realization that you will not have children. Some people find comfort in spirituality or religion. A variety of support groups help people cope with this type of loss through networking with others who have had similar experiences. (See Appendix B for information on how to contact these and other self-help groups and organizations.)

- **Stay close to your partner.** It's important for both of you to not be alone in your grief during this difficult time in your marriage. What's most important is that both of you come out of this period with a renewed vision of your relationship and a sense of how you are going to lead your lives.

  If one partner becomes withdrawn or distant, the other is likely to feel that he or she is being blamed for the disappointment that both partners are experiencing.

Women and men perceive the reality of a childless marriage in different ways. Although husbands may experience a deep sadness and feelings of inadequacy, wives are most vulnerable to feeling stigmatized by society and incomplete as human beings.

"I somehow feel that I didn't fulfill my destiny as a woman," one infertile client told us. "It's an emptiness I've never known before — and I feel it every time I see a mother with her baby."

✔ **Redirect your parenting instincts.** If "it takes a village to raise a child," everyone can participate in that village if he or she wants to.

More than anything else, being a parent is about nurturing and mentoring others. Whether or not you have children of your own, there is no shortage of opportunities to share your energies and gifts with those who need them.

Some people become "second fathers and mothers" to their nieces, nephews, or friends' children. Others become teachers, or volunteer to work with kids in schools, hospitals, or religious organizations. Still others mentor young people in the community or the workplace. The task for childless partners is to find a satisfying way of expressing their need to nurture.

Having children doesn't make a marriage (or a person) better or worse. We all have an opportunity to lead fulfilling lives, to have loving relationships — and to make the world a better place for all children!

Chapter 10
Women and Men at Midlife

. . . .

In This Chapter

▶ Coping with midlife anxieties

▶ Reassessing your personal and career goals

▶ Seizing the unique opportunities that midlife affords

▶ Recognizing a husband's midlife challenges

▶ Recognizing a wife's midlife challenges

. . . .

Marriage partners can experience an emotional crisis at any stage of *midlife,* which extends from age forty all the way to the mid-sixties. The problem often starts out as one partner's personal crisis, and may have little to do with the marriage. But before long, a once-good marriage can be in for a rough ride — especially if the other partner is experiencing an age-related crisis at the same time. That's why it's important to understand what you and your spouse are going through during this long and challenging transition.

In this chapter, we explore the problems and opportunities that you and your partner are likely to face during the midlife period. We look at how you can turn a potential midlife crisis into one of the most rewarding chapters of your life. We tell you what to expect during the various phases of midlife, and show how to use these predictable trouble spots as catalysts for personal growth and fulfillment.

Recognizing the First Stirrings of Middle Age

> *Silver threads among the gold. Ah, my friend, you're growing old.*
>
> — Traditional folk ballad

At forty, demographers consider you to be middle aged, although you may actually feel more youthful than you did in your twenties and thirties. You may sense that you've just reached adulthood at some point in your thirties — even though you may have already spent years raising one (or more) child.

Understanding why life extension occurs at middle age

In centuries past, teenagers were regarded as full-grown adults. However, as medical science has advanced, the life curve has stretched. Researchers have found that the increased ten-to-twenty years of life expectancy has been added to the middle, not to the end, of life. This means that men and women in their early thirties often experience a kind of extended adolescence, while those in their 40s, 50s, and 60s are also reaching certain milestones some ten years later than their counterparts in previous generations.

There are many advantages to gaining all this extra time. People are able to have children later in life; they have more years to reach their career goals — or to launch new, more-rewarding ventures.

How many times have we heard the thirty-something parents of a ten-year old say: "It seems like only yesterday that she was a baby taking her first steps." What these parents are also noting is the fact that, as their child has grown, they've somehow begun to feel the early stirrings of middle age.

By the time you reach forty, you're expected to conduct your life as a secure adult — someone who is settled in terms of both career and family responsibilities. At least that's what you've probably been told. That's why many people feel hemmed in by traditional expectations about what they're supposed to have achieved by a given age.

- ✔ Some men and women manage to meet these expectations in their thirties. If you're one of these people, you may be rising — but have not yet peaked — in your career. Your children are of school age — but not yet adolescents. You or your partner may be destined to have a midlife crisis down the road — but for now, your life seems to be well under control.

- ✔ Other wives and husbands in their thirties are struggling with themselves and with each other. You may feel anxious because you're not meeting your own expectations (or those of your family or society). And when these feelings of anxiety kick in, it often spells trouble for both you and your partner.

A crisis can occur whenever you feel trapped in your circumstances. When you're young, the world seems full of possibilities. But as the years go by, women and men often begin to feel frustrated about how their lives — and their marriages — are turning out.

Not so long ago, you and your partner were newly married and still passionately in love. In retrospect, those early years now look great. Chances are, you had a minimal number of responsibilities — and money left over after you paid the bills. Now, a few short years later, you have kids, mortgage payments — and more obligations than you ever imagined. Here's what can happen at midlife:

- ✔ You love your kids, but they now seem more interested in their peers and less responsive to you.

- ✔ Your spouse doesn't look as good to you as he or she once did. He's starting to lose his hair and is cultivating a belly; her waist is a little thicker than it was before she had children. Your partner may also feel stressed from life's pressures and responsibilities.

- ✔ You feel career pressures. Perhaps she gave up some of her most productive years to stay home with the kids. Now, she's wondering if she can pick up where she left off. Or maybe he's been working like a dog to make enough money for the growing family to have everything it needs. Lately, he's started to feel burned out.

To further complicate matters, that over-worked husband may not be so thrilled with his career — and wouldn't mind finding something more rewarding to do. Still, who can afford to quit when you'll have to face the escalating costs of sending your children to college — not to speak of your own eventual retirement? Considering all those colliding pressures and emotions, it's no wonder that both spouses feel frustrated and start taking it out on one another.

Wherever you are in your marriage, avoid blaming your partner for your frustrations. The following approaches can help you get out of the kind of the rut that people often experience in midlife:

- ✔ **Understand that you can't "have it all."** Every choice that you make in life precludes something else. For example, having children means that couples will have more responsibilities and less freedom than if they choose a child-free lifestyle. On the other hand, child-free couples miss out on the considerable rewards of parenthood.

- ✔ **Develop your own timetable.** Some things in life are time-sensitive; fortunately, most personal and career ambitions aren't subject to such strict time parameters. People write novels, start businesses, get advanced degrees, expand their horizons, and make contributions to the betterment of the world at all stages of life.

- ✔ **Avoid comparing yourself to others.** Advertisers make a handsome profit exploiting people by categorizing them according to certain simplistic expectations about how they're supposed to look, act, and conduct their lives at a given age. In reality, people are a lot more interesting (and a lot less predictable) than advertisers would have you believe.

The more you can march to your own drummer, the more fulfilling your life will be.

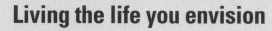

✔ **Manage time realistically.** Managing time is one of the most important ways to make the most of your choices. Do you want to pursue a business or career goal, spend more quality time with your family, undertake a creative venture, or simply have more hours in the week for leisure and relaxation? In order to accomplish any of these things, you have to understand how to use time in ways that reflect your particular lifestyle priorities.

Living the life you envision

As the years pass, it becomes increasingly more important that you spend time pursuing the kind of life you envision. If, for example, you decide that money and a powerful career are the most important values, the way you apportion your time will be different from someone whose priorities emphasize leisure or a rich family life. Here's how to attain the life you want:

✔ **Establish realistic goals in key areas of your life — including personal growth, family, career, spiritual life, and health.** Write down what you'd like to accomplish over the next year, five years, and ten years in each of these areas — and what you need to do to get there. Don't just go for high-sounding ideals. Be as honest with yourself as possible.

✔ **Discuss your goals and priorities with your spouse.** Tell him or her that your ultimate success requires his or her feedback and support.

Keep in mind that a goal must be *meaningful*. Unless you start out feeling that a goal has some intrinsic value to you, you won't have the drive to spend much time pursuing it.

A goal must also be *divisible*. In order to follow through on your goals, they must be divided into manageable steps that you can complete on a daily, monthly, and yearly basis.

A goal must be *tangible*. To realize a goal, you need to have a specific way to measure and observe your progress. If, for example, your goal is to spend more time with your partner, don't just say, "Let's put aside more time to be together." Set up regular date nights for the two of you to do things as a couple — and stick to that commitment.

✔ **Spend as much time as possible working on your priorities.** There are two keys to effective prioritizing: doing what's most important first, and devoting most of your time to your goals. Always be aware of what you're doing — and why. Take a minute to stand back and ask yourself: Is what I'm doing moving me toward my objectives? Or, would my time be better spent doing something else?

✔ **Don't waste your time.** Because time is limited, eliminate habits and people that drain your time.

✔ **Invest time in maintaining and improving your health.** Figure out a healthy diet that works for you. Schedule in times for regular exercise and relaxation. These affirmative measures are important in keeping you feeling young and making you less prone to illness, and also give you more positive energy to invest in your marriage.

Embracing the arc of life

Middle age is a time when women and men are forced to come to terms with their own mortality. The growth of your children tells you that time is marching on — as does the gradual aging of your body.

The death or illness of a parent is a sure sign that our own journey is finite. Your parents are said to belong to the "barrier generation to the grave." As long as they're alive, you may feel as if you'll live forever. With their death, you realize that you're the next to go. The death or collapse of someone close to our own age can serve as an even louder wake-up call.

There's a saying: In order to fully appreciate life, a person must come to terms with the inescapability of his own death. People who appreciate life's inevitable arc are better able to embrace the changes that come with age.

Meeting the Challenges of Your "Second Adulthood"

If you have to be somewhere, midlife is the place to be.

— From the conclusion of decade-long study on midlife

At forty, people have reached the statistical half-way point of life — a milestone some researchers have dubbed the "second adulthood." This is a time when the choices you've made start to feel more permanent. Career decisions are harder to reverse than they may have been ten years earlier. Couples who've postponed having children may find that it's too late to start. Most couples with children are already facing the formidable challenges that adolescents present.

In midlife, women and men have a unique opportunity to allow the hidden parts of themselves to blossom. A woman's midlife often focuses on self-fulfillment, self-discovery, and self assertion; a man's, on a heightened quest for intimacy. At midlife, wives and husbands both have greater freedom to be who they are and live the way they want.

Women and men in their forties and fifties may also be confronted with the demands and pressures of dealing with aging parents — who are often ill or dying. At this point, it begins to dawn on people that they're probably closer to the end of their lives than to the beginning. The following sections help you assess where you stand in key areas, so that you can become more effective in finding ways to meet the challenges of midlife.

Evaluating your personal satisfaction

Perhaps in middle age, one can, at last, be completely one's self. What a liberation that would be.

— Anne Morrow Lindberg, author

When a married individual experiences a personal crisis, he or she often shifts blame for disappointments to the spouse. That's understandable. You feel pretty much stuck with yourself, so you focus your dissatisfaction on the person closest to you. However, if you honestly reflect on what's really taking place, you're likely to find that your partner isn't the main cause of your problem.

If you allow your marriage to become a dumping ground for personal frustrations, you may wind up bickering and competing with each other.

Although it's human to do so, avoid blaming your partner for frustrations that are purely personal. That kind of venting may provide some short-term relief, but it only serves to alienate your partner. Plus, it takes the focus off of the one person who has the real power to make your situation better — you!

Pinpoint the problems and disappointments that have been bothering you. The following are some questions you may want to consider:

- ✔ Have you been preoccupied with thoughts about aging and mortality?

- ✔ Have you been distracted by issues involving your children or parents?

- ✔ Have you been feeling disappointed in your sex life?

- ✔ Have you been feeling disappointed in your friendships?

- ✔ Have you been having problems with — or second thoughts about — your career?

- ✔ Have you been having trouble sleeping?

- ✔ Have you been feeling ill or depressed?

- ✔ Have you been drinking more alcohol lately?

If you answered "yes" to one or more of these questions, talk to your partner about what's been bothering you. Ask if he or she is willing to work with you to make some changes.

If, for example, you're worried about aging, share your concerns with your partner. You may be able to help each other through such rough spots by being a good listener and offering support, perspective — and even a little humor. That won't happen if your spouse is unaware of your struggle, or feels blamed.

TRUE STORY

Janice and Jack at midlife

Forty-two-year-old Jack feels trapped in the job that he accepted ten years ago in order to meet the financial demands of his growing family. Now, he fears that it may be too late to realize his life-long ambition to start his own business.

"I'd love to quit my job, but that would put us in a financial hole," Jack told us. "It's depressing to realize that I may never have the chance to do what I really want."

Forty-year-old Janice also feels in a bind. She put her magazine editing career on hold for eight years so that she could stay home with the couple's two young children. Now, the kids are both in grade school, and she's ready to resume her career. However, Janice fears that she has lost too much ground.

"It's as though I'm back to square one," Janice told us. "I've lost all my seniority, and I'm too old to compete for an entry level position with recent college graduates."

Janice and Jack both have valid, age-related career concerns. Unfortunately, they've started blaming each other for their frustrations.

Jack wanted to wait a few more years before having children, but Janice felt that it was important to start a family while she was still young.

"I knew I should have launched my business before we had kids," Jack complained. "Now I'm trapped."

"Maybe if you had let me keep working, you could have gotten started sooner," Janice countered. "But you had it in your head that the kids would suffer if I didn't stay home with them. Now that things haven't gone the way you wanted, it's all my fault."

Eventually, they were able to acknowledge their mistakes and regrets, and come to understand each other's point of view.

WARNING!

Emotional problems — including those with sleep, depression, or alcohol abuse — may require medical or psychiatric consultation. However, these troubles are less likely to have as much of a negative impact on your marriage if you avoid the blame game and talk openly about them with your partner.

TIP

Good health tends to make you feel more energized — and more satisfied with life. Middle age is a great time for both men and women to take inventory of what they can do to optimize their health. The following questions can help you pinpoint areas where you can use some improvement:

- ✔ Do you exercise regularly?
- ✔ Do you practice good nutritional habits?
- ✔ Do you drink too much alcohol?
- ✔ Do you smoke?
- ✔ Do you get enough sleep?
- ✔ Do you make a conscious effort to relax?
- ✔ Do you engage in mentally stimulating leisure activities?

Evaluating your satisfaction with family-planning choices

> *Raising teenagers is like hanging wallpaper — just when you figure out what you're doing, you're done.*
>
> — Anonymous

It's not uncommon for wives and husbands who've enjoyed their young children to begin having problems as their kids grow older. Parenting adolescents can be difficult because it alters both partners' roles and foreshadows a time in the not-so-distant future when children will no longer be living in the house.

Asking the following questions and talking about them with your spouse can help you assess how you feel about your family-planning choices:

- ✔ What impact have children (or the absence of children) had on your marriage?

- ✔ What are your current feelings about the way you and your partner are dealing with your family?

- ✔ How have these interactions changed recently?

Adolescence has a well-earned reputation for being tough on everybody. This is partly because children are trying to forge their own independent identity at the same time that one or both of their parents may be re-considering *their* identities. Adolescence can also be a lengthy process, stretching from as early as age ten to as late as the mid-twenties. The longer a child's adolescence lasts, the greater the chances that it will collide with one or both parents' midlife identity crises.

As children grow into adolescence, parents start to have a lot less control over their kids' lives. Your child tends to be increasingly out of your sight and subject to the influence of peers. However, don't underestimate how much your child needs you — even though he or she rebels or accuses you of being "clueless."

You can exert a positive influence on the lives of your teenagers by taking the following steps:

- ✔ **Be prepared to listen — without being overly judgmental or dictatorial in asserting your authority.** Otherwise, your son or daughter may clam up and may have a hard time trusting you.

    Risk taking is necessary for an adolescent's growth and development — even if it makes you uncomfortable. It's up to you to help your teenager understand the difference between healthy and dangerous risk-taking.

✔ **Don't hesitate to make supervisory decisions.** Even though you no longer have as much control over your adolescent's day-to-day behavior, you can still make executive decisions involving his or her curfew and activities — as well as where the family resides and which school the child attends. We know of parents who've made the tough decision to move to a different neighborhood in order to get their adolescent away from troublesome friends or out of schools where drugs and alcohol are pervasive problems.

As your children evolve into young adults, they can become mirrors of your own self-doubts and unresolved conflicts. Mothers may begin to notice that men are paying more attention to their teenage daughters than to them. Fathers who've worked hard in less-than fulfilling careers to save money to send their kids to college may feel that they've sacrificed many of their own goals for teens who aren't motivated or appreciative.

Feelings of competition and resentment aren't unusual. However, if they become pervasive, they may signal deeper, unresolved emotional issues that require professional help.

Evaluating your career satisfaction

Change requires courage and determination. It holds the threat, as well as the thrill, of the unknown.

— Dru Scott, author and time-efficiency consultant

People in their forties and fifties often begin re-thinking their career options. Now that their older children need less supervision, spouses who've invested heavily in being homemakers may want to resume their former careers or pursue new opportunities. However, many fear that their age will be perceived as a negative.

Middle-age spouses, many of whom have already invested two decades in a single career, may fear being downsized just as the pressures of paying for college loom large. Others realize that they've put aside pursuing their true career ambitions to meet the financial obligations of their growing family. Now, they wonder if it's too late to make a change.

You may have chosen a career or job when you were very young — long before you were able to understand the impact of this decision. Most often, your choices were heavily influenced by parents, friends, and financial pressures. People in their "second adulthood" often think about forging new careers that better reflect their personalities and passions.

The following steps can help you select the career options that you'd like to pursue during the second half of your life:

- **Make a list of your talents, abilities and passions in a notebook or computer file that is devoted exclusively to your career.** This step signals that you're serious about pursuing new and more rewarding career goals. As you invest more time and energy in this self-assessment process, you will have a feeling of increased control over your choices.

  You may already be in a satisfying occupation. However, you may still want to take stock every so often. Even if you have no desire to switch careers, you may discover some changes that you can implement to make your work life even more challenging.

- **List three or more strengths that make you stand out.** We often hear people complain that the skills they use to earn a living don't draw on their greatest strengths. Unless you're applying those strengths in the workplace, you're probably not maximizing your true potential.

  Midlife career shifts force you to weigh your passions against your talents and your monetary needs. For example, you may have a love for jazz piano or abstract painting, but these may not be wise midlife career choices — especially if you lack exceptional talent or if you have bills to pay. On the other hand, you can always find creative ways to express your passions, even though many middle-aged people are shy about doing so.

- **Don't let age hold you back.** We hear people as young as thirty complain that they're too old to get another job or start a new career. Actually, you can find more opportunities for entrepreneurial businesses now than ever before — and age is almost never a factor when you're your own boss. Furthermore, research shows that older workers offer some definite advantages to employers. Highlight as many of the following benefits in your résumés and interviews that you feel give you an edge:

  - A level of maturity and judgment that younger people are not likely to possess.

  - Decades of life and work experience.

  - More developed skills at solving problems and handling interpersonal relations.

  - More highly motivated to do well.

  - A fat Rolodex containing lots of contacts.

  - Less likely to change companies.

In most states, it's illegal to fire or refuse to hire any employee because of their advancing age. This discrimination protection generally starts as young as 40.

Seek out the knowledge that you need. In order to plan new career moves effectively, you need to gather pertinent information — especially if you're pursuing unfamiliar goals. The following steps are particularly helpful in getting the information you need as you revise your career objectives:

- ✔ Determine what you need to know to achieve your goals.
- ✔ Make a written list of the questions that you want to ask.
- ✔ Attend seminars, take courses, and read extensively on relevant topics.
- ✔ Identify everyone you know who may have that information that you need — and contact them.
- ✔ Become familiar with the Internet and start using it.
- ✔ Don't rely solely on any one opinion or source of advice.

Ask yourself the following question: If I could do anything I wanted, what would it be? Set no limits on your thoughts — no matter how crazy they may seem. Then, be creative in coming up with different ways to reach your goal. Instead of looking at the big picture, pick out a small, achievable project and set it into motion.

Understanding Men's Midlife Concerns

Every man must grieve and accept the symbolic death of the youthful hero in himself, and then work through a process of reevaluation and reassessment.

— Daniel Levinson, microbiologist

When a man reaches his mid-forties, he often begins to fear that he's losing control over his life. At this age, a man often becomes anxious about work because he fears that he's reached the peak of his success. He may have recently been passed over for a promotion and senses that it's all downhill from here.

Many of the middle-age males we see are focused on their waning physical powers — though these losses are often more imagined than real. A 45-year old man may be just as vigorous as ever, but now there are some aches and pains after a workout at the gym. To compensate, he tries to play full-court basketball for the first time in 20 years, and winds up injuring himself.

Feelings of defeat and loss of control can decrease a man's testosterone levels, increase his performance anxiety, and cause him to act in ways that are troubling to his wife (see Chapter 7 for more information). Suddenly, the middle-age husband may find that he's unable to achieve an erection. So, he dyes his hair, or buys a sports car he can't afford, or starts looking lustfully at his secretary — or at his teenage daughter's friends.

Midlife crisis may be a myth

A landmark ten-year study on midlife development in the United States by the MacArthur Foundation disputes the notion that a midlife crisis is bound to happen. Instead, the researchers found that, "On balance . . . midlife is the best place to be." Their findings include the following:

✔ Over half of the 40- to 60-year-old women and men surveyed reported feeling better about their lives than they did ten years ago.

✔ Middle-age people find life to be challenging but rewarding. In general, they are less worried and nervous than people under 40.

✔ Most mid-lifers feel a growing sense of control over their careers and financial futures.

✔ Over 70 percent of those surveyed described their health as excellent, and were optimistic that they would stay that way in the years to come.

✔ For most midlife women, menopause isn't nearly the ordeal they feared. Some 62 percent of post-menopausal women expressed relief that their periods stopped.

Research shows that the loss of self-image and the injury to a man's ego in midlife can place him at greater risk for depression, heart disease — and even early death. The following five triggers appear to pose the greatest danger to a middle-age man's health:

✔ Death or serious illness of a parent or close friend

✔ Actual or potential job loss

✔ A major financial setback

✔ A recent physical checkup that reveals previously undiagnosed medical problems

✔ Erectile difficulty or sudden decrease in sexual desire

Men can counter the negative impact of these circumstances by taking the following steps:

✔ **Be open to new friends.** The death of a close friend can be a tangible loss to a middle-age man, as well as a sign of his own mortality. Women seem to be able to develop new friendships into middle age and beyond. However, many of the middle-age men we see haven't made a close friend since they were in their twenties.

You can find many opportunities to form new friendships. However, men need to understand the importance of cultivating these relationships, and become willing to reach out.

Midlife friendships can be based on common cultural or intellectual interests, such as music, films, or painting — as opposed to meeting people at work. Becoming active in mentoring or volunteer work is another good way to meet new friends. Political, social, or personal issues also serve to bring people together. These can include: working for political candidates, taking an active role in community affairs, and attending meetings of groups where people help each other cope with personal issues like alcoholism, surviving a heart attack, or grieving for a lost family member.

✔ **Start developing alternate career options.** As soon as you begin to feel dissatisfied with your career or fearful about losing your job, we suggest that you take the following steps:

- Reassess what work means to you. Do you really want (or need) to be working as hard as you're working now? If not, start designing a more comfortable and rewarding work style.

- Discuss your feelings with your partner.

- Begin assessing other, more-promising career options.

Your spouse's work issues may be much different than yours, so don't expect her to automatically understand or share your perspective.

✔ **Sit down with your wife and cooperatively start to re-evaluate your lifestyle.** Choices that you made 10 or 20 years ago may not work as well today — your wife may already be well aware of this.

✔ **Recognize age-related changes that can impact sexual performance.** Although men can remain sexually active into their eighties and beyond, it's not unusual for hormonal changes to impede a man's sexual performance in his fifties — or even his forties.

Most midlife male sexual problems are temporary responses that can be treated or controlled. Impotence can be caused by stress, high blood pressure, undiagnosed diabetes, too much alcohol, or a lack of exercise. Go to Chapter 7 for the lowdown on these illnesses. Your doctor can help you determine whether the problem is physical or emotional and come up with an effective treatment plan.

Understanding a Woman's Emotional Changes at Midlife

I try to see aging as a privilege. Aging allows me to do anything I want. It gives me freedom to speak up and tell the truth.

— Jeanne Moreau, actress

By the time most married women reach midlife, they have often spent a great deal of their time taking responsibility for the well-being of others. After devoting decades to caring for their husbands and children, many midlife women finally have a chance to pursue their own dreams and goals.

Women who don't seize the opportunity for the change and renewal that midlife affords often find this transition troubling. Some women have difficulty facing the loss of their youthful looks or their ability to bear children. Others feel trapped by aging and ailing elderly parents (or in-laws) who require their care and sap their energy.

Even with these losses and potential problems, midlife is a rich and exciting time for a woman. However, this doesn't just happen automatically. A woman has to work hard to re-shape her life, if she feels the need to do so.

Women today are more empowered than at any previous time in history to take advantage of the many opportunities that midlife affords. We see a growing number of women in their 40s, 50s, 60s, and 70s going for advanced degrees, starting new enterprises, pursuing artistic passions, and running for political office.

We suggest the following guidelines for women who want to make the most of the second half of life:

✔ **Focus on yourself for a change.** Women in western culture often fulfill their relationship needs by nurturing husbands, children, and parents. Midlife is a time for a woman to worry less about others and start following her own muse.

Whenever you change your approach, the people around you are forced to see you in a new light. Family and friends may greet the new you with confusion — or even anger — at first, but this is an unavoidable part of the process. It's going to take time for you — and those closest to you — to become accustomed to changes in your behavior. So, be patient with them and with yourself.

✔ **Move beyond the old stereotypes.** Some women feel that they have to follow the same paths as their mothers and grandmothers. In past generations, women usually built their lives around caring for their homes and families, although there were always some exceptions.

Today's midlife women have many more positive role models to inspire and support them. Seek out these women who've made it, and also others who are looking to break out of the traditional mold; get together with them on a regular basis; exchange life stories, plans, and dreams; and pool your resources.

✔ **Take your time finding a new balance.** Time becomes more precious in midlife, so it's important to make the most of it. Still, there's no hurry. Think about your options, catch your breath, and re-adjust your pace until you find a new balance that feels right.

✔ **Give yourself time to face the sense of loss that aging brings.** There's always a certain amount of grief that comes with any loss — including the loss of youth. You may grieve for opportunities that you may have missed or that you didn't take full advantage of. This is a perfectly natural response — one you should never ignore or resist.

The only way to move forward is to accept your past choices — and your losses — whether it's the loss of a loved one or the loss of your girlhood. Midlife is a time to accept all sides of yourself, to make peace with your past — and to begin taking full advantage of all the good years that lie ahead.

Understanding a Woman's Physical Changes at Midlife

Archie Bunker (to his wife): Edith, if you're gonna have a change of life, you gotta do it right now. I'm gonna give you just 30 seconds. Now come on, CHANGE!!

Edith Bunker (to her husband): Can I finish my soup first?

— from the TV series, *All in the Family*

At midlife, women have more well-defined physical changes than men. When a woman completes her last menstrual cycle, she enters menopause — a stage that is often referred to as *the change of life*.

Trying to look young

Sue: One of the most daunting losses women face at midlife is that they're no longer considered sexually desirable — at least not in the same way.

Steve: Men have lots of the same issues — like growing bald and having their hair turn gray.

Sue: Still, men aren't considered less sexy when they get older, the way that women are. Even very attractive women in their fifties will often say, "Men always flirted with me wherever I went. Then, suddenly, the flirting stopped!" A woman can suffer a real loss of identity when that happens.

Steve: When you were in your thirties and some guy whistled at you, you thought he was obnoxious. Now you miss it. As Freud once asked, "What do women want anyway?"

Sue: We'd like to have a choice!

Steve: I have to tell you that I was pretty uptight when my hair started falling out. It wasn't an easy choice, but eventually, I decided to shave my head, and I got to like it.

Sue: Any woman with a shaved head looks like she's in cancer chemotherapy. No matter what, we're expected to keep our youthful appearance as we age. At the same time, women who try to stay young by wearing certain kinds of clothes or spending a lot of money for plastic surgery get accused of being vain — and even ridiculous. You can't win!

Respecting the sacredness of later life

In Western society, women who reach menopause often fear that they're "over the hill." This stigma, which can cause a woman to feel depressed and "dried up," has more to do with cultural values than physical aging. We know this to be true because post-menopausal women rarely experience these symptoms in societies where they are valued and respected.

In some cultures, when a woman's periods have stopped, she joins in a ritual that endows her with the same respect awarded to the most powerful men in that society. In the Yanomamo tribe of South America, older women are considered sacred, and awarded far more power and status than their younger counterparts.

In cultures that value older women and offer them significant social roles, many of the troublesome physical and emotional symptoms associated with menopause are almost non-existent.

Many women have a difficult time dealing with the reality that they can no longer bear children. This transition is especially difficult for women who were brought up to believe that child-bearing is their primary role in life. The concept of the ticking biological clock can be especially potent for women who've never had children. But we've also seen many women who've completed their families get thrown into a midlife crisis by the *idea* that their child-bearing years are coming to an end.

We offer the following suggestions if you're having emotional and physical problems during this transition:

- **Accentuate the *pause* in menopause.** Use this passage in your life as a time to reflect on where you've been and to think about how you're going to enjoy all of the good years that lie ahead.

   Menopause is a bridge between youth and a midlife period that can last for decades. A woman's life expectancy was about 45 years at the beginning of the 20th century. It is now over 80 years. That means many women will be post-menopausal for over half their lives.

- **Obtain sound medical advice.** Your family doctor or gynecologist can tell you how close you are to menopause, and advise you on the best way to deal with it. Some doctors encourage women to begin estrogen replacement therapy several years before the actual onset of menopause. Others believe in waiting until a woman's menstrual cycle is about to stop. Still others encourage most of their patients not to use estrogen at all. Seek out information on the subject, and make your own assessment. If you have any doubts, we suggest getting a second — and even a third — medical opinion.

Your doctor can prescribe a variety of estrogen-based formulas. Every woman has to find her own particular amount and combination of drugs, so you may have to experiment for several months until you and your doctor find the best form and dose of estrogen for you.

Women also fear that, after their reproductive abilities are shut down, they'll no longer be sexually desirable, and that this will somehow make them less valuable as people.

The fact that a woman can no longer bear children doesn't make her less sexually desirable or less able to experience the physical and emotional joys of sex. Research shows that over 75 percent of women experience as much — or more — sexual satisfaction than they did before menopause.

Many women experience menopause as a catalyst for change, growth, and new-found freedom. Women describe themselves as feeling more confident and energetic — as well as sexually freer. Margaret Mead calls this phenomenon *postmenopausal zest,* which she credits to the energy and creativity that's released when a woman realizes that child-bearing and child-rearing are no longer her primary functions.

The pluses and minuses of estrogen replacement therapy

Estrogen, the reproductive hormone that occurs naturally in a woman's body, also strengthens the heart and bones. As estrogen levels decrease with the onset of menopause, a woman's risk of heart disease, osteoporosis, and memory loss increases. Estrogen replacement therapy significantly reduces those risks — and should be considered seriously if you're over forty, especially if you have a family history that increases your risk of any of these problems.

On the negative side, there is research suggesting that estrogen therapy may carry an increased risk of breast and uterine cancer, as well as gallstones and blood clots, especially in women with family histories of those diseases.

Doctors who are skeptical of estrogen sometimes suggest a variety of natural and pharmaceutical alternatives. For osteoporosis, calcium and vitamin D tend to strengthen bones, as does a regular program of weight-bearing exercises. There are also several promising prescription drugs on the market that control osteoporosis.

For women at risk for cardiovascular disease, some doctors recommend coenzyme-Q10, vitamin E, an increase of soy and fish oils in the diet — as well as a regular program of aerobic exercise.

A woman can begin feeling the effects of menopause as many as ten years before her menstrual periods stop. So-called *perimenopausal symptoms,* such as hot flashes, sleeplessness, and inexplicable periods of emotional distress, are signals that she is going through hormonal changes, and she's going to need support and understanding.

Don't get derailed by anxiety and negative stereotypes about menopause and middle age. Midlife women — and men — have a wealth of experiences and resources to draw on. This is the time to find activities that enrich your life, and to stretch yourself in new directions. Be good to yourself and to those you love!

Chapter 11

Making the Most of Marriage at Midlife

- -

In This Chapter

▶ Assessing your marriage at midlife

▶ Feathering the empty nest

▶ Restructuring the terms of your relationship

▶ Helping aging parents without hurting your marriage

▶ Getting ready for retirement

- -

*A*fter 20 or more years of marriage, it may seem a little late to ask yourself if you picked the right person. After all, it's way past the warranty period. Still, midlife is the time when wives and husbands are likely to ask that question.

Research shows that partners who've been together for between 20 and 30 years are at high risk for divorce. That's not surprising, considering the turbulent changes these wives and husbands face (see Chapter 10).

In midlife, married partners often find themselves sandwiched between two generations. Coming up behind the typical midlife couple are their adolescent children — who may require years of emotional and financial support before they become self-sufficient. Ahead of them are their are aging parents — who may be sick or dying. These changes come at a time when the partners are likely to be reflecting on their own mortality and on the choices that define their lives.

To further complicate matters, partners often find that they are moving in opposite directions in terms of occupational and social needs. Typically, husbands who've worked in the same career for almost 25 years may be looking forward to a time when they'll be able to travel and enjoy life. But wives who've devoted much of their lives to caring for a home and children often view this period as an opportunity to pursue unfulfilled work-related goals.

Couples facing this kaleidoscope of difficult circumstances must make special efforts to communicate openly and be sensitive to each other's needs. However, most marriages go through some kind of midlife crisis, just like most people do. For committed couples who pull together and negotiate these challenges as a team, midlife will be a rich and fulfilling time.

In this chapter, we show you how to handle the different issues and phases of this long transition so that you can be one of the couples for whom midlife is a peak period for happiness.

Evaluating Your Marriage at Midlife

There are three periods in life: youth, middle age, and "how well you look."

— Nelson A. Rockefeller, politician

Every man and woman goes through his or her own life cycle, and so does a marriage. These cycles occur simultaneously — sometimes in harmony, and sometimes not. Because midlife is such a critical period for both partners and the marriage, it's especially important to take stock during this phase.

The following questionnaire deals with the important midlife marriage issues. Circle the answer that best describes your current situation. This exercise is especially helpful when both partners complete it and then compare results, helping you see how close or far apart you are in the way you perceive key issues in your relationship.

1. **Has marriage met your expectations?**

   a. Yes.

   b. Not totally.

   c. We just stay together for the sake of the children.

   d. I would like to get out.

2. **Do you consider your spouse your best friend?**

   a. Yes.

   b. A good friend most of the time.

   c. A good friend under certain circumstances.

   d. No.

3. **Does your spouse listen to you when you discuss problems with him or her?**

    a. Yes.

    b. More often than not.

    c. Sometimes.

    d. I may as well talk to the wall.

4. **Our disagreements:**

    a. Generally end up getting resolved or at least understood.

    b. Usually end up in a standoff and keep recurring.

    c. Seem to be getting worse.

    d. We never discuss any disagreements.

5. **How are you making it financially?**

    a. We have more than enough.

    b. We're okay.

    c. We're always fighting about how to spend our income.

    d. There simply isn't enough.

6. **How do you feel about your work?**

    a. It's still exciting.

    b. I'm bored.

    c. I'm ready for a career change.

    d. I feel completely trapped.

7. **How do you spend your leisure time?**

    a. We have many shared interests and enjoy doing things together.

    b. We generally enjoy doing things independently.

    c. We have few shared interests, and that is a cause of conflict.

    d. We never seem to see one another.

8. **How is your sexual relationship?**

    a. Great.

    b. Getting better.

    c. Stagnant.

    d. We're both too tired.

9. **Has infidelity become a problem?**

   a. No.

   b. I think my spouse is having an affair.

   c. There have already been affairs, but we have survived.

   d. There have already been affairs, and it has hurt our marriage.

10. **Do you and your spouse have similar ideas about retirement?**

    a. Yes.

    b. We have some differences, but they can probably be worked out.

    c. We have substantial differences.

    d. We never discuss this issue.

Scoring: 4 points for each "a" response; 3 points for each "b"; 2 points for each "c"; 1 point for each "d."

In general, an "a" or "b" response indicates that the issue raised by the question does not present a problem at this point. A "c" response indicates a potential area of difficulty. A "d" response indicates a significant problem in your marriage.

Now add up the numbers. A score 30 points or more means you're doing very well. A score of 20 to 29 suggests that you may have some problems, which you can probably fix with the help of this book. A score of less than 20, or a wide disparity between your score and your partner's, suggests that you may need professional counseling. (Turn to Chapter 16 for getting outside help.)

Please pay close attention to those questions with an answer of "c" or "d". These are the areas that are of greatest concern. If your partner has also completed the exercise, look for those questions where your ratings are furthest apart. A careful analysis of the pattern of differences gives you a good idea where the most work needs to be done, individually and as a couple.

Becoming a Couple Again after Children Grow Up

You're getting old when you don't care where your spouse goes — just as long as you don't have to go with her.

— Anonymous

What happens to a marriage when teen-aged children evolve into young adults who go to college or go out on their own? One rather grim view pictures wives as becoming depressed or frantic in their efforts to fill their lives with meaning. The scenario for husbands is somewhat different — because a man's focus is often more on career and less on child-rearing. However, husbands too can be burdened by the fear of impending old age, and they sometimes miss the kids more than their wives do. Ironically, many men's mid-life hunger for intimacy turns them back to the family just when the kids are leaving. This is all part of what is known as *empty-nest syndrome*.

Even though husbands and wives can experience anxiety about their grown children leaving the home, many find this initially painful transition to be a positive force in their marriage. Research shows that mid-life couples who've launched their children have happier marriages and enjoy life more than those of the same age whose children continue to live with them, or those who've never had kids. Many couples actually look forward to their children leaving the house, and find that this is one of the happiest times for their relationships.

Here's how you can set the stage for a positive empty-nest experience:

✔ **Prepare yourself for the inevitable.** Some parents have trouble letting go of their children. Spouses who've spent their entire marriage caring for home and family sometimes fret over what they'll do after their last child leaves. The vast majority of parents readily acknowledge that their children's leaving is an essential part of the life process. Parents usually understand that their children don't need them in the same ways that they used to.

✔ **Think of new ways to re-channel your energies — both as individuals and as a couple.** Your children may not have required your physical attention for years. However, once they're out of the house, the sense of freedom may seem more real.

✔ **Lay the groundwork with your children for maintaining close ties.** Research shows that parents who have positive relations with their children are best able to cope with this transition.

If you don't stay close to your kids after they leave, the pain of missing them continues to linger. Staying close also smooths the way for positive interactions with your grown child's spouse and his or her family.

✔ **Consider downsizing to a smaller home, or renovating your present home.** This can give you the feeling that you're launching a new lifestyle.

✔ **Allow time for an adjustment period.** After investing so many years sharing your home with your children, you're bound to feel some sense of loss when they go. Part of your pain may date back to your own leaving home — and the stresses you may have had with your family of origin during that period. Give yourself time to reflect on those feelings, and share your thoughts and anxieties with your partner.

Studies show that couples often experience a kind of second honeymoon after the children are launched. With the kids out of the house, the partners now have an opportunity to re-focus their energies on each other — and on making their marriage more exciting.

Use the launching phase as an opportunity to develop a new intimacy with your partner. After all of your children are out of the house, you're both likely to feel less distracted and inhibited. If you and your spouse are able to support each other through this transition, you may soon discover that you are naturally becoming more affectionate and sexually responsive.

At this point, husbands and wives in a committed relationship have weathered many storms together and have grown closer than ever. They now have decades of shared history and have found ways to communicate and deal with their differences. This is the time when partners often find themselves falling in love with each other all over again.

Spouses who haven't dealt with their differences as a couple, or who have buried their negative feelings throughout their marriage, may not be able to re-group after their children are out of their house. Children often act as a buffer between husbands and wives. As a result, problems can get pushed under the rug, and resurface only after the last child has left. If this sounds like you, take a look at the communication and conflict-resolution techniques we discuss in Chapters 4 and 5, and use them to air out unresolved or long-buried issues. Couples therapy can also be helpful — but only if both partners are committed to working out their problems.

Redesigning Your Marriage

> *The person who views the world at 50 the same as at 20 has wasted 30 years.*
>
> — Muhammad Ali, professional boxer

In midlife, you and your partner are likely to discover that you have the opportunity — as well as the desire — to probe unexplored parts of yourselves. This often leads to a kind of gender role-swapping between married partners.

- ✔ Wives who've spent 20 years caring for a home and family may not have had time to pursue career goals and other outside interests. Midlife is a time when women in this position often become more confident, independent, and driven.

- ✔ Husbands who've spent their adult lives competing in the workplace may yearn to try something new. More often than not, that something involves adopting a more laid-back lifestyle, engaging in activities that are less competitive, and taking more of a nurturing role.

During midlife, wives and husbands often find themselves moving in opposite directions and at different paces. These changes can be confusing, because they force both partners to redefine their roles and the balance of power and expectations on which the marriage has rested for decades.

If only one partner changes, while the other one remains stagnant, there's sure to be conflict. Think of your marriage as a dance that you've both been doing for many years. Then, work at inventing a new dance — one that you and your partner can do together.

Married couples can deal with this process by using the following guidelines:

- **Help each other cope with change.** Whenever one partner attempts to make a lifestyle change or alter long-established roles, it's bound to create discomfort and conflict in the marriage. The way to move beyond this impasse is to be aware of yourself and the potential effect your unfamiliar attitudes and behaviors can have on your partner — and find constructive ways to deal with these changes.

  It's human nature to resist leaving familiar comfort zones, and you may have to encourage your partner to do so. A spouse who acts like he doesn't want you to change and grow may be acting out of his own fear of change. You can help your partner (and your marriage) by showing empathy for this resistance, while gently encouraging your spouse to explore dormant parts of him- or herself and to join you in some new adventures.

- **Find things that you can do as a couple — and alone.** The two of you may find some kind of joint venture. If you both love books, for example, perhaps you can start a study group or run a workshop at your local library. If you share a passion for politics or the environment, you can join forces in taking an active role in promoting those causes.

Naturally, you and your spouse will want to pursue some activities on your own. This is every bit as essential as doing things jointly because, especially in midlife, the two of you will find yourselves moving in new, sometimes opposite, directions to address your respective needs.

Midlife presents both partners with an opportunity to redesign their marriage. However, both spouses must be willing to take an active role in the process — or the marriage may not survive.

Caring for Aging Parents

Children despise their parents until the age of 40, when they suddenly become just like them — thus preserving the system.

— Quentin Crewe, travel and food writer

The aging and eventual death of your own mother and father and your partner's parents is an expected part of midlife — but that doesn't make it easy. Studies show that middle-aged couples can expect to spend as many years caring for their parents as they do caring for their children. Aging parents often become ill and require help. This can put a strain on a marriage, especially if that person has to move into the family home.

When an infirm parent enters what is often an already complicated generational mix, the added stress on a marriage can be overwhelming. The following suggestions can help married partners who are caring for aging parents:

- **Think of the added responsibility as an opportunity for growth.** Most married couples are already up to their neck in responsibilities. The extra time and effort it takes to care for an aging parent may be a major burden, but the experience can add depth and value to your lives. Spending time with an aging parent can give you an opportunity to become closer with a loved one — and to resolve earlier conflicts that have persisted for years. This kind of caregiving can also increase your capacity for patience and understanding. However, this may not be a solution for every family, and some elderly people are too confused or physically ill to be kept at home.

Your family's relationship with an aging parent doesn't have to be a one-way street. Senior family members often have much love and wisdom to impart — especially to children in the home. If they are financially secure, grandparents may also be able to contribute to the family's material well-being. They also make great and loving babysitters.

Adults who care for elderly parents report symptoms of depression almost four times more often than the person they're caring for. One reason for such a reaction is that the caregiver is forced to confront her or his own aging and fear of death. Another tough emotional issue is the role reversal that takes place when you care for a parent who is no longer capable of living independently. A mother may enjoy feeding and bathing a helpless child. However, a grown daughter who has to dress and bathe her now-helpless elderly mother may feel profound sadness and confusion in having to play the parental role to a mother who has become dependent. Wives and husbands who feel depressed or overwhelmed by these emotions should consider seeking out a support group.

- **Make certain that your spouse shares the responsibility.** Caring for an older parent needs to be a joint effort — regardless of whether that parent is yours or your partner's.

In the vast majority of families, it's the wife who does most of the caretaking for aging relatives — both hers and her husband's. However, it's important that both partners share the responsibilities equitably. Children and young adults who are still in the home should also be encouraged to participate in the caretaking process.

✔ **Prioritize, prioritize, prioritize!** Adding an aging parent to your already full plate can be stressful and time consuming. Taking care of a home, a job, parents and children can result in *role overload,* which often leads to feelings of inadequacy and depression. One way to deal with this is to make a list of all the things you do in a given week. Rate each one in order of priority. Then, start at the bottom of the list, and eliminate everything that you consider to be non-essential.

You can't do everything. Caring for an elderly relative can burn you out — both physically and emotionally. This is not a time to take on any new commitments that sap your energy. However, it's a good idea to devote some time to activities that sustain you physically and emotionally.

Encourage the senior relative to live independently as long as possible, if that's what he or she wants. Be careful about taking an aging or ailing parent into your home if he or she is capable of independent living. Sometimes, a well-meaning attempt to move an older person out of familiar surroundings can be devastating to that person.

✔ **Don't let guilt drive your care-taking decisions.** Many conflicting emotions come into play when a parent needs your help. You love that person and want to do your best, but that doesn't mean you should have to jeopardize your marriage because of guilt or a false sense of duty. You can help your senior relative remain autonomous by doing the following:

- **Find out which services your relative requires and the best way to access them.** Some communities provide free or low-cost meals for seniors, shopping assistance, and a variety of other supports. Contact your local social services agency to determine your relative's eligibility. Supplement these with paid services, as your family budget permits. Devote your time to helping your relative with those tasks that *really* require your personal attention.

- **Be respectful, but set limits.** Older parents sometimes make unrealistic demands on their adult children. They may claim that allowing strangers to shop or cook for them is unacceptable, which can leave you holding the bag. You must determine which tasks you should do and which can be hired out. More often than not, what your parent or in-law needs most is to be treated with dignity and included in family activities and decisions.

- **Be mindful of safety.** Keep an eye open for certain red flags that indicate the need for certain security precautions. Is it still safe for the person to be driving a car? Has he or she recently become forgetful? Do you see other behaviors that tell you that your relative may be a danger to him- or herself or others?

As your parents or in-laws get older, be watchful of how they're conducting their lives. Are they keeping up with their bills? Are they able to shop and are they eating enough? Have you noticed that the mail is piling up? It's important to take an interest in how they're holding up.

✔ **Be prepared to make some hard decisions.** However much you love your parent and want to provide personal care, you may have circumstances in which your best alternative is to place that senior in an assisted living facility. If, for example, the relative becomes incapable of doing anything for him- or herself, or if he or she starts verbally abusing your spouse or your children, the relative may need the kind of around-the-clock care that most families are unable to provide.

Placing a parent or in-law in a nursing home is never an easy choice. However, it's one that couples sometimes have to make — for the senior relative's sake, for the other members of the household, and to preserve their marriage. If there is serious disagreement about how to proceed, seek out a social worker with geriatric expertise to help you make a decision.

In addition to the emotional turmoil that nursing homes entail, they can also be very expensive. Without careful planning, an older person's lifetime savings can be wiped out in a few years. Seniors in assisted-living facilities are also easy targets for thieves and looters. An elder care attorney can be invaluable in helping your family sort out the financial details of a nursing home placement.

Planning for Retirement

I really think that it's better to retire . . . while you still have some snap left in your garters.

— Russell B. Long, United States Senator

Not long ago, 65 years old was considered the end of a person's productive working life. Many companies would force people of that age to accept mandatory retirement. They'd hand you the proverbial gold watch and wish you a pleasant time playing shuffleboard in some sunny retirement community. As with many other long-standing traditions, the retirement picture has undergone some radical changes during the past two generations.

On one side of the retirement coin, you have men and women who either want or have to continue working throughout their lives. Some of these people need the money; others simply want to remain productive — though not necessarily in the same line of work they've been doing most of their lives.

On the other side, you see financially secure people as young as 50 who want a change in lifestyle. They may seek to be involved in something they consider more meaningful than work, or to spend the bulk of their time traveling and pursuing leisure activities. Here are two examples:

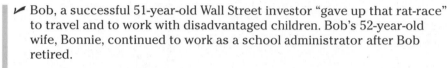

- ✔ Bob, a successful 51-year-old Wall Street investor "gave up that rat-race" to travel and to work with disadvantaged children. Bob's 52-year-old wife, Bonnie, continued to work as a school administrator after Bob retired.

- ✔ Allison, a 54-year-old attorney who was a partner in a large law firm, recently resigned after a 20-year tenure. A few months later, she and her husband, Sam, moved to Arizona. Allison now spends her time painting and working part-time at a free legal clinic. Sam, a freelance journalist, had no problem going along with his wife's retirement plans, because he was able to continue working much as he did before.

- ✔ Jack was a 40-year-old successful salesman who spent a great deal of time on the road. He and his wife recently had a second child. Because he had missed a great deal of his four-year-old son's early years, he decided to retire after his daughter was born. He quit his job, and his family managed to live on his retirement money, which he calculated would last about 15 years. At that time, he and his wife planned to go back to work, until they had saved up again for their "real" retirement at age 70.

The changing landscape of elder care

In most cultures, grown children have traditionally cared for their aging and ailing senior members. However, the demands are greater now because of the following circumstances:

- ✔ As a result of increased life expectancy and continuing breakthroughs in geriatric medicine, more and more seniors are mentally and physically capable of living independently throughout their lives. Still, your involvement can help them live a richer existence — even as it strengthens your own sense of family commitment.

- ✔ Today's seniors had fewer children than their predecessors, so fewer family members are available to share the responsibility.

- ✔ Many middle-aged couples had children later than their predecessors. Therefore, it's not unusual to have youngsters or adolescents living in the house that now has to accommodate an ailing senior.

- ✔ Children are leaving the nest later. Plus, so-called *boomerang kids* have become increasingly common. These are young adult children — most often sons — who "temporarily" return to their parents' home after a few years on their own. The usual reasons for this return are a lack of money, delayed or quashed marriage plans, or extended schooling.

- ✔ Women, who have traditionally assumed most of the hands-on responsibility for elder care, are more likely to have full-time jobs outside the home.

Unfortunately, not all married couples are in agreement about their visions of retirement. When one spouse decides to stop working, the other may feel that he or she is being forced to go along with the new lifestyle.

One common scenario is that of a husband who wishes to retire after thirty years of working in the same career. The wife would not consider retirement, because she started her career much later in life. "I married him for better or for worse . . . but not for lunch," quipped one busy woman who no longer wanted to have two-hour midday meals with her retired husband. When husbands leave the workforce before their wives, the following marital problems can surface:

✔ A husband, especially one who has had a successful career, may suffer a loss of status and identity after he retires. The wife, who comes home tired after a hard day at the office, may have trouble empathizing with her husband's boredom or depression.

✔ A husband whose primary social contacts were in the workplace often wants more of his wife's attention and companionship after he retires. A working wife may not be able to fill that need, because so much of her time and energy are focused on her career.

✔ A recently retired husband who has been accustomed to his wife maintaining the house may expect her to continue that caretaking role. Meanwhile, the working wife sees no reason why the retired husband can't do more of the shopping, cooking, and cleaning.

Couples can anticipate and avoid these problems by taking the following steps:

✔ **Plan ahead.** Retirement involves significant lifestyle changes for both partners that can have an impact on a marriage for years to come. Instead of waiting for the day one of you retires, start brainstorming as far ahead of time as possible.

Financial planners recommend that people start putting money away for retirement in their 20s. A similar principle applies to planning for the emotional impact of this phase of life. Couples should start talking to each other about retirement 10 to 15 years ahead of time. This gives you and your partner plenty of time to anticipate some of the issues that you need to work out.

✔ **Start experimenting now.** Sit down with your spouse and talk about how you may want to change your lifestyle in the coming years. Would you like to travel? Would you like to move to another area, start a new career, or pursue a dream you've been neglecting? Would you like to play golf every day? Retirement gives you the opportunity to do some or all of those things — if you are emotionally and financially prepared.

Some people look forward to retirement; others dread that prospect. Some want to spend most of their time traveling; others want to continue working full time. As with all phases of marriage, partners need to strike a balance between their retirement needs as individuals and their needs as a couple.

Chapter 12

Remarriage and Stepfamilies

More than one out of three Americans will find themselves living in a remarried or stepfamily situation at some point in their lives.

Remarriages occur after divorce or death, and often take place against a background of grief, hurt, or disappointment. This partly explains the high divorce rate for remarried couples. One out two first marriages eventually end in divorce, while almost two out of three remarried couples divorce within the first five years.

Many of the problems that remarried couples and stepfamilies experience come about when the partners fail to recognize that different guidelines are needed to support these complex situations.

In this chapter, we spell out the key differences between first marriages and remarriages, and show you how to use your past experience as a positive force in your new relationship. We also talk about the additional complications that stepfamilies face, and share guidelines for balancing the needs of children (his, hers, and both of yours) with your needs as a loving couple.

Understanding the Emotions of Remarrying

First-time spouses are often driven by romantic passion and go to the alter with unrealistic expectations of how great things are going to be. However, people rarely enter second marriages with the same fantasies, because these relationships necessarily follow a divorce or the death of a first spouse. After going through divorce or widowhood, remarried partners tend to be more realistic and less bright-eyed than first-timers.

Many people go into a second marriage terrified of messing up and getting hurt again. These husbands and wives are often so afraid of causing conflicts and alienating the new partner that they bury feelings that couples need to deal with if their relationship is going to last. If you're considering remarriage, we strongly suggest that you give some thought to the following questions:

✔ Do you consider yourself and your prospective partner ready for a permanent commitment?

✔ Are you and he or she finished mourning the divorce or death of your first spouse?

✔ What are the three main reasons that you want to remarry?

✔ What do you think are the three main reasons that your prospective partner wants to marry you?

✔ Do you and he or she share similar values?

✔ Do you and your prospective partner share a similar vision of marriage?

✔ Have you and he or she discussed possible alternatives to marriage?

✔ Have the two of you had a serious and open discussion about finances — and whether or not you want a prenuptial agreement?

✔ Have you prepared your children for what will very likely be a drastic change in their lives?

Alternatives to a conventional marriage — such as living together or living separately in a committed, permanent relationship — are sometimes better options, especially for people who've been previously married.

Remarrying after the death of a spouse

The death of a spouse is one of most stressful events a person can suffer. If the surviving partner intends to remarry, he or she must first deal with the unavoidable feelings of guilt, sadness, or anger, so that these emotions don't destroy the new relationship.

We offer the following advice to people who are considering remarriage after the death of a husband or wife:

✔ **Don't rush into a new relationship.** After the unspeakable trauma of the loss of a spouse, you must allow yourself sufficient time to grieve and regroup before entering into another serious relationship. People sometimes try to short-circuit this process by seeking out a new love interest before they are anywhere close to being ready. Such unions are very risky.

Recognize the lingering effect your deceased spouse can have on your new relationship. For example, widows and widowers who are burdened by feelings of guilt often deal with these emotions by turning the deceased spouse into a saint. Unfortunately, the new partner is a flawed and living human being who can't possibly live up to the idealized memory of someone who is no longer present in the material world. When a widowed partner carries the unseen but controlling presence of the deceased spouse into a new marriage, the new relationship doesn't stand a chance.

✔ **Honor the memory of your deceased spouse, but don't live in the past.** Talk to your new spouse about your former relationship — acknowledge that the person will always have a unique place in your heart. Do, however, focus most of your energies on your new partner, and do everything possible to nurture that relationship.

✔ **Don't sanctify your deceased partner.** We know of people who actually keep their dead spouse's ashes in a vase on the mantel. This is usually not helpful for widowed spouses who are living alone, and it's an especially bad idea for those who are remarried. Acknowledge that your deceased spouse also had faults, and make it clear that you love and accept your new partner for the person he or she is.

Remarrying after a divorce

Many a man owes his success to his first wife, and his second wife to his success.

— Anonymous

Estranged partners go through a great deal of pain after a divorce. This can drive them to "fall in love" with the first appealing prospect that comes along. Quite often, this new love interest is perilously similar to the last spouse.

Studies show that partners who enter second marriages too quickly are heading for trouble. This is especially true of remarriages that start out as affairs during the first marriage. Over 70 percent of those relationships don't work out.

If your first marriage failed, we strongly recommend that you do the following before tying the knot again:

✔ **Take your time.** Before you jump into a new marriage, try to understand why things didn't work out the first time. Give yourself plenty of time before making a commitment again. Talk to your prospective partner about the possibility of a long courtship or engagement before you get married.

✔ **Understand your past mistakes — and take responsibility for them.**
Acknowledge that you and your estranged partner both contributed to
your first marriage not working out. You may find yourself focusing on how
that no-good-so-and-so destroyed the marriage. However, it's much more
important to understand what *you* did, so you can avoid doing it again.

Research shows that the single greatest risk for divorced partners who
remarry is repeating the same mistakes in choosing a new partner. This
happens because the identical impulses that attracted you to your first
spouse are likely to influence your choice of the next one. If you're not
careful, you can end up with a new mate who is a carbon copy of the last
one. Even if you find another kind of person, you may unwittingly repeat
the same patterns. If that happens, the problems that undermined your
first marriage may wind up sinking the new relationship.

✔ **Write a brief history of your first marriage.** This gives you a better
understanding of what brought you to this point, and helps you recognize how you can do things differently this time. Be sure to answer the
following questions as you write:

- What attracted you to your first spouse and what went into your
decision to marry that person?

- What were the positive and negative aspects of that relationship?

- How did each of you contribute to those dynamics?

- Are you aware of any feelings of anger and guilt that you may be
carrying into your new relationship?

- What can you do to increase the probability that this new marriage
will work?

✔ **Don't bring negative feelings from your first marriage into your new
relationship.** An estranged wife or husband often carries a great deal of
anger towards her or his first spouse after a divorce. It's important not
to allow those lingering negative impressions to contaminate your new
relationship.

If, for example, a wife was often angry at her first husband for never contributing to housework, she may rail at her second husband if he
inadvertently forgets to close a drawer. Venting your anger at your ex-
spouse, and misdirecting it to your new one, is unfair and
counterproductive.

It will be hard — if not impossible — to fully commit to a new marriage if you
haven't yet completed the "emotional divorce" from your estranged spouse.
Sometimes professional help is needed to help you let go of your old marriage, and all the strong feelings you still have about it.

Making a Second Marriage Work

I don't worry about terrorism. I was married for two years.

— Sam Kinison, comedian

In second marriages, one or both partners have already gone through a marriage that ended in a painful way. When you've been hurt, it's hard to let yourself be vulnerable again. Paradoxically, a willingness to expose yourself is the key for remarried partners who want to develop a true intimacy with their new spouses.

Here are some suggestions for achieving the kind of closeness that may have been lacking in your first marriage:

✔ **Truly get to know each other.** Perhaps you and your former spouse never fully opened up to one another. Now you have a second chance to know someone on a deeper level — and to allow that person to know you.

✔ **Don't be afraid to share your most important thoughts and feelings with your partner, and encourage him or her to do the same.** Listen carefully to what your spouse tells you, and allow that person to open up at his or her own pace.

✔ **Develop new routines and rituals that don't mirror those of your previous marriage.** When wives and husbands have been married for a number of years, they develop certain patterns that come to define the relationship. People who've been single for a long time often become set in their ways. It's quite natural to want to continue these routines and rituals — and to expect your new spouse to follow suit. These expectations can be a source of conflict — especially if your spouse is also bringing in a completely different set of expectations from his or her former marriage. It's important to sit down and rewrite the rules in a way that reflects both of your needs and desires.

It takes time to change your expectations about how things are supposed to get done. You probably had to make similar adjustments in your first marriage — remarriage is an opportunity to be more flexible in how you and your partner negotiate the terms of your relationship.

✔ **Make a fresh start.** It's usually a good idea not to live in the home where either partner resided with the former spouse. These are places where ghosts can haunt your new relationship. If at all possible, move into a home where neither of you have lived before. This gives each of you the sense that you're truly starting over.

Remarried couples often have the maturity to form deeper, more-intimate relationships than first-time partners. Hopefully, you and your new spouse have both profited from your experiences and mistakes. If so, you have a much better chance to make marriage work this time around.

Remarried wives and husbands on housework and infidelity

In a study called "Entitlement, Obligation, and Gratitude in Family Work," published in *The Journal of Family Issues,* a team of researchers from the University of California interviewed 193 remarried men and women about their views on housework and infidelity. Their study turned up the following results:

✔ Remarried wives often complain that their second husbands don't help enough around the house. However, many of these same wives acknowledge that they are more helpful than their first husbands were.

✔ Remarried wives spend twice as many hours on housework each week as their husbands.

✔ Only ten percent of remarried husbands devote as much time to housework as their wives.

✔ Remarried men who had affairs during their first marriage feel that their second wives should be grateful that they are now remaining faithful.

✔ Some formerly adulterous husbands actually believe that their new-found fidelity should excuse them from doing very many household chores in their new marriage.

✔ Wives who had unfaithful first husbands are, in fact, grateful to their second husbands who don't cheat on them. However, these wives don't believe that this should excuse them from contributing to household chores.

Understanding the Complex Issues That Stepfamilies Face

> *Children . . . whose parents float in and out of their lives after divorce, are the most precarious little boats in the most turbulent seas.*
>
> — Hillary Rodham Clinton, political figure

When a childless couple divorces, the partners generally go their separate ways — unless they voluntarily choose to remain in contact. However, when children are in the picture, estranged husbands and wives have to negotiate any number of financial and emotional issues with each other for many years to come.

There's no way they can get rid of each other. Should one or both spouses subsequently remarry, the cast of characters can expand dramatically — and so can the potential complications. In the following sections, we discuss the best way to navigate these complexities.

Understanding remarriage finances

I'm an excellent housekeeper. Every time I get a divorce, I keep the house.

— Zsa Zsa Gabor

Remarried partners tend to see money differently than first-time spouses. In the majority of first marriages, the partners agree to pool their money. However, second marriages have a different set of realities — especially when children are involved. The following are some of the most common financial issues remarried spouses face:

- ✔ **Remarried families are often strapped for funds.** A remarried husband may be paying alimony and child support to his former family, while assuming part or all of the financial burden for his new wife and her children. An estranged wife may have to deal with an ex-spouse who is unable or unwilling to pay his child support and alimony, even though he has been ordered to do so.

- ✔ **Child support arrangements can be tricky — even when both spouses have money — because of the many different ways that custody is shared.** There are some situations where one parent has primary custody, and the other has visitation. Custody can be split or shared in a number of ways. Most custody agreements have a financial component that the estranged partners must negotiate — often while they're in the midst of a scorched-earth battle with each other.

- ✔ **Remarried partners usually want money accumulated during the first marriage to be passed to their own children.** You may be in love with your second spouse and care deeply for that person's kids. Nevertheless, money traditionally flows according to blood lines, and it's generally accepted that a parent's primary financial obligation is to his or her own biological or adopted children, as opposed to stepchildren.

You can avoid many misunderstandings about money if you set down some ground rules early. We recommend that remarried couples take the following steps, preferably before getting married:

- ✔ Be aware of all of the financial implications of entering into the new marriage. Start out by having a series of discussions about the exact amount of money each of you plans to contribute to maintaining the household.

- ✔ Talk about any monies that you're not willing to contribute to the common pool, as well as any legal ties and obligations each of you may have to your former spouse or major pre-existing debts.

- ✔ Be sure to take notes and make calculations so that you can make accurate decisions about your financial future.

✔ If either or both of you have children from a previous marriage, talk about how each child will share in assets accumulated in the first marriage, as well as assets the two of you accumulate together.

✔ Consider drawing up a marital agreement. *Prenuptial agreements* are legal documents that are signed before a couple marries. *Postnuptial agreements* are signed afterwards. These contracts, which spell out the financial arrangement between a husband and wife, are far more common in second and third marriages than in first-time unions.

Veterans of the divorce wars are unlikely to go into another marriage with the same trustful innocence they had the first time around. Also, second-time partners have had more time to accumulate assets, which means that they may have more to lose financially.

Marital agreements can address a wide variety of issues. They can define which property belongs exclusively to one of the spouses, which is owned jointly, and which property spouses and children from former marriages are entitled to. Marital agreements can spell out the terms of a possible divorce — including alimony and child support. They can also provide for the education of children, and the distribution of property upon the death of either spouse.

Bernard Rothman, author of *Loving and Leaving: Winning at the Business of Divorce*, suggests that both spouses retain separate counsel when drawing up a marital agreement. He also recommends that any agreement should adhere to the following guidelines in order to hold up in court:

- The agreement must be in writing, and it must comply with any other legal and technical requirements of the state in which it is drawn.

- The contract must be fair and reasonable — when both partners sign the document, as well as at the time of its enforcement.

- Each party must make a complete and honest financial disclosure — including all assets and obligations — before signing the agreement.

In a sense, a prenuptial agreement can serve some of the same purposes as premarriage counseling, because both require couples to engage in a frank and open dialogue about the realities and potential difficulties that can impact their marriage.

Forming a new family unit

There's only one way to have a happy marriage, and as soon as I learn what it is I'll get married again.

— Clint Eastwood, actor

When two people marry, and one or both have children from a previous marriage, a complex unit called a *stepfamily* is formed. Although there are many similarities between stepfamilies and first-time families, there are also important differences.

Wives and husbands in a first-time family can draw tight boundaries between their family and the outside world. However, if you're remarried and either you or your spouse has children from a previous marriage, the boundaries have to be much more fluid.

In stepfamilies, children often spend time in both the mother's and father's house. If one or both of their biological parents are remarried, those children may also have to share those homes with stepsiblings. This makes it nearly impossible to maintain the same degree of control or influence over your children as in a first-time family.

This change requires some delicate ongoing negotiations, as well as an extended period of adjustment for all concerned. Although the change from a first-time family to a stepfamily is never easy, you can make the process less stressful by allowing sufficient time for all the stepfamily members to form caring relationships, and to develop a comfortable family unit. There's no such thing as an instant family. This is a process that can take years, but giving it enough time is the only way for it to work.

In a first marriage, the bond between the husband and wife has time to develop before children are brought into the picture. However, in a remarried family, the child/parent relationship predates the marital connection. This can lead to the following problems for the various players:

- The new spouse may find himself competing with one or more of the partner's children for the partner's loyalty and affection. In a very real sense, that husband or wife is entering the parent-child relationship as an outsider — one who can easily feel excluded.

- The children, who have already suffered the loss of their once-intact family, may have to suffer a series of additional losses. They may be forced to move to a new neighborhood, attend a different school, and make new friendships. Children also feel the loss of simple family traditions and rituals that they once took for granted.

- Biological parents have an entirely different set of problems. In the context of a newly structured family, they are likely to find themselves torn among their child's need for attention; their wish for a stable home life; their new partner's need for intimacy; and the demands of an ex-spouse, who may be hostile to the new relationship and otherwise unsympathetic to the estranged spouse's problems.

Families who recognize that all these difficulties are part and parcel of step-family life, are able to ease this transition. You can communicate your understanding by using the following techniques:

- **Encourage an open expression of feelings.** Instead of becoming defensive when family members express their concerns, show that you understand what they're going through.

  For example, if your spouse indicates that he feels jealous or competitive with your child, don't say, "That's ridiculous," or "You're crazy." Instead, say something like, "I can understand how that could happen. Let's talk about it."

  If your young child — who is having problems adapting to his new home and accepting his new stepparent — complains that he misses his dad, don't try to convince him how much nicer your new partner is than your estranged spouse. Instead, ask the child what he misses most, and talk about how he can spend more time in person and by phone with his father.

- **Don't ever badmouth your child's absent parent — however much you may despise that person.** Research shows that children of divorce have a much harder time adjusting to a stepfamily when their parents are in open conflict.

  One of the most hurtful things estranged spouses do is to use their children to deliver hostile messages to one another, such as: "Tell that no good so-and-so that he'd better send this month's support payment on time."

- **If you are a stepparent and your partner admits that he or she feels torn between you and her biological or adoptive child, don't accuse her of being disloyal.** Instead, acknowledge her conflict by saying, "That must be tough. If I were in your position, I might have the same kind of mixed feelings."

- **Foster open lines of communication among ex-spouses, children, their biological parents, stepparents, grandparents, and other relatives.** The more cut off people feel from those they love, the more conflict and hostility there will be between family members, and the more difficult it will be to have a smoothly functioning stepfamily.

Children need the love and support of both their parents. You and your estranged spouse have an obligation to maintain enough civility to provide for those needs.

My children, your children, our children

I'm lucky! I've got two moms, two dads, four grandmas, and four grandpas.

— Lily, a six-year-old girl who is part of a new stepfamily

A growing number of stepfamilies are constructed from both spouses' first marriages. For example, the mother may have primary custody of her biological or adopted children, while the estranged father has the children on holidays and weekends. Meanwhile, the father in the newly formed family may share custody of his own children with his former wife.

Having a house full of kids with mix-and-match parents and stepparents (with visits from each of their extended families) can be a complicated business. You may find a built-in ambiguity of roles and relationships that has little resemblance to a traditional first-time family.

While you won't find a model for how each uniquely structured family is supposed to operate, try sticking to the following guidelines:

- **Take the primary responsibility for raising and disciplining your own children.** A remarried wife often make the mistake of assuming that their new husband will automatically be able to assert his authority over her children. Remarried men often expect their new wives to be an instant second mother to his kids. In reality, a stepparent has to gradually earn the child's respect and, hopefully, love.

It's a mistake for a stepparent to come on too strong — no matter how intense he feels about disciplining children. Stepparents may feel that, because they are adults, they have a right to assert their authority over children who are living under their roof. Studies show that it takes at least two years — and sometimes much longer — for a child to accept a stepparent's authority and affection. Until that happens, the primary responsibility for disciplining and caring rests with the biological or adoptive parent. Whatever authority the stepparent has derives only from the original parent.

Stepparents can play many rewarding roles, other than that of an authority figure, in the lives of their stepchildren. These include that of a friend, an older sibling, a good aunt or uncle, a coach, or a mentor.

- **Keep your expectations modest.** Remarried spouses often find that the relationship between their children and new partner is not what they'd hoped it would be. The children may be distant and hostile, and you may not be able to do anything about these feelings — at least not in the short term. The best strategy is to recognize that you can't control some things, and the best you may be able to do is to foster a cooperative attitude among all concerned.

Research shows that a person who has never been married has the hardest time adjusting to the rigors of a stepfamily. A person who has always been single hasn't had the opportunity to experience married life firsthand. When a single man or woman enters someone else's ready — made family, he or she is likely to feel overwhelmed.

✔ **Be prepared to deal with unfamiliar situations.** Stepfamily relationships have many sides to them — some of which can cause unanticipated complications.

For example, the oldest child in your family may suddenly find that he is no longer the oldest child in the new family. A reshuffled birth order can create unexpected conflicts among the children, as well as the remarried partners. Still, that's far from the most troublesome complication that stepfamilies can face.

Adolescent children are tough enough for any parent to handle. But, when you have adolescent stepsiblings living under the same roof, you can have constant and intense bickering. Even more tricky is the very real possibility that a romantic or sexual entanglement can develop between teenage stepbrothers and stepsisters.

There is no incest taboo to inhibit sexual contact between stepsiblings, and no guidelines that tell adults what they can do to slow down a teen's raging hormones. The best advice we can offer is to be watchful and talk to your adolescent children about the potential discomfort and complications that such entanglements can cause.

Your chances of forming a cohesive stepfamily improve dramatically if you develop patience in dealing with unfamiliar situations. That means allowing each member of your new family the space and time to adjust to a complex mix of personalities and circumstances.

✔ **Hold regular family conferences.** Every family can benefit from a forum where each member has an opportunity to air concerns and express feelings. These conferences can be especially helpful to stepfamilies, in which you have more players with different needs, backgrounds, and viewpoints.

The goal of a family meeting is to improve communication and make the family environment more nurturing and cooperative. The following guidelines may help you plan family conferences:

- Set a regular time and place for the meeting that everyone agrees on. These should not be framed as rules that are set in stone. However, a consistent schedule helps give all family members a shared sense of structure and participation.

- Make sure that each family member has a turn. It's important not to let any one member dominate the conversation — especially if that happens on a regular basis. Try changing the order of who starts and who ends the session. Give everyone an opportunity to lead the discussion. Set a limit on the total time, as well as the time allowed to each member.

TRUE STORY

A stepfamily success story

Jess and Meg are both divorced and in their forties. After dating for two years, the couple married and moved into a new home, along with Meg's three children, ages four, seven, and ten. Jess had a son and daughter from his previous marriage; both attend colleges out of town.

Jess felt he'd done a good job raising his children, and had strong views on what Meg's kids needed from a dad. Jess felt that Meg's kids were disrespectful to her and too undisciplined for their own good. Meg welcomed Jess's help, because her ex-husband was irresponsible and often unavailable when his children needed him.

Meg's children didn't respond well to Jess's attempts to influence them, and Meg also thought his approach was too harsh. Jess felt he was trying his best. But the more he tried, the more resistant the kids became. On those rare occasions when Meg's ex-husband did show up, he was openly hostile to Jess. This led to a series of arguments. The children defended their father, no matter how outrageously he behaved. What hurt Jess even more was the feeling that Meg didn't support him in these battles.

Meg felt caught in the middle. She was upset that Jess didn't show more patience with her children. At one point, she decided that he didn't like them very much.

"How can I live with a man who doesn't love my kids?" Meg wondered. Meanwhile, Jess kept asking himself, "How can I go on living in a family where I'm treated like an outsider?"

It took lots of hard work on both Meg's and Jess's part for them to understand and accept the realities of stepfamily life.

Meg finally realized that she'd have to accept the major responsibility for nurturing and disciplining her own kids. The relationship between the children and Jess would have to develop slowly, and Meg couldn't force it to be the way she'd once hoped to.

Jess understood that he couldn't have the kind of control he had with his children, and that there was a bond between Meg and her three kids that didn't include him. Jess came to accept that a loving relationship with his stepchildren was possible, but it would come at its own pace.

Jess and Meg made a commitment to talk about the issues, work on their problems together, and to give things time to get better. They started having regular family conferences, during which each family member shared his or her feelings and concerns. Meg and Jess also carved out time for the two of them to be alone so that their relationship could grow deeper and more intimate.

There were times when this couple thought they might not make it. But after five years of marriage, their hard work and commitment to each other has begun to pay off. There are still issues to work out, but Meg, Jess, and the kids have become as strong and loving a family as any we know.

- Make a rule that each member must talk in "I" statements. What's most important at these meetings is that everyone be given an opportunity to express his or her feelings. Blaming and finger-pointing should be avoided at all costs. (Turn to Chapter 4 for a complete discussion of the power and effectiveness of using "I" statements when you attempt to communicate your feelings).

✔ **Make special time for the two of you to spend alone.** Remarried partners sometimes become so involved in dealing with parenting issues that they neglect their own relationship. You and your spouse need intimate time together. That can mean planning a dinner alone at a favorite restaurant, taking quiet walks together several times a week — even going away for a romantic weekend without the kids.

Separate stepfamily problems from other issues. Don't attribute every difficulty that a child may have to the stepfamily. All children can have problems related to school, peers, social life, and just plain growing up.

There are many pluses to being part of a stepfamily. Children can come to appreciate being part of an extended family circle that includes two sets of caring parents, more siblings, more aunts and uncles, and several sets of grandparents.

Most girls and boys feel fortunate to be members of such large extended families. They recognize that their new families are different from their first families, better in some ways, and worse in others. Still, after they make the adjustment, these kids feel good about their lives.

Part V
Maintaining a Healthy Marriage

The 5th Wave   By Rich Tennant

"My wife and I were drifting apart. We decided to go back to doing what we used to do when we were first married. So we called her parents and asked to borrow money."

In this part . . .

Stress, money, infidelity, and therapy. These may sound like strange bedfellows. However, each of these factors plays an important part in keeping a marriage healthy.

In Chapter 13, we talk about two kinds of stress: healthy, positive stress (the kind that drives you to move forward and face new challenges) and negative stress (the kind that can lead to depression, heart attacks — even early death). In this chapter, we show you how to cut down on negative stress in your marriage, and how to turn positive stress into a healthy force in your marriage.

In Chapter 14, we explore the multiple meanings of money — and the ways it can impact a marriage. We show you how to resolve your differences about money, and help you avoid some common disputes about family finances.

Chapter 15 explores the reasons that wives and husbands cheat. We detail the warning signs that your spouse may be having an affair, and offer advice on how to rebuild your marriage after a partner has been unfaithful.

In Chapter 16, we explore the circumstances where outside help is necessary. We describe the different kinds of groups, counselors, and therapists, and point you to the ones that can best address your problem.

Finally, in Chapter 17, we offer some alternatives to divorce, and show you how to proceed if divorce turns out to be your best option.

Chapter 13

Reducing the Stress on Your Marriage

- -

- -

Doctors define *stress* as a hormonal response to pressure, and there is an upside and a downside to it. The right amount of stress is healthy, because it can drive you to face new challenges, and provides an adrenaline jolt that helps you move forward. We call this *positive stress*. Without a certain amount of it, life would be predictable and boring.

On the downside, too much pressure can seriously compromise your physical and emotional well-being. We call this *negative stress*. Stressed-out people are at greater risk for heart attacks, cancer — even early death.

Marriages are also subject to stress. A moderate amount of positive stress keeps the relationship vital and promotes growth. But too much negative stress can hurt — or even destroy — the relationship.

In this chapter, we explore the different ways each partner's tension level impacts a marriage. We show you how to reduce negative stress and how to turn positive stress into an engine that propels your marriage — and you — to new heights.

Understanding Negative and Positive Stress

Everyone experiences tension — in both good and bad times. Even eagerly awaited events like the birth of a child can be highly stressful. The same is true of a promotion at work or a move to a bigger home.

Positive stress can act as a stimulant that focuses your concentration and enhances your performance. But positive stress can also cause anxiety or sleeplessness while you're adjusting to new circumstances.

A more damaging kind of stress comes about from changes that amount to emotional and physical body blows. Some of these stressors are fleeting — like when another driver cuts you off or a stranger pushes ahead of you on line. Most negative stressors are more substantial — like those caused by a financial setback or feeling stuck in a job you hate.

Too much stress has been linked to headaches, digestive problems, back pain, insomnia, anxiety, chronic fatigue, depression, and feelings of perpetual anger — as well as a variety of potentially fatal conditions like cancer and cardiovascular disease. Research shows that stress-related illnesses are at least partially responsible for almost two-thirds of all visits to family doctors.

The highest levels of negative stress come from devastating events, like the death or serious illness of a close relative. Taken together, all these large and small hits to your system can put your life — and your marriage — in turmoil.

Dealing with Your Own Stressors

It's the puddle that drowns you, not the flood.

— Alexander Solzhenitsyn, author

In order to reduce the negative stress on your marriage, you first have to understand and manage your own personal stress.

You can begin doing that by utilizing the following guidelines:

✔ **Identify the real sources of your stress.** Make a written list of the people or situations that you think are causing you the most tension. Then write down how you're dealing with those people and situations. Try to answer the following questions:

- What is the source of the stress?

- How are you affected by it?

- How are you coping with the stress?

- What do you plan to do about it?

For example, you may feel frustrated and anxious about being stuck in an unsatisfying career. But, instead of dealing with the problem head-on, you take your frustrations out on your spouse or your kids. This only winds up creating more negative stress.

For each stressor that you name, write down the list of possible ways you can deal with it. If, for example, you've been stoically and quietly suffering with your job, think about how you can handle the problem more productively. Consider asking your spouse for his or her thoughts about your frustrations at work. Does your spouse think that you should talk to your boss? Should you consider looking for a new job — or even changing your career?

✔ **Talk to a friend.** Research shows that one of the best ways to reduce stress is to communicate with a close friend at least twice per week. Women tend to do this better than men. We believe that if more people made it a point to turn to their friends for support, they would be better able to cope with adversity.

✔ **Slow down.** Even though you may have to function in a fast-paced world, you can relax yourself internally. The following techniques can help cushion the stressful hits that undermine your well-being and compromise your relationships.

- Listen to your body talk. Find a quiet time in your day, when you can be alone and without distractions. Sit down, close your eyes, and listen to your internal rhythms.

  As you become more aware of your body rhythms, you can actually begin to control them. Research shows that people who focus attention on the cadence of their breath and pulse for as little as ten minutes a day can reduce their blood pressure and heart rate.

- Use deep breathing to relax your mind and body. Inhale slowly, drawing air deep into your lungs. Hold for a few seconds. Try to take twice as long to exhale as you do to inhale. As you exhale, imagine that your breath is carrying all of the stress and anxiety out of your body.

- Use positive visualization. When you're feeling tense, try closing your eyes and mentally transporting yourself to a peaceful, beautiful place. Can you remember a lovely beach or forest that you went to as a child or with your spouse? Transport yourself there now by forming a mental picture of all the sights, sounds, and smells of that place.

You can complete a positive visualization in as little as two or three minutes. When you return, the tensions of the day will seem less important or overwhelming.

- Take a power nap. People whose lives are hectic often don't get enough sleep at night. This makes them tired, irritable and less able to deal with the pressure. One effective way to reduce this problem is to take one or two short naps during the day.

  A power nap can last anywhere from 10 to 20 minutes, sometimes even less. Lie down on a couch or sit in a comfortable position. Close your eyes — and allow your mind to drift away from the worries of your frantic life.

✔ **Find time in your day to do something that makes you feel good.** Some people relax by playing the piano, or tennis, or chess. Others enjoy listening to music or taking walks. You can reduce your stress level by devoting some time each day to enjoyable, relaxing activities.

✔ **Discover the joy of physical activity.** You don't need to be a professional bodybuilder or an avid jogger — simply keep a set regimen of physical exercise. Regular physical activity helps keep stress levels in check, while promoting good general health.

Instead of thinking of exercise as a chore, make it part of your daily stress-reduction program. Leave your car at home, and walk to the store. If you live or work in a high-rise building, use the stairs instead of the elevator. Just putting that little piece into your daily routine (and sticking to it) may be as beneficial to your health and your mood as a more formal exercise program.

Most people who stick with a long-term exercise program find it to be a great source of pleasure. Ask your spouse to join you for a walk every day. Find a friend who can jog or swim with you on a regular basis. Some people stick to one form of physical activity they enjoy; others prefer switching among several different activities. Experiment until you find the combination that's best for you.

✔ **Keep your sense of humor.** It's possible to find humor, even in the midst of highly stressful circumstances. The ability to laugh when things are rough comes more naturally to some people than to others, but it's a skill that anyone can cultivate.

Whenever you find humor in a difficult situation, and even laugh at yourself, the people around you are likely to respond in kind. This tends to make your life less stressful.

✔ **Don't let your mistakes derail you.** Dwelling on past mistakes generates a lot of negative stress. Plus, it's a waste of time. Mistakes are unavoidable in your personal life, your career — and in your relationships.

Whenever you make a mistake, reflect on how you can better handle the situation the next time. Allow yourself to feel regret. Then move on.

✔ **Don't bite off more than you can chew.** Every person tolerates stress differently, but everyone has a limit. Some people can't stand a lot of noise and confusion in their lives; others are stimulated by that kind of environment. Some people thrive on pressure; others function better in more relaxed situations. Understand your own limitations and factor that assessment into how you structure your life.

If the non-medical approaches we discuss in this chapter don't work, your physician may suggest anti-anxiety or anti-depressant medication. (Anti-depressants like Prozac or Zoloft are quite beneficial for some types of nervous tensions.) This does not mean that you're emotionally unstable or that you're going to become dependent on a drug. It simply means that bio-chemical factors play a major role in generating your stress.

Keeping Stress from Undermining Your Marriage

> *There are three specific ways that stress has a negative effect on marriage. It saps us of the strength we need to renew our love. It turns us from allies into adversaries, as we blame each other. And stress makes us hostile competitors for each other's sympathy.*
>
> — *Marriage Partnership Magazine*

Marital problems become magnified when the partners take their personal stresses out on each other. The resulting problems can get so complicated that they become very difficult to unravel.

Your spouse is a handy scapegoat for stress-related problems that really have nothing to do with him or her. Still, your partner is often the most available (and least risky) target. It's only a matter of time until your spouse will retaliate by directing his or her stress-related anger and frustration right back at you.

You can avoid this vicious cycle by taking the following steps:

✔ **Take time to decompress.** After a stressful day at work, many people need time alone to decompress before they're ready to talk. One spouse has had a horrible day at the office and a rough commute. The other's been stuck at home all day with two sick kids. A 15-minute period of calming down, reading the paper or looking at TV, may be necessary before any meaningful conversation can begin. Of course, the less-stressed partner must take over so that the more-stressed one can reconstitute.

✔ **Allow each other time to gripe.** Psychologist John Gottman recommends a daily "sanctioned whining session," where "each person gets to complain about any catastrophes that occurred, while the other is understanding and supportive."

✔ **Find out what's upsetting your partner.** Now it's time to talk about the details of your day — your successes and your disappointments. If your feelings are out in the open, you'll be less likely to vent your frustrations on each other.

Talk to your partner about what's been troubling you, and encourage your spouse to do the same. You can help each other by listening attentively and figuring out how you can be supportive. The best way to do this is to ask your partner what he or she needs — not to try to read that other person's mind.

Your spouse isn't a mind reader. Don't assume that you know what he or she is feeling. It's up to you to make your feelings known and to recruit him or her as an ally to combat the real cause of your stress. This is a process that takes time and careful listening.

When married partners become obsessed with their own stressors and don't communicate with each other, the very foundation of the relationship begins to crumble:

✔ **Recognize the different ways that you and your partner deal with stress.** Some people keep their stresses hidden — often even from themselves. Other people complain loudly when they're under pressure. It's important to understand the differences in how you and your partner handle stress, and not get competitive about whose way is better.

✔ **Don't take it personally.** Try not to take it as a personal attack when your spouse is grumpy or preoccupied when under stress — as long as these mood shifts aren't too frequent or severe. On the other hand, if he or she seems irritable all the time, you may need to come up with some specific help. It's not supportive just to listen quietly if your partner is always stressed out. Then you're dealing with a chronic condition, not just with a time-limited acute crisis.

✔ **Ask each other for what you need.** Husbands and wives require different things from each other when they're stressed. Your partner may want to talk about what's on his mind, or she may want to take a walk or cuddle up in bed. Other times, your partner may prefer to be left alone.

The more direct and specific you are about what you need, the more likely your husband or wife will be able to respond. Men seem to have an especially hard time asking for support. Some men (and women) fear that such requests are interpreted as signs of weakness. It's important to trust your partner enough to say, "I'm having a really hard time and I feel overwhelmed. What I need from you is . . . [state specifically what you actually need]."

✔ **Forgive yourself and your partner.** A lot of marital stress is caused by relatively small incidents. One couple we know had a major fight after they discovered that one of them forgot a piece of luggage at an airport on their way to a Caribbean vacation. The husband and wife started to blame each other, and the two-week vacation was ruined.

Assigning blame never helps a marriage. In the end, it really doesn't matter who is at fault. What's most important is that married partners don't allow the good feelings between them to be destroyed by finger pointing.

✓ **Don't expect perfection — from your partner or yourself.** Perfectionism almost always ends up creating unnecessary stress because it's impossible to achieve.

There's no such thing as the perfect spouse or the perfect parent. It's also self-defeating to expect a trip — or even an evening out — to come off without a hitch. Something can always go wrong — even though it's usually inconsequential.

✓ **Find ways to take care of your partner — and yourself.** Take turns massaging each other. Take a hot bath together. Go out for a special dinner. Buy tickets to a show or concert you've both been wanting to see. Be thoughtful and creative when you select the kind of special care that most effectively addresses your situation.

✓ **Change the scenery.** Planning some time away from your normal routine can help both of you relax and approach your stressors more productively.

You don't have to go on a lengthy or exotic vacation. One night in a hotel in the country — or even across town — can recharge both your batteries and give you a fresh perspective.

Forgiving yourself and each other

Sue: A number of years ago, I drove into Manhattan to visit a friend. I actually found a parking space on the street. I was in the midst of taking my doctoral exams, so I had a lot on my mind.

At the time, I had one of those burglar-proof radios that you pull out of a slot in the dashboard and take with you. I always remembered to do that — except this one time. When I returned to my car at the end of the evening, I found the window shattered and my radio gone.

Steve: I was pretty upset when you told me about the incident, and I guess I put you down for being careless.

Sue: I was pretty angry with myself as it was. What I really needed was some understanding — which you weren't in the mood to give. So, I called my friend and told her what happened.

Steve: What did she say?

Sue: She told me, "Look, you do a good job most of the time, but occasionally, things just spin out of control. Sometimes, we get distracted and make poor judgments. You're only talking about a few hundred dollars. It's not the end of the world. Just take the financial hit and stop worrying about it." Nobody had ever said anything like that to me before, and I never forgot how good those words made me feel.

Steve: When you told me what your friend said, I realized that she was absolutely right. I had to own up to the fact that nobody is always on top of things — not even me! That stolen radio turned out to be a useful lesson about why it's so important to forgive yourself — and each other.

Dealing with Stress in the "Red Zone"

When a computer memory is full, it shuts down. But since we're human, we just keep trying to stuff more in.

— Susan J. Kraus, psychotherapist

R-r-r-ing!!! It's the obnoxious noise of your alarm clock signaling the start of a new day. But you've been up for hours, too anxious to go back to sleep. How can you expect to sleep when your spouse is worried about money and your child is running a high fever? As if that's not enough, the transmission on your car died last night — and you have no other way to get to work. You feel like your head is about to split wide open, when you suddenly discover that you can't find your keys. How much stress can one human being take before he or she starts to break down?

Each person can tolerate only so much pressure before the stress level reaches the *red zone,* a toxic combination of accumulated stress and feelings of anger about that stress.

We suggest the following techniques for fending off and relieving red-zone stress:

✔ **Give yourself a stress checkup.** Go through each source of stress, and ask yourself if it's a positive or negative force in your life.

We know couples who are both exhausted from working 60-hour weeks. Nevertheless, their stress levels stay out of the red zone because both partners find their work challenging and rewarding. We also know people who work 35-hour weeks at jobs that they hate. These are the men and women who are most likely to have stress-related breakdowns.

The stress you experience is determined not so much by what exactly happens by how you interpret the various events and circumstances in your life. A large home with five noisy kids may be one couple's ideal and another couple's worst nightmare. These things can only be judged by the meaning that you and your partner give them.

✔ **Rethink your day-to-day life.** Many people take commuting in stride, but others seethe with rage because they hate spending hours traveling to and from work. For some people, the problem is solved by moving closer to the office or finding a job closer to home. For others, a lower-paying job and scaled-down lifestyle prove to be the best answer. The key is to find a solution that works best for you and your family.

Understanding the link between stress and pain

Physical pain is one of the most common symptoms of red-zone stress. Dr. John Sarno, author of *My Aching Back*, has discovered that people unconsciously generate much of their own pain. According to Dr. Sarno, back pain is the brain's way of deflecting angry stress.

When you can't face your feelings, your nervous system responds to this negative energy by reducing the blood flow to whatever part of the body is most vulnerable. For many people, the hot spot is the back. For others, it's the neck, hand, or ankle. Whatever the site of the pain, relief comes only after the sufferer faces — and eventually lets go of — the anger.

Alexa is a very successful lawyer who was suffering from a stress-related depression. She lived almost two hours away from her office, and was upset because she couldn't practice law and still spend as much time as she wanted with her two young children. We suggested that Alexa ask her employer if she could work from home one or two days per week, and he agreed. This was meant to be a short-term solution. However, when Alexa came out of her depression, she realized that her restructured work arrangement provided a richer, less-stressful lifestyle, and she continued the arrangement with her firm.

✔ **Find positive ways to re-direct negative stress.** A great deal of marital tension is generated by relatively insignificant things that put you over the edge. Did your husband forget to hang up his clothes — again? Did your wife buy the wrong brand of coffee — again? Don't assume it means that he or she doesn't care about you. Assumptions about the meaning of another person's behavior are a continuous source of stress.

Before you fly off the handle, ask yourself if this will be important in a year, a week — even an hour. Take a deep breath and think about what's really bothering you. Then invite your spouse to sit down and discuss the matter with you.

People who are great at standing up in the face of a real crisis are often unable to deal with the most minor annoyances. Yet blowing up at the smallest provocation rarely provides any relief. These individuals only increase the stress on themselves, their partners, and their marriage.

Understanding the Connection Between Stress and Control

Happiness is the ability to receive the [good] things in life without grasping, and the [bad] without condemning.

— Mark Epstein, psychiatrist

A lot of stress and anger are generated when people feel out of control. We would all like to believe that we can exercise choice over our lives. But sometimes, circumstances leave us feeling that we have no options — at least none that we like.

The following techniques can help you when you're stuck in difficult circumstances:

✔ **Don't allow yourself to get boxed in by temporary plights.** If you've ever been caught in a monstrous traffic jam, you know what it feels like to have no control. Unless you're ready to abandon your vehicle and walk, you're pretty much stuck in that place for however long it takes to get out.

Even though you may not be able to master a particular circumstance, you always have a choice of how to respond. For example, while you're trapped in that car, you can seethe — as your blood pressure goes through the roof. Or, you can try one of the following stress-reducing diversions:

  •Listen to some calming music.

  •Listen to an audio book.

  •Meditate.

  •Think about an upcoming activity that you're looking forward to.

  •Use the time to enjoy a positive visualization.

✔ **Develop strategies to deal with long-term stress.** Sometimes, life forces you to cope with an extraordinarily stressful situation that has no end in sight. Imagine what would happen, for example, if your spouse or your child became seriously ill. Certainly, you'd be forced to make some major changes in your life. Many of these changes would be out of your control.

Still, that wouldn't necessarily make you a victim of circumstance with no options. You almost always have choices. Stress increases dramatically when you feel hopeless and utterly helpless. Research shows that even cancer patients with advanced disease do better when they feel that they still have some control over their lives.

✔ **Keep your perspective.** When people find themselves in dire circumstances, they have a tendency to look at everything else in a negative light. For example, men who lose their jobs often feel that their wives are no longer sexually attracted to them and that their children don't acknowledge their authority.

When one part of your world seems out of control, don't allow your disappointment and anger to contaminate the more positive aspects of your life.

Every setback offers new opportunities, although you may not see them at the moment. For example, the loss of your job can give you more time with your family — at least in the short run. It can also motivate you to look into new career options. Answering the following questions can help you cope when you're confronted by a situation that threatens your sense of control:

- Are you seeking support from your spouse, your family, and your friends?

- Can you think of any new skills or ideas that can come out of this difficult circumstance?

- Are you looking for joy and fulfillment in other areas of your life?

- Can you foresee an end to the stressful situation?

- Are you taking care of yourself — physically, emotionally, and spiritually?

✔ **Don't let stress place you in the middle of a vicious cycle.** When circumstances make you feel that your life is out of control, you may be tempted to overeat or overuse alcohol. This, in turn, creates additional stress — on your body and your emotions. What you wind up with is a whole new set of problems that generate even more pressure.

When people are overwhelmed, alcohol seems like an easy escape. One or even two drinks can have a soothing or tranquilizing effect. But anything more than that on a regular basis can increase stress and lead to a chronic depression.

Assessing the Impact of Stress on Your Marriage

The secret of a happy marriage remains a secret.

— Henny Youngman, comedian

Recognition is always an important first step in making positive changes. Table 13-1 helps you recognize how you and your partner deal with the stressors that cause the most conflict in marriage. After you pinpoint the areas of greatest concern, you can begin a dialogue on how these stressors may be affecting your relationship.

This exercise is especially helpful when both partners complete it and then compare results. This will help you see how close or far apart you are in the way you perceive the stressors in your marriage.

Choose a rating for you and your spouse in each of the ten areas that cause marital stress. Then enter the number in the appropriate box.

Table 13-1	Stress-Response Test			
Life Area	*Stress Score*	*You*	*Your Spouse*	*Difference*
1. Your marriage	2=Constantly under stress 1=Alternating periods of comfort and stress 0=Most of the stress is positive			
2. Personal satisfaction	2=Often feel dissatisfied about how things are going 1=Alternating feelings of satisfaction and dissatisfaction 0=Generally comfortable with how things are going			
3. Finances	2=Money is a constant source of negative stress 1=Money is an occasional source of negative stress 0=Money is generally not a source of negative stress			
4. Career	2=Work is often stressful and provokes anger 1=Work is occasionally stressful and sometimes provokes anger 0=Work is generally satisfying			
5. Health	2=Frequent or chronic health problems 1=Some health problems 0=Few or no health problems			

Life Area	Stress Score	You	Your Spouse	Difference
6. Children	2=Children are a frequent source of stress 1=Stress from children is both positive and negative 0=Stress from children is mainly positive			
7. Friends	2=Frequent feelings of dissatisfaction about isolation from friends 1=Moderately satisfied with quantity and quality of friends 0=Enjoy positive relationships with friends			
8. Family of origin and in-laws	2=Frequent conflict with family and in-laws 1=So-so relations with family and in-laws 0=Mostly positive relations with family and in-laws			
9. Your home	2=Unhappy about your home and neighborhood 1=Moderately comfortable withyour home and neighborhood 0=Generally happy with your home and neighborhood			
10. Aging and mortality	2=Frequent feelings of anxiety about growing old and dying 1=Occasional feelings of anxiety about growing old and dying 0=Acceptance of growing old and dying			
Totals				

To score the test in Table 13-1, do the following:

1. **Calculate your own cumulative score in the first scoring column, and your spouse's in the second scoring column.**

   • A total of 0 to 5 indicates a healthy stress level.

   • A total of 6 to 10 indicates a moderately healthy balance between positive and negative stress.

- • A total score of more than 11 indicates that you or your spouse is experiencing a great deal of stress.

2. **Enter the difference between your rating and your spouse's rating in the last column.**

3. **Add up the differences and rate yourselves according to the following scale:**

   - • 5 or fewer points: You have similar ideas about the stressors in your lives.

   - • 6 to 10 points: You have reasonably similar ideas about the stressors in your lives.

   - • Over 11 points: You have major areas of disagreement that can lead to conflict.

Please pay close attention to differences in individual categories, especially those with a score of 2. If your partner has also completed the exercise, look for those areas in which your ratings are furthest apart. A careful analysis of these differences gives you a good idea of where more discussion and better communication are needed.

Chapter 14

Exploring the Role of Money in Marriage

*M*oney is one of the most common causes of marital problems. Couples argue about who will earn it, who can spend it, and who is better at dealing with it.

In this chapter, we show you how your attitudes about money were formed, and help you recognize how they are impacting your marriage. We help you understand what's behind many of the disputes that married couples have over money, and show you how to start resolving them.

Recognizing How You and Your Partner Deal with Money

> *In some way, all financial behavior stems from what we experienced as children. It's either a reflection of what we learned or a rebellion against it.*
>
> — Emily Card, author and financial expert

Handling money is no easy task, even when you don't have to worry about someone else's feelings and choices. But when a person who is loose with money (a spender) marries someone who is tight with money (a saver), you're bound to have constant struggles over managing household finances.

Spenders find that they are always running out of money — though this may not stop them from continuing to spend and building up even more debt. Savers are forever squirreling cash away for rainy days — even though they may have already saved more than they can possibly use in a lifetime.

We often hear such value differences regarding money aired in disagreements like the following:

- ✔ I want to put away funds for retirement; my spouse wants to spend it while we're still relatively young.

- ✔ I want the children to earn what they get; my spouse believes in showering them with gifts and money.

- ✔ I hate owing money; my spouse feels that carrying a certain amount of debt makes good financial sense.

Here are some suggestions for resolving style differences in dealing with money:

- ✔ **Sit down with your partner and have a frank discussion about the way your respective families of origin dealt with money.** Discuss the family's actual financial situation versus their values in terms of spending and saving.

- ✔ **Talk about ways that your past experiences may be impacting the present situation.** Ask yourself and your partner if your current attitudes and behavior make sense. An honest approach here can be an important step in making positive changes. How do each of your past experiences impact your present-day attitudes and behaviors? If you or your partner seems too frugal or too extravagant, an open discussion of feelings sometimes helps people recognize these patterns and the need for change.

- ✔ **Talk about your short- and long-term financial goals.** Do you both envision yourselves eventually living in a penthouse? Or do you want to save enough money to retire to a relaxing but modest lifestyle in the country? Are you planning to send your children to expensive private colleges? Or do you feel they ought to work to pay for their own higher education?

- ✔ **Talk to each other about how each of you envisions these and other aspects of your lives.** How do you picture your lifestyle in a year? In 10 years? In 20 years? Be as specific as possible, and pay careful attention to those areas where you disagree.

In order to achieve a meeting of the minds, you first have to express and acknowledge your differences.

Do your best to negotiate and compromise in as many areas as possible. It's not unusual for couples to have different lifestyle goals and different ideas about how to deal with money. But even big differences about money management can be resolved if you're willing to negotiate and meet somewhere in the middle.

Linking your spending to your past

People have a tendency to form ideas about money and how to spend it at an early age (long before they actually have any money to spend!). For example, those who grew up in a family where finances were tight often develop a survivalist mentality in adulthood. No matter how much wealth they possess, there is a nagging fear that it may all be gone tomorrow.

The attitudes about money that you carry over from childhood, very often don't realistically reflect your current financial situation. As both partners come to understand how their approach to money is linked to past experiences, they can begin a constructive dialogue that's free of blame.

Frank and Joyce had been married for three years. Both were in their early 30s; both had good jobs. They had recently bought an expensive condo. As a result, there was only a small amount of money left after all the monthly expenses were paid. Frank wanted to put that money into savings, while Joyce wanted to spend it on entertainment and vacations. They were able to resolve their immediate problem by using the following guidelines:

- **Understand that your different values and ideas about money require constant negotiation.** There is no quick fix for couples like Frank and Joyce, so it's important to recognize that the same differences over money are bound to come up again and again.

- **Respect each other's feelings and preferences.** Joyce and Frank were able to recognize that their different ideas about money were not questions of right and wrong. They never attacked or demeaned each other for the choices they wanted to pursue.

- **Brainstorm solutions that address both partners' comfort levels.** Frank and Joyce spent hours discussing various ways of reaching a compromise. At one point Joyce came up with an idea: "Instead of simply putting money into a savings account, why don't we find out more about investing in the stock market? That way, we'd have a better chance of generating more money in a shorter amount of time. Then we could use some of that money to do the things I like to do. If we lose money, I'm willing to put off our vacation."

Frank was receptive to Joyce's idea and agreed to her suggestion that a certain portion of the profits would be used for travel and entertainment. However, he pointed out that investing in the stock market involved risk, and it was important that they get as much information as possible. They started exploring a variety of investment options together (a good resource is *Investing For Dummies* by Eric Tyson [IDG Books Worldwide, Inc.]). After they had some idea of their investment strategy, they consulted a financial planner for direction and technical advice. They found that investing in the stock market was something they enjoyed doing together, although they sometimes disagreed about how much risk to take.

As long as both partners are more emotionally invested in having a viable marriage than in saving or spending money, most couples are able to negotiate their money differences.

Recognizing How Money Problems Can Threaten Your Marriage

There are more important things in life than money. The trouble is, they all cost money!

— Milton Berle, comedian

As is the case with all marital differences, there isn't one right or wrong way to deal with money. However, extreme behavior in the direction of either spending or saving can erode — and eventually destroy — a marriage.

Disputes about money can cover up deeper emotional issues — like depression, lack of self-esteem, and power struggles within the relationship.

As a rule, we judge a person's way of dealing with money as extreme if it's out of line with his or her actual financial situation. For example, in a poor family — or one that's experiencing a financial crisis — a spouse who watches every cent may be acting appropriately. However, we would question the same attitudes and behaviors in a wealthy family. At the same time, it's also important to look at the reasons for the extreme behavior.

What's your choking point?

Sometimes, disputes over money stem from what we call *choking points* — amounts that far exceed your idea of how much something should cost. If, for example, your spouse comes home and announces that he spent $50 for a coat, you're likely to consider that a reasonable amount — or even a bargain. But what if your spouse spent that same $50 on a pair of socks? In that case, the issue wouldn't be whether or not you have the money, but how that money was spent.

One choking-point issue for many people who live in a big city is the cost of parking a car. A midtown parking lot can cost 25 dollars or more, and this fact sometimes motivates people to drive around for hours looking for one of the precious few available free spaces on the street. It's not that they're particularly cheap or can't afford the cost of a lot. They simply consider the price to be outrageous.

Understanding what's behind compulsive spending

Eat, drink, and be merry, for tomorrow they may cancel your credit cards.

— Anonymous

A compulsive spender who wastes the household budget on things he or she can't afford poses a very real danger to the family. A wealthy spouse who spends extravagantly may be well within the boundaries of his or her financial means. However, if the excessive spending is used to ward off depression or to compensate for low self-esteem, we still consider it problematic.

Generally, compulsive spenders can't admit that they have a problem until a crisis — like divorce or bankruptcy — forces the spender's world to come crashing down.

If you or your spouse is a spending too much, and that behavior is undermining your financial security, the following tips can help:

✔ **Cut up your credit cards and throw them away.** Whenever people talk to us about their spending being out of control, they invariably mention the irresistible lure of credit cards. There's something about those little pieces of plastic that make overspending too easy for many people. When you have to pay for what you buy in cold cash, the expenditure seems a lot more real.

✔ **Keep a log of every dollar you spend.** This is a good practice for anyone who wants to gain more financial control. In reality, most people find it unpleasant to have to write everything down. For compulsive spenders, however, this is an important step because it provides a moment-by-moment accounting of what's going out.

Reducing expenses and getting rid of credit cards are helpful short-term solutions for the excessive spender. However, if the need to spend is a true compulsion, the afflicted partner needs to address the compulsive behavior directly in order to find long-term answers to his or her pathological spending behavior.

✔ **Consider seeking outside help.** In general, the support of a spouse is not sufficient to stop a compulsive spender. This behavior is considered a disease, similar to substance abuse. As with alcohol and drugs, compulsive spenders are often helped by groups like Debtors Anonymous, which use the same 12-step approach that works for any addictive behavior. You can also find therapists and counselors who specialize in treating this kind of problem.

Like most addicts, compulsive spenders are usually driven by feelings of low self-esteem. They over-spend in a futile attempt to fill their inner emptiness. Unfortunately, that strategy rarely works and the person continues to spend more money because he or she still feels empty. This often creates guilt feelings — which the compulsive spender deals with by going on an even more destructive spending spree.

Understanding what's behind miserly behavior

There's one reason you can't take it with you. It leaves before you do.

— Milton Berle

Misers are usually cheap in ways that go far beyond money. They withhold affection and support — as well as cash. An overly frugal partner's unwillingness to give often makes the relationship feel empty and unsatisfying to his or her spouse.

A miser's negative impact is more subtle than that of a spendthrift. However, the long-term effect on the marriage can be just as devastating. A middle-class or wealthy family who has a compulsive saver calling the financial shots may be forced to endure a more humble lifestyle than families who are really poor — and this can become oppressive.

Misers generally don't seek counseling because their extreme behavior doesn't get them into debt or bankruptcy. Therefore, they rarely perceive themselves as having a problem. In a culture that encourages over-spending and conspicuous consumption, a compulsive saver may argue that frugality is a healthy and practical way to achieve financial security. Maybe so, but when this seemingly responsible behavior becomes extreme, it can leave the other spouse feeling economically deprived and emotionally impoverished.

Most money-related disorders are rooted in emotional, not practical, issues. A well-off person who obsesses over every penny is often acting out of a fear of giving up control.

Everyone is vulnerable to many things in life — illness, accidents, natural disasters, and death. However, money is relatively easy to control — and that has an irresistible appeal to an overly frugal spouse.

This type of person is expert at accumulating and holding onto money, which provides a sense of power that's hard to find in other areas of life. Unfortunately, this need for control and domination often makes life miserable for the compulsive saver's partner and his family.

Spouses married to misers sometimes appear to go along with their partner's extreme behavior — although they'll try to spend on the sneak if they can get away with it. Others find it intolerable and eventually file for divorce. If you're stuck in such a marriage, we suggest redefining the hoarding behavior as a piece of personal pathology that's undermining your relationship, not as a prudent use of money. Insist that the compulsive saver seek professional help so that he or she can understand why it's so difficult to spend anything.

You can never completely undo the impact of a person's early experiences with money. This is part of the emotional package each individual brings into a marriage. With the support of a therapist or a self-help group, an overly frugal person can begin to uncover how he or she relates to money and develop more productive attitudes toward saving and spending.

In time, a miser can make positive behavioral changes — but only under the following three conditions:

✔ If he or she comes to understand the attitudes and childhood experiences that are driving the behavior.

✔ If he or she is able to recognize the effect that the frugality is having on other people.

✔ If he or she is able to make a conscious choice that the marriage is more important than holding onto money.

Recognizing How Money Impacts the Balance of Power in Marriage

Money is like a sixth sense . . . without which you cannot fully enjoy the other five.

— Anonymous

In Western culture, money is power. That may not be fair, but there's no getting away from that reality. Traditionally, it was the husband who earned it, and that gave him a great deal of power and control over the relationship. Today, both partners work in 60 percent of all marriages — with the wife outearning the husband in more than 25 percent of those marriages.

Western culture devalues the wife's contribution to the family in economic terms. This is not the fault of either men or women. Mostly, it has to do with the way boys and girls are socialized, through the messages they receive — from parents, TV commercials, and traditions that go back to the Bible. These traditional gender roles are still changing, but it's a slow — and sometimes painful — process.

Marriage theorist Betty Carter has done extensive research on the impact of each spouse's financial contribution to a marriage — and the resulting power battles. At one end of the spectrum are very wealthy couples with two financially independent partners. At the other pole, there are very poor couples who are barely able to make ends meet. Carter finds that almost every married couple between these two extremes fits into one of the following four categories:

- ✔ **One spouse earns most or all of the money, while the other spouse assumes the role of a full-time caretaker.** In such marriages, the working spouse (generally the husband) often takes control of all of the major financial decisions, and may try to control the non-working spouse's ability to make even the smallest monetary decisions.

    The wife in this type of marriage may have a hard time retaining any control of her life unless she has independent money or some marketable skills. However, if she is completely dependent on her husband's income, she can lose all autonomy and have little power to negotiate.

- ✔ **Both spouses work, but one earns far less money than the other.** In this kind of situation, higher-earning spouses may decide that they have a right to make financial decisions, because they bring home most of the money.

- ✔ **A spouse stops working to care for the family.** This spouse has marketable skills, however, and could support him- or herself if necessary. Partners in this position have choices, which give them more power to negotiate and make demands. For example, if the working spouse wants financial control, this spouse can always return to the workplace and generate his or her own money.

- ✔ **The wife works, and earns more money than her husband.** One or both partners may become anxious over the husband's failure to be the primary provider. This "affront" to a man's masculinity can have a negative impact on his self-confidence, as well as his sexual performance.

    A wife in this situation may end up trying to prevent her greater financial contributions from driving a wedge through the relationship by turning down promotions or accepting lower-paying positions so that her husband won't feel threatened.

There is a cultural stereotype that a powerful woman who brings home a fat paycheck is less desirable to a man than one who embraces more traditional feminine roles. For a man, success in the workplace is a sign to everyone that he has made it. But women often find that those same achievements are not so happily received by her husband or by society in general.

If one spouse chooses to use his or her greater income as a lever for gaining power in making financial decisions, the other spouse may eventually become angry and resentful in a way that will negatively impact the relationship. Married couples can avoid most conflicts over money and power by taking the following steps:

✔ **Discuss your respective roles and contributions.** The stereotype of the hero-husband who goes out into the workplace to support his stay-at-home wife has largely faded over the past few decades. Still, one or both partners may still cling to these traditional expectations of how a marriage is supposed to operate.

The only way to make certain that you're both in agreement about who does what is to have an open discussion of what your roles are going to be. Even if you've been married for many years and have never had this kind of discussion, you should have it now.

It's important for married partners to develop a shared vision of the relationship and to negotiate (and renegotiate) differences as they come up. In many long-term marriages, spouses assume that they know what their partners want — and they're often dead wrong.

If either spouse is unhappy with his or her role, burying that dissatisfaction will lead to built-up resentment, which makes the problem worse.

✔ **Respect each other's contribution to the marriage as equal.** It's impossible to judge the value of each partner's contribution in strictly monetary terms. For example, how can you compare the value of a husband who's a corporate executive earning a six-figure salary to that of a wife who is a full-time homemaker?

We've seen many husbands attempt to calculate that value by adding up the costs of hiring outsiders to perform his wife's traditionally low-cost care-taking services. But that doesn't begin to reflect the real value of the wife's contribution to the family.

Many divorce courts now value a homemaker's contribution as being equal to that of the so-called *monied spouse* — even if she has no tangible income. However, the need for mutual respect goes beyond that. If either partner feels disrespected or undervalued, a power struggle will almost certainly erode the good will and intimacy between the partners.

✔ **Make sure that you and your partner both have access to the money.** Most married couples set up joint bank accounts. But all too often, the funds in those accounts are under the control of the spouse who earns them so that, in reality, there isn't a common pool. We suggest that you take the following steps to ensure that you and your partner both have an equal say in how the money is spent:

- Agree on an amount that each spouse can spend without consulting the other. The actual amount of discretionary money will, of course, depend on a couple's financial situation, their budget, and their comfort level. For example, a middle-class couple may agree that both partners can spend up to, say, two hundred dollars a month on anything they want, without conferring with the other. Every couple needs to negotiate the details of such an arrangement. But, if there is discretionary money available, both partners should have some authority to spend a certain amount without having to ask.

- Put some assets in each partner's name. In marriages where one partner earns most of the money or comes into the marriage with substantial assets, it's not unusual for that monied partner to keep all those assets in his or her name. Placing some of the funds in the non-monied partner's name helps to equalize each spouse's power over financial decisions.

Whenever either partner feels that there's an imbalance of power in the relationship, both spouses — and the marriage — suffer.

Understanding How a Flexible Marriage Protects Your Financial Future

A successful man is one who makes more money than his wife can spend. A successful woman is one who can find such a man.

— Lana Turner, actress

We believe that role flexibility is one of the best financial insurance policies a married couple can have. Does that surprise you? Think about it: In relationships where each partner is willing to take on only certain specific roles, an unexpected financial setback can throw you for a loop.

Picture a marriage in which the husband always worked and the wife always cared for the home. Suddenly, the husband gets fired or gets sick, and he can no longer work. What happens then?

Certainly, this unexpected change would generate more than a little stress and anxiety in any marriage. However, in a flexible relationship, the wife would be ready and willing to take up the slack by attempting to generate as much income as possible. Meanwhile, the husband would not feel resentful about doing housework and assuming other caretaking functions.

THE MARRIAGE DOCTORS SAY

Money matters

Steve: We had lots of disagreements about money when our two oldest children were small. I felt that I was working very hard and you were spending too much.

Sue: You were spending money as freely as I did; you just spent it on different things. When you wanted to spend money, that was fine, but when I wanted to spend it in ways you didn't like, you objected. I thought there was a double standard.

Steve: That was probably because I was earning most of the money at that point. I felt that this gave me greater authority when it came to making financial decisions, even though our marriage was supposedly 50/50.

Sue: There were only two years in our 30 years of marriage that I didn't work. At the time, we had decided that I would stay home and care for our two small children. I was responsible for running the household and all of the childcare. As far as I was concerned, the work I was doing in the home worth as much as your work outside the home.

Steve: I still think that I was working harder.

Sue: You always said that my contribution was as valuable as yours, but you sure didn't back up those high-minded words. I think that we were having a power struggle that neither of us fully understood. You would get angry and complain about the way I spent money. I would often agree, but then go ahead and do what I wanted — either openly or secretly. Eventually, you'd find out, and we'd have an argument.

Steve: I'd really get angry when you went behind my back. It took us a while to find a comfort level for both of us, but once we found it, we rarely fought about money again.

REMEMBER

Financial setbacks and other turbulent changes test both partners' adaptability and their willingness to work as a team. In a flexible relationship, these apparent blows can present opportunities for growth and change. However, partners who are inflexible and cling to rigid roles endanger the financial — and emotional — viability of their relationship.

TIP

The following steps can help you create a marriage with more role flexibility:

TRUE STORY

- ✔ **Keep up your skills.** One of the best ways to stay flexible is to maintain the job skills that you bring into a marriage. For example, Andrea was a successful attorney who decided to take a few years off to raise her two children. However, she still volunteers her services at a free legal clinic on a part-time basis. "I'm good at what I do," she recently told us, "and I enjoy it. Plus, when I'm ready to go back to work, I won't be rusty."

- ✔ **Talk about why you chose to divide responsibilities in a particular way.** Are your financial and work-related arrangements the result of carefully thought-out decisions reflecting choices and abilities? Or are you dividing these responsibilities on the basis of outdated gender stereotypes? That no longer apply?

The more openly each of you can express your goals and preferences, the better you will understand each other's perspective.

✔ **Help each other understand what your day is like.** Talk to each other about what's going on. If possible, try changing roles every so often. For example, let your husband stay with the kids for the evening while you go out drinking with your friends.

Many couples harbor resentments about what they imagine their partner does all day. A stay-at-home wife may envision her spouse taking long lunches and spending hours socializing with attractive woman. Even though he may do a certain amount of socializing, the husband resents this characterization, because he mostly feels that he works hard.

A working husband may think his wife has it easy. He resents the fact that she doesn't have to commute, doesn't have a boss, and can stay home. Meanwhile, that wife feels her husband has no appreciation for the hard work she does managing the house and supervising the kids. She feels certain that her husband couldn't cope with her responsibilities — not even for a day.

Talking to your partner and putting yourself in your partner's shoes will give you a new perspective and appreciation for what he or she is contributing to the welfare of the family. At the same time, it may help you envision what it would be like for you to take on that role.

In the best marriages, partners are committed to a working as a team. This principle applies not only to money, but also to dividing up household tasks, raising children, and making lifestyle decisions. There may not be a 50/50 balance between partners at every given point in time. Still, the structure of the relationship is based on equality and common interests.

Chapter 15

Examining Extramarital Affairs — and Knowing What to Do about Them

- -

In This Chapter

▶ Defining an affair

▶ Recognizing when cheating is most likely to occur

▶ Dealing with infidelity

▶ Keeping your marriage together after the affair is over

- -

Some marriage experts see an affair as a sure sign that the relationship has begun to come apart. Others view infidelity as an attempt to save — or even revitalize — a marriage. Some affairs have more to do with a husband or wife's personal problems than with the marriage itself. But whatever provokes it, an affair is bound to create strife in a marriage.

Researchers differ about what percentage of married spouses have affairs. The numbers range anywhere from 20 to 60 percent — and this is only one bone of contention. Mental health professionals argue about whether it's wise for a husband or wife to own up to having an affair. And, if the cheating spouse does confess, how much detail should he or she reveal?

In this chapter, we help you recognize what an affair says about you, your partner, and your marriage. We talk about how to deal with a cheating spouse — as well as how to handle your own temptations and infidelities. We then explore the steps couples can take to begin healing the pain of infidelity.

Understanding What an Affair Is — and Isn't

If love is blind, marriage is a real eye-opener.

— Anonymous

When people discuss marital cheating, they are generally talking about having sexual intercourse with someone other than a spouse. However, the issue is more complicated than that — as the Bill Clinton-Monica Lewinsky case demonstrated. President Clinton was accused of perjury when he denied "having sex" with Ms. Lewinsky. Eventually, the president indirectly admitted to having oral sex, but claimed that this type of physical intimacy did not constitute sexual relations as the term is generally understood.

We leave it to others to decide which acts do and don't meet the legal standard for adultery. However, as we see it, engaging in any kind of sexual behavior with someone other than your spouse is cheating. That includes petting and passionate kissing. Moreover, cheating, in the broadest sense, can sometimes include an ongoing relationship in which you and another person have strong sexual vibes — even if there never is any actual physical contact.

It's not always easy to draw a line between fantasizing or flirting and actual cheating. But the following are signs that you or your spouse is getting dangerously close to crossing that line:

- **Secrets and lies:** There's someone at work with whom you share a mutual attraction. Before long, the two of you start having lunch every day. Soon, you add weekly dinners after work. You don't tell your spouse about these meals. Instead, you talk about business lunches with colleagues, or occasional dinner meetings with clients. You tell yourself that these are innocent omissions — white lies. But, if that's the case, how come you can't discuss these get-togethers with your partner?

- **Friendships that are too close for comfort:** There's no harm in having opposite-sex friendships, but there can be trouble when people start getting more intimate with a friend than they are with their spouse.

  If, for example, you feel that your mate is neglecting you, while, at the same time, you complain to an opposite-sex friend about your love life, there's likely to be trouble. A spouse who turns to someone else for understanding about his or her marital problems is developing a level of intimacy with that person that can threaten the marriage.

Lying about purely emotional relationships outside the marriage can be destructive — even if they don't involve sexual intimacy. You may not have committed adultery in the biblical sense. Still, when you start directing your emotional passion to someone other than your spouse, you're getting dangerously close to what one popular song describes as "the cheating side of town."

✔ **Erotic use of the telephone and the Internet:** In recent years, phone sex and cybersex have become increasingly popular. While you may not share any direct physical contact, sharing sexual fantasies with someone other than your spouse can cross the line — especially if the communication is ongoing and in secret.

If you're not certain whether or not a particular act constitutes cheating, try asking your wife or husband what she or he thinks!

Understanding Why (And When) Spouses Cheat

Eighty percent of married men cheat in America. The rest cheat in Europe.

— Jackie Mason, author and comedian

Married partners cheat on each other for a variety of reasons, including personal reasons that have little to do with the marriage. An affair can be:

✔ The result of anger toward the partner

✔ An attempt to find intimacy, excitement, or passion that's lacking in the marriage

✔ The result of a fear of intimacy within the marriage

✔ From a fear of getting older

✔ The result of career problems

✔ An attempt to find a way out of an unhappy relationship

✔ A way to avoid conflict in the relationship

✔ Motivated by unresolved issues from one's family of origin

✔ An effort to fix the marriage

Some cheating spouses have relations with the same lover for years. Others get caught up in the heat of the moment, and have a single one-night stand. Still others have a pattern of cheating with a variety of partners.

Husbands and wives can cheat at any point in the marriage cycle. However, there are certain danger zones when spouses are more likely to stray. The following sections explore those zones.

Warning signs that your partner may be cheating

Look for the following warning signs. Your spouse may:

- ✔ Stop having sex with you, without offering a believable explanation

- ✔ Suddenly start acting a lot more attentive — or completely inattentive

- ✔ Call frequently to say he or she has to stay late at work

- ✔ Go on a sudden spending spree that includes expensive clothes, cars, and other flashy items, or start running up credit-card charges that can't be readily explained.

- ✔ Become indifferent to family events, such as holidays and birthdays

- ✔ Suddenly become intensely religious, or abandon a lifelong commitment to religion

Danger zone 1: Shortly after the wedding

When a couple first starts having sex, the electricity can be incredibly intense. But, as soon as the excitement starts to fade, a husband or wife may turn to someone else in an attempt to recreate those early fireworks.

We know of spouses who've started cheating months — even weeks — after the wedding ceremony (as well as some who cheat during the engagement). People in this category often experience a kind of "'buyer's remorse," a feeling that sometimes kicks in before they even walk down the aisle. It suddenly strikes them that they're trapped in a relationship for life, and cheating provides what looks like an easy way out.

During the early stages of marriage, people are prone to wonder if they made the right choice. Issues of intimacy and commitment are particularly pronounced at this time.

Still, you can deal with the temptation to cheat by doing the following:

- ✔ **Develop the habit of turning toward your partner, rather than away.** When husbands and wives feel unhappy in their marriages, they often keep it to themselves, or complain to someone else. It may be hard at first, but talking to your partner about what's bothering you makes it more likely that the two of you will become closer and find a way to work out the problem.

    It's important that both of you are committed to sharing big and small intimacies on a regular basis, including those topics that can create tension in the relationship.

Talking about what's upsetting can help husbands and wives grow closer. Keeping these issues hidden creates more distance.

✔ **Make a conscious choice not to act out your impulses.** Let's face it, there is an element of risk and fun in cheating. The question is, are you willing to risk your marriage to satisfy your need for excitement?

We once heard someone say that adultery is for adults. The truth is, marriage is an enterprise for grownups — notwithstanding the childish way that many high- (and not-so-high-) profile people treat it. A committed marriage partner may feel attracted to — or even flirt with — other people. However, acting on those charged-up feelings almost invariably puts a marriage in danger.

It's not unusual to feel nervous about being locked in to one sexual partner for a lifetime. And, while it's true that your initial feelings of passion will change and become less intense, research shows that the potential for having better and more meaningful sex is greatest in a long-term, committed marriage because of the bond that can develop over time. (See Chapter 6 for help with developing a great sex life with your partner.)

Danger zone 2: When a baby enters the family

The birth of a first child is a time of great joy, but it can also be very stressful. (See Chapter 9 for a complete discussion of the impact of a first child on a marriage.) Extramarital affairs are common at this stage, because both partners are suddenly forced to deal with a raft of new issues that include the following:

✔ Financial pressures mount, as do arguments about dividing the child-care responsibilities. Partners who are unwilling to discuss their resentful feelings and conflicts may look elsewhere for understanding, emotional intimacy, or sex.

✔ A new baby can be bad for a couple's sex life. Couples may find it hard to have sexual relations during pregnancy — and this pattern continues after the baby is born.

New mothers sometimes feel hesitant about having sex in the weeks and months after giving birth. They may still be sore from the delivery, or they may have put on weight and feel unattractive to their husbands. Meanwhile, new dads often have trouble seeing their wives in a mothering role — particularly if they are breast feeding.

✔ Some men are upset because their wives seem to be giving them less emotional attention. They end up feeling as if they're in competition with the new baby. Under the circumstances, it can be far easier for a man to find a lover than to try to deal with all the problems at home.

There is a very high risk of divorce during the third and fourth years of marriage. It's no coincidence that these years often correspond with the birth of a first child, and the dramatic changes that accompany this event.

The following guidelines can help couples in this danger zone reduce the risk of an affair:

✔ **Tackle unfamiliar changes together.** No matter how many books or articles you read about raising an infant, you and your spouse will be in for many unexpected surprises. Some of these will be wonderful — like the way you feel when your baby utters his first words or takes her first steps. Other surprises will test your ability to cope — like being forced to deal with your baby's high fever at 3:00 a.m. and then having to face a critical deadline at work a few sleepless hours later.

✔ **Make time for each other.** Some new mothers become so invested in their babies that they virtually ignore their husbands. This kind of maternal bonding is natural. However, if the husband feels abandoned by his wife, who seems to have time only for child-related concerns, he will be far more likely to seek companionship outside the marriage. A man like this needs attention and respect for his feelings.

At the same time, husbands have to exercise patience and understanding during the first few months after a baby arrives, and to recognize the physical and emotional exhaustion that new mothers experience. Show in your actions that you respect and support what your wife is going through. Ask her how you can give her more love and attention.

✔ **Talk frankly to each other.** If you're having trouble adjusting to your new responsibilities, don't be afraid to say so. If you're anxious about the state of your sex life, it's usually a good idea to raise that issue — but gently!

Many things change when a first child enters a family — sex included. It's likely that sex will be less spontaneous than it used to be — at least for a while. Still, that doesn't mean it can't be enjoyable and passionate. The addition of a child can make your marriage stronger, but that's not likely to happen if one of you runs into someone else's arms.

The workplace is one of the most fertile breeding grounds for affairs — especially when spouses are trying to cope with a baby. At work, relationships start out in a non-threatening way, but they can cross the line in a hurry. There's an element of danger in having an affair with a co-worker that many people find seductive. The workplace gives people an opportunity to dress up and look their best. Plus, the conversation rarely includes unsexy topics, like whose turn it is to calm a crying baby in the middle of the night. Before long, the attractive, attentive co-worker appears to have of all the qualities that your spouse is lacking. Under the circumstances, it's easy to lose perspective, to avoid directly communicating negative feelings, and to and give in to a short-term temptation that can seriously harm your marriage.

The 7-Year Itch

The seventh year of marriage has long been recognized as a peak period for extramarital affairs. But the term *seven-year-itch* became a household expression after it was used as the title for a hit film in 1957.

The 7-Year Itch is the story of a 30ish New York book editor named Sherman who sends his wife of seven years and son to the country for the summer. Meanwhile, he's stuck in the family's Manhattan apartment, alone with his work — and his vivid sexual fantasies.

Sherman is determined to lead a sensible life during the summer and not be like the other men he knows, who start playing around the minute their wives leave town. But on his very first night alone, Sherman's resistance is tested by a sexy summer tenant who has just moved in upstairs — a beautiful blonde, played by Marilyn Monroe. This character is never given a name. She is simply called "The Girl."

When he can tear himself away from his fantasies about making love with The Girl, Sherman pores over the manuscript he's supposed to be editing. It's a book by a psychiatrist about the repressed sexual urges of men just like him. Its title: *The Seven-Year Itch*.

At one point, Sherman's editing is disturbed by a knock on his door. It's The Girl, complaining that it's too hot in her apartment to fall asleep. Sherman isn't sure that he can resist temptation — but he does. Our hero lets The Girl use his air-conditioned bedroom, while he sleeps on the living room couch.

The next day, Sherman flees to the country to spend two weeks with his wife and son. Somehow, he has managed to stop himself from scratching an itch that could have destroyed his marriage.

Danger zone 3: The seven-year itch

This danger zone is marked by two critical events:

- ✔ One or both spouses have passed their 30th birthday
- ✔ A second child has entered the family

Either of these events can be upsetting to husbands and wives, because they are beginning to feel that time is slipping away. "Did I really choose the life I'm living," a man or woman might wonder. "Or has it been thrust upon me because I wasn't sure about what I really wanted?"

After age 30, people begin to feel their youth fading. Suddenly, you look in the mirror and realize that you're no longer a kid. It's not that you've changed much physically. But, when you were 20 or 25, you kind of went with the flow — figuring that there was lots of time to right the ship if it veered off course. But now, things seem more serious. You start asking yourself the following kinds of questions:

- ✔ Is this the career I really want?
- ✔ Is this the spouse I really want?
- ✔ Is this the life I really want?

When people feel stuck in one or more aspects of life, they often find that their marriage is the most convenient scapegoat. It's hard to leave your job and nearly impossible to overhaul your life — at least in the short run. However, it's relatively easy to find sex outside the marriage — and that's the course many dissatisfied spouses take.

The divorce rate for persons aged 30 to 34 is about twice as high as for older couples. In this danger zone, it's easy to allow career problems and personal disappointments to undermine an otherwise solid marriage.

The following guidelines can help decrease the chances of that happening:

- ✔ **Try to pinpoint the source of your dissatisfaction.** Because there are so many stressful issues that converge around the seventh year of marriage, it's easy to lose perspective about where the real problem lies. You may be feeling stuck in your career, having problems with your kids, or going through what some researchers refer to as an *early midlife crisis.* (You can find more about midlife changes in Chapter 10.)

- ✔ **Recognize that your work/fun ratio may be temporarily tilted in the wrong direction.** The seven-year-itch comes at a time when both spouses feel pressures and responsibilities mounting. Consequently, they tend to do more work and have less fun in day-to-day living — and they resent it. Husbands — as well as a growing number of wives — may seek to cheat at this point in order to put more fun in their lives.

Danger zone 4: The midlife marriage crisis

You might expect that as husbands and wives mature, they would become more reserved and less likely to cheat. Not so. Research shows that almost 25 percent of married partners in their 40s have affairs. That's more than any other age group — except for 18- to 24-year-olds. Furthermore, over a third of people in their 40s believe that extramarital sex is sometimes justified.

These statistics come as no surprise to anyone who understands the emotions that middle-aged wives and husbands go through. At this point in life, people are often at their peak of financial responsibilities and emotional turmoil. Plus, there are issues of changing sexual appetites, aging, and mortality that can cause lots of *angst* at this stage. (For a complete discussion of personal and marital midlife issues, go to Chapters 10 and 11).

A frequently cited study by the MacArthur Foundation research network finds that the incidence of what's commonly known as a *midlife crisis* has been greatly exaggerated. Still, even those researchers recognize that finances and sexual activity are the areas that middle-aged people feel they have least control over. As a 46-year-old client who read the study sarcastically remarked: "That's right. Everything is going great guns in my life — except for sex and money!"

Other, less-optimistic studies show that a growing number of people over 40 fear that their lives are becoming more tedious and less exciting. Under the circumstances, it's not surprising that husbands and wives are prone to seek out extramarital affairs.

The husband in search of his fading youth

Research shows that middle-aged husbands are more likely to cheat than their wives. Many cultures heap scorn on an unfaithful wife, but view an older man taking a young lover a normal exercise of the male prerogative. However, as the film *An Unmarried Woman* reveals (see "*An Unmarried Woman*" sidebar), middle-aged men who become embroiled in such affairs are often pathetic souls who can wind up losing everything.

A husband's midlife affairs often stem from his own panic about aging. This doesn't mean that a wife should ignore her own devastation and simply accept her husband's wrongdoing as par for the course. Still, it's useful for a wife to recognize her husband's midlife panic, so that she can protect herself and her marriage.

An Unmarried Woman

When the film starts out, the audience is introduced to an attractive, affluent couple who've been married for about 20 years. At least from the outside, this marriage appears to be happy. Erica and Martin seem to have an easy rapport with each other and their 15-year-old daughter. Suddenly, with no apparent provocation or motivation, 40-something Martin announces that he's leaving Erica for his much younger secretary. Erica proceeds to throw up. She then begins the tough business of reconstructing her life. What ultimately happens between Erica and her estranged husband is all too commonplace.

Within a few months, Martin's young lover dumps him. Suddenly, he realizes how much he had with his wife and begs her to take him back. But it's too late. As a result of her estrangement, Erica has been forced to become more independent and self-assured than she ever could have imagined.

After 20 years of marriage, many husbands fear that they are starting to lose their competitive edge — both sexually and in the workplace. The easiest way to prove to themselves that they're still virile and vital is to have sex with a younger woman. This is often easy to accomplish, because women in their 20s often find middle-aged men attractive. But, in the end, men who indulge this impulse often do irreparable damage to themselves and their families.

The wife in search of a dashing prince

A growing number of wives are having affairs in midlife, and they are motivated by many of the same forces as their wayward husbands — loneliness, boredom, feelings of being unloved and unappreciated, anxiety about their fading youth — as well as a search for sexual excitement. There has also been a backlash in recent years against the double standard that says adultery is acceptable for husbands but taboo for women.

In an apparent attempt to turn the tables, feminist writers like Dalma Heyn have attempted to frame marital cheating as "a revolutionary way for women to rise above the conventional." Heyn calls on wives to break out of the "rigid institutional cage . . . that imprisons their sexual selves." This view has been applauded by articles in women's magazines touting the benefits of women's infidelity, and films such as *The Bridges of Madison County* (see *"The Bridges of Madison County"* sidebar).

The Bridges of Madison County

In this film, Francesca (played by Meryl Streep) is a middle-aged farm wife, whose husband and children are away for a long weekend. She breaks out of her tedium by having an affair with Robert, a handsome photographer (played by Clint Eastwood) who happens by the house.

The liaison between Francesca and Robert is no sleazy one-nighter. Instead, it turns out to be what one critic termed "an aching affair of heart and mind — and flesh." This is the kind of wife's affair currently being promoted by some as "a sexual recharging, an escape from a worn-out relationship, a way into something better."

When Francesca reveals her unrealized dreams to her lover, he says, "I think I know how you feel." Then, he offers to help her cook dinner — and clean up! All of that non-husbandly behavior and a Hollywood-star's physique to boot. What neglected middle-aged wife could refuse that kind of offer — at least in her fantasies?

In the end, Francesca decides to stay with her husband because breaking up her family would cause too much pain. Still, in a letter to her children discovered years later after her death, Francesca confesses the affair and tells them that it gave her the strength to endure the remaining years of her marriage. She also beseeches them to, "Do what you [must] to be happy in this life."

The fantasy of an affair can be highly alluring, but acting on these desires is likely to weaken or destroy your marriage. Often, an affair starts out as a "fling," but then grows into an emotionally complicated relationship, in which the cheating spouse feels he or she is in love with both spouse and lover.

We offer the following advice to any woman or man who wants to resist the temptation of an affair:

- ✔ **Talk frankly and openly to your spouse about your feelings that something is missing in the marriage.** Tell that person about your urges to seek intimacy elsewhere. Find out what your spouse is thinking. Don't assume.

- ✔ **Recognize that the reality of living with your spouse cannot compete with the fantasy of the unknown.** Remember that by acting by acting on your impulses, you prevent your marriage from growing.

- ✔ **Flirt, and agree that it's okay for your partner to do the same.** The vows of fidelity that you took at your wedding are serious business. Still, it's helpful for both spouses to admit that there are other attractive people in the world. Flirting can be a healthy release — if it doesn't happen very often or focus on one person. Both partners need to give each other permission to do it. Such permission, as lawyers like to say, should not be unreasonably withheld.

Understanding What to Do about a Cheating Spouse

He who goes out of his house in search of happiness runs after a shadow.

— Chinese proverb

Cheating breaks a sacred bond of marriage and generates a great deal of pain, whether the wife or the husband has been unfaithful. We are well aware that, human nature being what it is, a certain percentage of wives and husbands will always cheat. Nevertheless, that is little consolation to a betrayed spouse.

We recommend the following course of action to husbands and wives who discover that their spouse has been unfaithful:

- ✔ **Assess the seriousness of the affair.** If you suspect (or know) that your spouse is cheating, determine whether it was a brief fling, a long-term liaison, or a pattern of philandering. In general, affairs fall into the following categories:

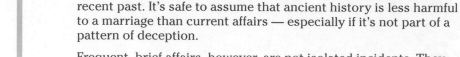

- **The one-night stand:** There is a difference between a brief dalliance that occurred years ago and one that took place in the recent past. It's safe to assume that ancient history is less harmful to a marriage than current affairs — especially if it's not part of a pattern of deception.

  Frequent, brief affairs, however, are not isolated incidents. They are patterns of infidelity that have far more serious consequences for a marriage than a true one-night stand.

- **The long-term outside relationship:** This type of liaison can be very threatening, especially if the deceived spouse eventually finds out that her spouse has been having an intimate relationship that parallels the marriage. Frequency can be an important issue in this type of a affair. There's a difference between long-term liaisons that take place once a year, and those that involve weekly contact.

- **The chronic cheater:** Many husbands and wives cheat more than once in the course of a marriage. However, the situation is extremely serious if the spouse engaged in a pattern of cheating with a variety of partners. The chronic nature of the behavior points to a deep-seated problem in the marriage — or in the cheating spouse's emotional makeup.

The meaning of the infidelity depends largely on the unresolved issues — both individual and marital — and their significance to each partner. The same circumstances can provoke radically different responses, depending on each spouse's personality, the nature of the relationship, and the facts surrounding the infidelity. All of these elements will relate to the whole issue of "do you tell" or "don't you tell."

✔ **Don't get trapped by your spouse's guilt-driven excuses.** Cheating spouses who get caught may employ one or more of the following tactics:

- **"I'm a sex addict."** Mental health professionals are still debating whether or not the compulsive need for sex is a true addiction. In any case, when an unfaithful husband or wife offers it as an excuse, you can bet that it's a way to avoid responsibility for hurtful behavior.

- **"I'm a terrible person."** A cheating spouse may genuinely feel guilty, but he also wants you to believe that his guilt is more profound than your hurt feelings. This attempt to cry on your shoulder may be driven by a real need for your indulgence and understanding. It make take some time to sort it out, but you have to decide if the cheating spouse is sorry about what he did, or just sorry that he got caught.

On the other hand, a display of remorse may be based on a fear of your ultimate retribution in divorce court. Technically, adultery is not a legal ground for divorce in most states. As a practical issue, however, evidence of cheating weighs heavily in decisions courts make when awarding alimony, child support, and child custody. Although it is not supposed to matter, a father who is branded as a "philanderer" has very little chance of being awarded custody of his minor children.

- **"I don't deserve you."** Women and men are both capable of resorting to this tactic. Middle-aged husbands who cheat with younger women often use this approach to try to win their wives over. Such a husband may applaud you for your maturity and sterling character — even complaining that his lover is selfish and flighty. "You are every man's dream," he might say. "She can't even make a sandwich. You're the mother of my children, a mountain of strength and loyalty. She is shallow and irrational."

  This strategy is especially tricky, because it often contains the not-so-subtle excuse that your husband's young lover needs him more than you do. In complimenting you, your husband is also conveying the message that you have everything his better nature wants — but his lover appeals to his childish vanity, which he's too weak to give up.

Research shows that women are far more likely to forgive their unfaithful husbands than husbands are to forgive their unfaithful wives. Some studies suggest that this is due in part to financial considerations and to the greater difficulties that middle-aged women often have in finding new mates. However, we encourage women not to allow these statistics to weaken their position when confronting a cheating husband.

✔ **Make sure the betraying spouse understands your suffering and rage.** Cheating spouses often make light of their actions. They may say something like, "Let's put this all behind us and move on." This approach doesn't promote healing. A betrayed spouse needs her partner to understand her pain, suffer her anger, and agree to do the hard work of restablishing trust.

✔ **The betrayed spouse should take responsibility for his or her role in the relationship.** Of course, you're entitled to feel pain, rage, and a host of negative feelings. There comes a time, though, where you must work to forgive and stop punishing the person who betrayed you. Otherwise, there will be no healing.

✔ **Give everyone lots of time.** Working though profoundly hurt emotions takes lots of time. Don't expect just to kiss and make up.

To tell or not to tell

Sue: We used to have major differences about confessing an affair. I've thought that it's usually helpful to come clean if that knowledge is going to help the marriage.

Steve: At one time, I believed that nobody should ever confess to an affair if at all possible. You once got really upset when I said that if a husband gets caught in bed with another woman, he should explain that she's selling mattresses. At least that shows more respect for the wife than saying: "Okay, you caught me. I'm in bed with my mistress because sex is a lot better with her than with you."

Sue: Respect is the wrong word. At best, that kind of denial is a misguided attempt to protect the wife from pain. I mean, who is really being protected in that situation?

Steve: My thought was that the cheating husband would essentially be saying: "This person means nothing to me, and I'm willing to discard her just like that! You are the person who is important." I've come to see that this is unrealistic, because denying reality doesn't help in the long run.

Sue: I think that we're both pretty much in agreement on this issue now.

Steve: Our positions are definitely much closer now than they once were. I am very aware that honesty is essential in maintaining intimacy. Still, I think that too many people blurt out their painful secrets instead of thinking long and hard about what's best for their marriage.

Sue: The other side of that coin are people who harm their marriage by rationalizing their cheating behavior. You can't just say, "What my wife doesn't know won't hurt her." What someone doesn't know can wind up hurting them a great deal — because it undermines and poisons the relationship.

Admitting versus Denying Infidelity

When trying to decide whether to admit to marital cheating, we believe that no hard-and-fast rule fits all situations. Sometimes you're better off — and more considerate — keeping quiet about a long-ago affair, particularly if your spouse has no idea. In other situations, admitting an affair is the only way to preserve the marriage — and the emotional stability of both partners. Many experienced therapists believe that guilty secrets in a marriage interfere with intimacy and that it's essential for a spouse who crossed the line to come clean.

Evan Imber-Black, family therapist and author of *The Secret Life of Families*, states: "To consider the impact on a relationship of a secret you are keeping, ask yourself two questions: What are the effects of my keeping this secret on our relationship? In what ways would our relationship change if I were to open this secret? . . . You begin to see that there can be no simple formula for making your decision, and no guarantee that it will be risk free."

We suggest that you consider the following factors in making that decision:

- **Recognize your goal in confessing the affair.** Let's assume that you had a one-night stand many years ago, and your spouse doesn't suspect anything. What purpose would be served by telling him or her at this point? If your only goal is a clear conscience, you may want to consider confessing to a priest or talking to a mental health professional. Ask yourself the following question: Will telling your spouse create unnecessary pain and problems in the relationship, or will it enable you to be truly intimate and learn how to communicate and connect?

    On the other hand, you might have some reason to feel that your spouse has a right to know about your cheating — even if she's not suspicious. For example, one client who had a short-term fling later found out that the woman he was sleeping with was both promiscuous and a drug abuser. He felt that his wife had a right to know that he may have contracted a sexually transmitted disease and passed it on to her.

- **Recognize the dangers of denying an affair.** If your spouse directly asks you if there is another person in your life, it's best to admit it. Most wives or husbands who ask that question have good reasons for their suspicions. At that point, denying the affair can do further damage to the relationship — and to your spouse.

    Don't try to manipulate your partner's perceptions and emotions. When you continue to deny the existence of an affair after your spouse has confronted you with proof, you're inflicting a level of hurt that amounts to cruel and unusual punishment. It's like trying to drive him or her crazy. Few things are more hurtful than continually telling someone that his or her correct perceptions are inaccurate.

- **Revealing an affair can help you and your partner begin addressing your individual and marital problems in a more honest and constructive way.** Some people decide not to tell and attempt to work out the problems on their own. However, any issues that involve your spouse will be harder to resolve without his or her cooperation.

Rebuilding a Marriage After an Affair

Because a man is unfaithful to you is no reason to leave him. You should stay with him and make sure the rest of his life is sheer hell.

— Roseanne Barr, actress and comedienne

When recovering from an affair, there is good news and bad news. The good news is that most healthy marriages can survive and thrive after an affair. The bad news is that the road back to a warm, trusting relationship is almost always long and hard.

The pain that results when one partner has an affair may never completely go away. Still, rebuilding your marriage is likely to be faster and less painful than the agony of a divorce. Research shows that 70 percent of couples who divorce because of infidelity come to regret that decision.

So, before you call a divorce lawyer, we suggest that you see if the following steps can help you and your spouse rebuild your marriage:

- ✔ **The person who cheated must agree to stop immediately.** This is not always as easy as it sounds — especially if the affair has been going on for a long time. Nevertheless, it's essential that the cheating spouse agree to cut off all communication — including all contact in the workplace. This may mean transferring to another department — or even changing jobs. One way or another, the adulterous relationship has to end if the marriage is going to survive.

If the affair occurred in the workplace, and the "other person" is your employee or under your supervision, you're caught in a real dilemma. You need to be very careful about how you cut off contact, or you may get sued for sexual harassment. You can't fire or transfer an employee, just because he or she has become an embarrassment to you or a problem in your marriage. You should consult with an attorney before you make any decisions about this sticky problem.

A wife or husband may be able to hide an affair, especially if it is short-lived. However, after one spouse finds out that the other has been unfaithful, both must go through a recovery process if they intend to stay together.

- ✔ **The spouse who betrayed the relationship must be sincerely remorseful — and forthcoming about his or her actions.** The betrayed partner may have a lot of questions to ask, and the cheating partner needs to be prepared to answer them. Some spouses will want to know every single detail of the affair, such as: Where did you meet her? How many times did you sleep with her? Did you talk to her about our sex life?

In general, it's a good idea for the betraying spouse to let the hurt partner take the lead in determining how much information needs to be revealed. Some people in that position want to know a lot less detail than guilt-ridden spouses feel compelled to unload.

The level of pain that a betrayed partner feels is partly a function of how much deception he or she has suffered. If, for example, a wife confesses to a one-time fling, that's likely to be less painful than a confession of a two-year affair, especially if it involved an ongoing series of secrets and lies.

- ✔ **Expect your spouse to distrust you in the wake of the revelation that you've been cheating.** One spouse may ask the other to call several times a day. He may want to drop into her place of work unannounced. These demands may seem excessive and unreasonable. Still, giving into them — at least initially — can help to slowly rebuild trust. Resisting them can hurt the chances for recovery.

✓ **Recognize your equal obligation to protect your children.** No matter how much hurt there is and who is to blame, you and your spouse must enter a pact that you will not put your children in the middle of your disputes or subject them to the gory details of what went on. Note, however, that children who are kept completely in the dark by their parents are at risk for repeating infidelity in their adult lives.

✓ **Slowly begin to broach the history of the relationship and the problems that led to the affair.** This is a difficult phase of the rebuilding process, because it means that the betrayed partner must accept part of the responsibility for the conditions that led up to the affair.

Couples who can eventually agree on the problems in their marriage, with each seeing his or her own part that led to the cheating, usually have an easier time regaining trust and solidifying their relationship.

Don't confront long-term marital problems until the initial hurt and anger begin to subside. The person who had the affair is often surprised at the level of shock his partner expresses when the truth is revealed. The cheating spouse has lived with that knowledge for a while, but the other needs time to put it into context.

✓ **Don't pass the buck.** The spouse who cheated should not look to blame the deceived spouse for his or her own poor choices — even if the deceived partner contributed to some of the overriding difficulties in the marriage. There are other ways to deal with marriage problems aside from cheating. The spouse who took this road bears the primary responsibility for his or her actions.

✓ **Work together at forging a new and stronger bond.** The idea that adversity can lead you to a better place may be hard to accept while you're still in pain. Nevertheless, if you plan to keep your marriage together after an affair, it's important to try to view things in that light.

In order to create a stronger bond, the partner who had the affair must demonstrate in his attitudes and actions that his apology is genuine — not just lip service. At the same time, the spouse who has been betrayed must be willing to forgive — even though some of the hurt is likely to linger for years.

True forgiveness is the hardest part of the rebuilding process for the deceived spouse. However, it's the only way to express your commitment to your partner — and the marriage.

It's true that if you choose to forgive your spouse and attempt to rebuild trust, you leave yourself open to the possibility of being hurt again. At the same time, you also open yourself up to the very real possibility that, with time, you can use this painful experience as a way to begin creating a stronger and more loving marriage.

Why do people have affairs, anyway?

Psychologist John Gottman believes that most extramarital affairs aren't about sex, but rather are "about seeking friendship, understanding, respect, attention, caring and concern — the kinds of things that marriage is supposed to offer." Gottman points out that 80 percent of divorced men and women said their marriages ended "because they gradually grew apart and lost a sense of closeness, or because they did not feel loved and appreciated." Family thera-pist Emily Brown makes the same point in her book, *Patterns of Infidelity and their Treatment.* She says, "Affairs have little to do with sex. They are about fear and disappointment, anger and emptiness. They are also about the hope for love and acceptance. . . . Affairs occur when one is feeling restless, fed up, ready for change, and doesn't know how to effectively manage these feelings within the context of the marriage."

Chapter 16

Getting Outside Help

● ●

● ●

*A*ll married couples experience difficulties at one time or another. Fortunately, many problems can be addressed by using the techniques we explore throughout this book. However, some marriage troubles aren't likely to improve without seeking some kind of outside intervention.

The question many people ask is: "How do I know if my problems require outside help?" There is no easy answer to this question. However, as a rule, couples tend to seek help too late — not too soon.

In this chapter, we help you determine when outside help is *likely* to improve your marriage — and when it's a *must*. We talk about the different kinds of therapists, groups, and counseling options available, and show you how to make the choice that best addresses your needs.

Recognizing Problems that Require Outside Help

> *Marriage is our last, best chance to grow up.*
>
> — Joseph Barth, painter

Seeking outside help isn't a sign of weakness, nor does it mean that something is seriously wrong with you, your spouse, or your marriage. People often believe that they have to handle every problem on their own. That's a mistake. In fact, seeking help is often a sign of self-awareness and strength. The sooner you reach out for intervention, the better your chances of working your troubles out. Too many individuals wait until their problems get out of hand before they look for counseling. Similarly, married couples often wait until they're on the verge of divorce — which may be too late — before they start working seriously on improving their relationship.

There are few hard-and-fast rules about when an individual or a married couple has reached the point where problems require some kind of outside intervention. A growing number of individuals and couples use counseling or self-help groups as a kind of preventive medicine to keep problems from getting out of hand. In a way, this is like going to your doctor on a regular basis for a physical checkup. We understand that this approach isn't practical for most couples. As an alternative, we strongly suggest that you always watch for trouble signs, which we cover in the following nine sections.

Problem drinking

Alcohol is as much a drug as cocaine or heroin. However, unlike those substances, alcohol is legal, widely available, cheap, and socially acceptable. These conditions make getting hooked on alcohol and denying problem drinking easier for a potential alcoholic.

There's no way to tell exactly when a social drinker becomes a problem drinker, but a number of red flags warn you that a person has crossed the line into problem drinking. These include:

- ✔ Drinking alone.
- ✔ Drinking in the morning to shake off a hangover from the night before.
- ✔ Drinking as a way of increasing self-confidence.
- ✔ Needing to have a bottle or a drink close by.
- ✔ Being arrested for driving under the influence.
- ✔ Missing work.
- ✔ Behaving erratically.
- ✔ Hiding bottles or sneaking drinks so that others won't know.

Research shows that people whose parents and siblings are alcoholic are much more likely to become problem drinkers. This doesn't mean that you can't ever drink safely. Still, people with this kind of family history need to keep a close eye on their drinking habits.

Some tips for getting outside help for you and your spouse include the following:

✔ **Confront the alcoholic's denial.** If your spouse is a problem drinker, you must challenge his or her insistence that there is no problem.

 Denial is at the core of all addictions. It's not that the alcoholic literally denies the he consumes alcohol. He or she just says that everyone drinks socially, and then spends hours trying to convince you that drinking isn't a problem.

✔ **Arrange an intervention.** Sometimes, you have to plan a formal intervention with the help of an alcohol treatment center. An *intervention* is a carefully scripted confrontation between the alcoholic and his family members and closest friends. Each plays a part in telling the alcoholic that he or she must get help immediately. A bed has already been arranged at the detoxification-rehabilitation facility and transportation has been planned for. Everyone will go there together to be sure the alcoholic family member does not back out.

✔ **If you're a problem drinker, get help; if your spouse is alcoholic, insist that he or she get help.** The most inexpensive, effective, and widely available form of treatment is Alcoholics Anonymous (AA), a 12-step self-help group based on fellowship and self-help principles. Other effective treatments for problem drinking include prescription medications, as well as individual and group therapy. If your partner won't get help, attend an Al-Anon to find ways to cope with your spouse's refusal. See the "What to do if you're married to an addict" sidebar.

Drug abuse

Getting hooked on illegal drugs is much the same as becoming an alcoholic. In addition, the use of many unlawful substances like heroin and cocaine can lead to a criminal conviction and a prison term. The high cost of obtaining these drugs sometimes causes addicts to commit financially irresponsible or criminal acts that endanger themselves and their families.

Confront your spouse, and encourage him or her to begin attending meetings of a drug-treatment program or Narcotics Anonymous (NA). NA is a 12-step self-help group based on the principles of Alcoholics Anonymous. A physician may also be able to prescribe a number of highly effective medications that help with detoxification and abstinence. Drug-dependent individuals sometimes require a period of in-patient detoxification and rehabilitation.

Certain prescription drugs are just as addictive and dangerous as their illegal cousins — even though they're prescribed by a doctor. People may begin taking pain-killing drugs like codeine and morphine for temporary relief after surgery or an injury and wind up with a full-fledged addiction. In addition, addicted individuals often mix illegal drugs, prescription drugs, and alcohol.

What to do if you're married to an addict

Wives and husbands of addicts often facilitate or *enable* their spouse's addictive behavior by choosing to ignore trouble signs or making up stories to other family members and friends in the name of protecting the person they love.

In the long run, enabling winds up undermining the non-addicted spouse's self esteem, even as it makes it easier for the addict to continue the addictive behavior. Instead of enabling, do the following:

✔ **Become an active participant in your spouse's recovery.** All 12-step programs have parallel groups to help families deal with the problems of living with an addict. Al-Anon is designed for the spouses of alcoholics, and Al-a-teen for their children. Online AL-Anon (www .ola-is. org) is now available on the Internet.

In all cases, these groups help the non-drinker understand the alcoholic's actions and behaviors, and to develop strategies to aid in the recovery. Even more important, Al-Anon helps non-drinkers maintain their personal integrity and to draw appropriate boundaries to protect their own lives. ACOA (Adult Children of Alcoholics) is a group for adults who have grown up in alcoholic households.

Each of the other addictions has a group for family members. For drugs, it's Narc-Anon; for gambling, Gam-Anon. The strategy in all cases is the same: to protect the non-addicted partner, to prevent enabling behaviors, and to help develop effective rehabilitation plans.

✔ **Recognize that you may have to leave your spouse** — at least temporarily — to convince him or her of how seriously you take the addiction.

You will likely find issues to deal with even after your partner has overcome the addiction. Couples often neglect other problems in their marriage while they are dealing with drinking, drugging, and gambling. As your spouse's problem behavior ceases to be the main focus of your lives, long-buried marital disputes may begin to re-surface. You may also find that you're relating to each other in different ways, and that can create anxiety and discomfort. One or both of you may need counseling to help you get through these transitions.

Compulsive gambling

Millions of families have been thrown into financial ruin because of compulsive gambling. The problem has been aggravated by the explosive growth of gambling casinos and state-sponsored lotteries. Gamblers often start out by looking for a quick fix to pull themselves out of financial difficulty and wind up in far more serious trouble.

Compulsive gamblers are forever certain that they're just one bet away from changing their luck. In fact, they've become risk junkies — people who are addicted to the thrill of staking all they have on an impossible long shot. The inevitable loss is followed by a period of depression that can only be relieved by placing another bet.

Compulsive gamblers often try to hide their problem from family and friends. Some telltale signs to look for include the following:

- ✓ Your spouse suddenly wants to take care of household finances, without offering a good explanation.

- ✓ Your spouse becomes irritable or agitated for no apparent reason, particularly when you question him or her about gambling.

- ✓ Money is disappearing from your joint bank accounts.

- ✓ Unexplained cash withdrawals begin appearing on your credit card bills.

We suggest that you take the following steps if these or other signs lead you to suspect that your spouse is a compulsive gambler:

- ✓ **Protect your assets before they're all gone.** You may have to take money out of joint bank accounts, reopen bank accounts in your name, and cancel your credit cards.

  You may be legally responsible for your spouse's debts — especially if the money he's spent was drawn against a joint credit card or bank account. It's possible that you may need an attorney to inform you of your rights and liabilities and advise you on how to proceed.

- ✓ **Alert other family members and friends to your spouse's problem so they don't give or lend him or her money.** These people may be completely unaware that your spouse is a gambler. It is unlikely that they will ever get their money back.

- ✓ **Confront your spouse with evidence of his or her gambling, and help your spouse seek treatment from a support group or a qualified professional who is experienced in dealing with pathological gambling.** One of the most effective treatment programs is run by Gamblers Anonymous (GA), a 12-step self-help group based on the Alcoholics Anonymous model.

Domestic violence

We consider physical abuse a deal breaker in any marriage. It's essential for the abused spouse to obtain advice about how to physically remove herself (or in some cases, himself) from the situation. As Marian Bentancourt advises in *What To Do When Love Turns Violent*:

Making a safety plan

Women in abusive relationships must set up a safety plan to protect themselves. A safety plan includes the following steps:

- Obtain the numbers of local telephone hotlines that deal with domestic abuse.

- Identify your partner's violent tendencies so that you can leave before things get out of hand.

- If possible, remove all weapons from your home.

- Ask a neighbor to call the police if he or she hears unusual or suspicious noises coming from your home.

- If you have children who are old enough, teach them how to call 911 and give your correct name and address.

- Know the location of the closest battered women's shelter. Visit that facility in advance, and discuss your situation with the people in charge.

"When you are ready to leave for good, two things should be foremost in your mind. First, you will be at increased risk of retaliation now, so safety planning and caution are critical. Never leave an abusive relationship without being sure that you have enough protection and help from others. Second, the laws are changing so fast that it is imperative that you get legal help from people who are knowledgeable about the current status of using evidence of domestic violence in divorce and child custody proceedings."

The violent use of words may be a more subtle form of intimidation than a physical attack, but can be just as destructive to a marriage. Seek professional help if you and your spouse are engaged in a pattern of constantly insulting each other, or if one spouse uses sarcasm and verbal intimidation to bully the other. When physical abuse is involved, the first step is for the abused spouse to protect herself (see the "Making a safety plan" sidebar). Family counseling can come later.

Unresolved grief

It's appropriate and natural to grieve for any significant loss. Bereavement can cause changes in a person's mood, motivation, and physical health, but for most people, these changes are temporary. There is no standard timeframe for how long a person is supposed to mourn a particular kind of loss. However, if your spouse is (or you are) unable to function or continues to obsess over the loss for an extended period of time, we strongly recommend that you arrange for a consultation with a mental-health professional.

The following circumstances are likely to generate varying levels of grief:

- Death of a spouse, parent, sibling, child, or friend — even a fetus or a pet

- Job loss or retirement

- Physical illness or disability

- Aging and its accompanying physical and emotional changes

- Infertility

- Loss of financial security

- Loss of a home due to fire or other natural disasters

- Loss of a dream

- Loss of sexual desire

- Loss of familiar roles as parents or children

Some losses — like the death of an elderly parent or the emptiness that mothers and fathers often feel when a child goes out on his own — are expected events in the life cycle. Even so, these events can create turmoil — especially if one or both spouses carry unresolved emotional issues. You will have an easier time finding closure when you feel good about the relative than when you're burdened by anger and regret.

Events that aren't a normal part of the life cycle — like the death of a child — can drastically change the way a person sees the world and sometimes lead to unbearable feelings of guilt and blame. Many marriages break up after these terrible things happen. Therefore, we strongly urge couples who've been through a tragedy to seek professional help. Still, the vast majority of people recover from the ordeal, and go on to find meaning in their lives.

Depression

In the wake of a setback or a loss, people often experience adverse changes in mood, outlook, and energy level. Alterations in sleep and appetite patterns are also common under these circumstances. Clinically depressed people may not be aware of the specific circumstance that triggers these changes — and the problem may be even more daunting if it's not linked to a particular event or loss.

Depression can have serious consequences if the condition remains unchecked. Depressed people are at high risk for substance abuse and suicide attempts. The following ten signs are warning flags that you or your spouse may be depressed:

- A loss of interest in work, family, and daily activities

- Difficulty sleeping or chronic oversleeping

✔ Loss of appetite or chronic overeating

✔ Chronic fatigue

✔ Frequent digestive problems or headaches that have no apparent physical cause

✔ Chronic sadness and pessimism about life

✔ Loss of sexual desire

✔ Recurrent feelings of frustration or irritation

✔ Crying spells without any apparent cause

✔ Pervasive feelings that life is no longer worthwhile

People who aren't clinically depressed can experience some of the symptoms on this list at any given time. However, if you or your spouse have a combination of two or more of these symptoms, and they last for over a month, seek outside professional help.

If you or your partner appear to have a problem with depression that isn't linked to a particular setback or loss, schedule a complete physical examination with your physician to rule out the possibility that a physical problem may be causing the condition. Common medical problems linked to depression include hypothyroidism, viral illness, hidden cancer, neurological disease, and alcohol or drugs, to name a few. Many medications also produce depression as a side effect, particularly the anti-hypertensive agents. If your doctor finds no medical problem, he or she may then refer you to a psychiatrist to rule out a biologically-based depressive disorder and to prescribe a medication, if appropriate.

Researchers aren't certain about the exact cause of depression. Some studies link the condition to genetics or brain chemistry. However, in many cases, biochemical factors appear to play only a minimal role. Whatever its cause, many depressed people can be treated successfully with psychotherapy and/or anti-depressant medication.

When a child has a serious physical or emotional problem

Parenting is never an easy job, even under the best of circumstances. But when a child has a serious physical or emotional problem, the foundation of a marriage can be undermined.

We suggest that parents in these circumstances take the following steps:

✔ **Seek out a support group that addresses your child's particular condition.** For example, you can find groups for parents of children with physical diseases like cancer or cerebral palsy. You can also find groups for parents of children with emotional and behavioral disabilities, ranging from autism and mental retardation to dyslexia and attention deficit disorder. Often, these groups can also direct you to organizations, resources, and specialists that can provide invaluable help for your child.

✔ **Don't let the compelling needs of your sick or disabled child prevent you from caring for the rest of your family — and yourself.** Children with special needs place an extraordinary amount of stress on a marriage. You may acquire added financial and emotional pressures that are bound to have an impact on your whole family. You and your spouse need to look at the short- and long-term impact that the situation may be having on your marriage. Consider the effect of the child's condition on the other siblings, who are often resentful that they're not getting their fair share of attention. We suggest consulting with a therapist or counselor who specializes in dealing with couples with special-needs children.

When the two of you are unable to resolve differences

All married couples have differences. Those who say they don't are often not revealing their true feelings or are in marriages where little open and honest communication is actually taking place.

Research shows that the most successful couples are those who can argue respectfully and effectively, reach solutions, or agree that it's sometimes all right to disagree.

Couples who have trouble resolving their disputes will find a great deal of specific guidance in Chapters 4 and 5. However, if one or both partners are totally unable to express feelings and viewpoints, or the couple has a great deal of anger, contempt, criticism, or withdrawl, there may be serious underlying communication obstacles that require third-party intervention.

When one or both of you has decided to seek a divorce

Wives and husbands who've decided to proceed with a divorce sometimes ask the following question: "Why should my husband and I talk to a therapist when we've already decided that the marriage is over?"

This kind of attitude is understandable, given the fact that spouses who've chosen to end the marriage don't usually consult their spouses beforehand. Nevertheless, we believe that it's *always* a mistake to separate or divorce without first attempting to achieve some emotional closure.

Think of pre-divorce counseling as an opportunity to gain greater insight into what went wrong with your marriage. This knowledge increases the chances of future relationships working out.

Therapy slows down the break-up process, by giving both spouses time to think about what they're doing — and the potential consequences for everybody. Even if a husband and wife ultimately proceed with the divorce, things always go more smoothly when you develop a thoughtful plan of action. (See Chapter 17 for more on divorce and its alternatives.)

Don't let the divorce process become more contentious than necessary. Divorce is an intense experience — one that can bring out the worst aspects of both of your personalities. Before you get into an all-out war, consider ways that you can hammer out solutions to the most difficult issues. Divorce mediation is a method that helps many couples do this. A person trained in mediating disputes can help you set objectives and reach solutions that make sense for the whole family. Each spouse still needs to retain a lawyer to be sure that the proposed solution is fair to him or her.

Finding the Right Kind of Outside Help

> *The point of therapy is to get unhooked, not to thrash around how you got hooked.*
>
> — Marianne Walters, psychotherapist

You can find plenty of professional and non-professional help in the community. However, there is a wide variation in the type and quality of the counseling — as well as in the time and costs that are involved. The places you can look for outside help include the following:

- **Friends and relatives** can be helpful for confiding everyday complaints — and their counsel is cost-free. Don't underestimate the value of friends and family for emotional support. However, these well-meaning people are often too close to the situation to offer the advice you need.

- **Clergy members** often provide counseling services, and those who've been trained to work with married couples can be especially effective in this work. In general, their services are free to congregation members.

✔ **Twelve-step programs** can help women and men cope with a wide variety of difficulties that impact a marriage. These include Alcoholics Anonymous, Narcotics Anonymous, and Gamblers Anonymous. These groups are free and run by the members, who form a supportive fellowship. (Twelve-step groups now exist for a variety of addictive behaviors, both chemical and non-chemical. These include Overeaters Anonymous, Emotions Anonymous, Sex Addicts Anonymous, and many others. Most of them have counterparts, like Al-Anon, for the non-addicted spouse.)

✔ **Targeted support groups** help wives and husbands deal with issues like infertility, the death of a parent, and a wide variety of children's problems. Most of these groups are run by not-for-profit organizations that require little or no payment. They are good sources of information and also put people in contact with others who are experiencing similar difficulties.

✔ **Psychiatrists, psychologists, social workers, nurse practitioners, marriage and family therapists, sex therapists and other qualified practitioners** can offer help and guidance to individuals and couples.

Psychiatrists have to graduate from medical school and complete a lengthy course of post-graduate training. Many psychiatrists are skilled at providing therapy, and all of them understand the role of medical and biological factors. Only psychiatrists (or other physicians) can prescribe medication.

Psychologists, clinical social workers, and nurse practitioners complete a prescribed course of training and are licensed by the state. *Marriage and family therapists* and *sex therapists* can have any of the above credentials, but also have special training in helping couples.

In most locales, you don't need a license to call yourself a *therapist*. Anybody can put up a shingle and call himself a counselor or therapist — so the buyer of these services needs to beware.

To make certain the person you're considering is properly trained and certified, consult a professional organization such as the American Psychiatric Association, the American Psychological Association, the National Association of Social Workers, or the American Association for Marriage and Family Therapy. These organizations can verify the credentials of the therapist and also refer you to qualified individuals in your community.

Exercise as much care in choosing an individual or couples therapist as you would in selecting a surgeon to perform a major operation. When you think about how much you have invested in your marriage, it would be foolhardy to put yourself in the hands of someone who isn't experienced and well-qualified.

✔ **Ask people you trust for referrals.** If you have a friend or relative who was helped by a particular therapist, you may want to consider seeing that person — after you check out his or her professional qualifications. Don't hesitate to interview more than one person.

Even the best therapists can't help every couple. A therapist who did a great job helping your friend save her marriage may not be able to do the same for you. Each married couple has a different package of issues and problems to deal with — just as each therapist has his or her particular areas of expertise and skill.

✔ **Set up an initial consultation.** Some therapists spend a few minutes talking with you on the phone prior to making your first appointment. However, we believe that you should have at least one in-person consultation before you decide if you can work together. In the course of that first meeting, ask the following questions:

- First and foremost, ask about the therapist's professional credentials, training, and certification, how many couples in a situation similar to yours he or she has worked with, and so on.

- What is the fee? The fees therapists charge vary widely, depending on the locale and the person's qualifications and experience.

- Does the therapist accept health insurance? This is a question that you can ask over the phone. More specifically, you want to know if the person accepts *your* health insurance policy or healthcare provider as full or partial payment.

- Does the therapist offer a sliding fee scale based on the client's ability to pay? Therapists will sometimes accept patients at a reduced rate — depending on their calendar and interest in the case. People who cannot afford these rates can often find free or low-cost counseling through a local university or medical school psychology or psychiatry department. Free or affordable services are also available through church-sponsored agencies, such as Catholic Charities, Federation of Protestant Welfare Agencies, or Jewish Family services. Although the sponsoring organizations are identified with particular faiths, the treatment services are non-sectarian. They are offered to everyone, regardless of race or religion.

- How many sessions will there be each week? In general, therapists and marriage counselors see their clients once a week or once every other week. Couples in crisis may have to be seen twice a week or more.

- What is the therapist's telephone policy? During a crisis, are you able to call for support and guidance while waiting for the next session?

- How long will each session last? Most individual therapy or counseling sessions are between 45 minutes and one hour, although
couples' sessions commonly last 1½ hours.

- What is the projected timeframe for completing treatment?
Depending on the nature of the case and the therapist's training,
the process can last anywhere from a few weeks to several years.
In general, the length of couples therapy is between three months
and one year — but it can be more.

- Will you be seeing the therapist alone, with your spouse, or both?
A therapist may begin by seeing the spouse who presents the problem. However, if a husband's or wife's problem is related to the
marriage, the therapist may want to see the other partner — either
alone or as a couple.

Research shows that marriage problems usually have better outcomes (as do individual problems, like depression) if both spouses
are seen. A therapist who is uninterested or unwilling to meet with
your spouse is probably not the right person to help you deal with
your marriage.

- Does the therapist have experience treating your particular problems? Married couples can have difficulty for a wide variety of
reasons. In one marriage, the wife may be depressed or alcoholic.
In another marriage, the husband may be sexually dysfunctional or
a compulsive gambler. Find a therapist who has experience dealing
with your most troubling issues — as individuals and as a couple.

- Does the therapist share your and your spouse's views on marriage? Some therapists believe that couples should stay together —
even when there's physical abuse. Others are quick to encourage
spouses to leave a troubled marriage without exploring possible
avenues for keeping the relationship intact.

We generally look for a way to save a marriage, but we don't count
ourselves among those who believe that all couples should stay
together no matter what. We strongly suggest that you avoid therapists who have any rigid philosophy or an inflexible approach.

Deflating Six Common Therapy Myths

*A psychiatrist is [someone] who asks you a lot of expensive questions [that]
your wife asks for nothing.*

— Joey Adams, comedian

New clients often ask, "Will couples therapy really help improve my life and
my marriage?" In the majority of cases, a competent therapist can help a great
deal. Just how much help is hard to say. However, a successful outcome is far

more likely when the person or couple entering therapy comes in with realistic expectations about the process. To that end, we'd like to deflate six myths that often keep people from getting the most from professional help.

One school of therapy is better than another

Research has shown that a therapist's effectiveness in dealing with marriage-related problems has more to do with the person's experience, skill, and caring, than with the theories that he or she subscribes to. Therapists have different approaches. Some do a lot of talking and offer direction or highly structured advice. Others allow the client to take the lead and are less willing to offer opinions about behavior.

There is no one best approach. Success depends largely on a good match between the client and the therapist. If a therapist has a laid-back style and the client needs a lot of direction, that kind of fit probably won't work. However, you should consider yourself at least as responsible as the therapist for deciding if the sessions are helping.

Successful therapy has more to do with the therapist than the client

Someone once compared a therapist to a car mechanic this way: When you bring in a car to be fixed, the mechanic does the work. But in therapy, it's up to you to do most of the work.

> ✔ **Therapists and marriage counselors are primarily consultants and coaches.** They are not miracle workers. Neither is a therapist your boss — or your judge!
>
> We find that therapy is most successful when clients become active collaborators in finding the best way to deal with the issues at hand.
>
> ✔ **Don't go into therapy expecting to sit back while the therapist does all the heavy lifting.** You must take an active role in the process, ask questions, and express your concerns if you feel that things aren't going well.

If you're unhappy with a therapist, you have a right to bring up your doubts and to expect satisfactory responses to your concerns. You can discontinue the sessions at any point. Do, however, discuss your feelings with the therapist before you make a final decision.

A therapist's job is to make you feel good

Clients sometimes want to dump their therapists the minute they're confronted with some truths they're not prepared to accept. This is almost always a mistake.

Part of a therapist's job is to challenge your attitudes and behaviors and tell you things you may not enjoy hearing. At that point, you're not likely to feel much affection toward that person. Even when you have a good relationship with your therapist, you're bound to find pockets of tension.

Be prepared to be angry at your therapist. Depending on the nature of your problem, a therapist may have to generate a good deal of tension and unpleasantness before he or she can help you. This is often a critical point in the process, so hang in there and work through these feelings.

A therapist is supposed to champion your cause

Picture the following scenario: Your spouse has recently admitted having an affair. The two of you have started couples therapy to deal with the repercussions. You automatically assume that the therapist will side with you and condemn your husband for being unfaithful, but that's not what happens. You're mortified when she gently asks him to explain why he sought sex outside of the marriage. It's as if she thinks he had a right to cheat on you. She actually seems to be taking his side!

In individual therapy, there is only one client. Therefore, the therapist normally remains focused on that person's point of view. However, in couples therapy, the counselor has three clients to consider: you, your spouse, and the marriage.

During the first few sessions, a therapist may start out by listening to each partner's viewpoint, usually without making judgments. During subsequent sessions, he or she finds a way to shed light on the overall situation, and may never come down on one side or the other.

There may be times when the apparent interests of the spouses are at odds with each other — and with the best interests of the marriage. At that point, the therapist has to walk a fine line in order to balance those competing interests.

Don't use your therapist as a co-conspirator. When you see an individual counselor he or she is absolutely pledged by law and professional ethics to keep what you say confidential. However, when you and your spouse see a therapist together, the rules are far less clear.

Several years ago, we treated a couple, in which the husband was a compulsive gambler. After several months, he appeared to have overcome his gambling problem, and the marriage was improving. But then, in an individual session, the husband revealed that he had started gambling again and was dipping into the couple's joint bank account. We told this husband that he needed to reveal the truth to his wife if he wanted us to continue seeing them. We offered to help this man disclose his behavior to his wife, but we refused to participate in his deception and still see them as a couple.

A therapist's views and values don't matter

In theory, therapists are supposed to be objective and neutral. But in reality, all therapists bring their views and values into the session. In some cases, a therapist's underlying beliefs are more important than his training or professional experience.

All human beings — including therapists — have very strong feelings about good and bad, right and wrong, best and worst. For example, a pregnant wife and her husband who are arguing about seeking an abortion aren't likely to get balanced advice from a therapist who happens to be a devout Catholic. Discuss these matters with your therapist as soon as possible to find out if you're going to have a clash.

Generally speaking, the gender, ethnicity, or individual background of a therapist doesn't make much difference. However, personal preferences and special needs should be respected. For example, some women only feel comfortable working with women therapists, just as some African-American couples may only be willing to see an African-American therapist.

Most people don't require a counselor of the same gender or race. Nor do your values have to be totally in synch with those of your therapist. On the other hand, you want to make sure that you work with someone whose values and subjective feelings don't stop him from taking a clear-eyed look at what's in your best interests as individuals and marriage partners.

The goal of therapy is to solve all your problems

When you begin seeing a therapist, it's important to set the short- and long-range goals that you want to achieve. Those goals need to be specific — and they never include solving every problem or completely revamping your (or your spouse's) personality.

Therapy is a purposeful encounter. Therefore, the goals must be made explicit. There should also be some way of determining when you reach those goals so that the therapeutic process isn't open-ended.

It is the client — in collaboration with the therapist — who determines the goals of therapy. Some couples come into treatment with a different agenda than the one they present to the therapist. For example, some wives and husbands have already decided to divorce. She or he will drag the other spouse into therapy and immediately announce that they are here in a last-ditch effort to save the marriage. In fact, that wife or husband has already concluded that divorce is the way to go. She or he is essentially using the therapist to help get that message across.

A therapist can help you work on your marriage only if you and your spouse are both committed to putting forth an honest effort. If one of you has made up your mind that divorce is the resolution you want, it's doubtful that any counselor is going to change your mind — nor should that necessarily be the therapist's objective.

A good therapist can help couples who are genuinely committed to strengthening their marriage achieve the following goals:

✔ Greater insight into what is and isn't working in their relationship

✔ A more positive attitude toward your partner

✔ Effective techniques for relating and communicating with each other more constructively

✔ Avenues for identifying realistic and unrealistic expectations of themselves and the marriage

Hopefully, a couple can come out of therapy with added skills and new insights — and a better feel for what each partner needs. Then they may decide that they have the basis to rebuild their marriage. If so, the husband and wife can look in the mirror — and at each other — and feel that it makes sense for them to go forward together. Even if their relationship is imperfect, at least it's good enough to build on. For many couples, that's good enough!

Chapter 17

Understanding Divorce and Its Alternatives

Divorce isn't an option that any wife or husband should choose without first considering all they have invested in the marriage. Younger spouses sometimes want to opt out of a marriage when they discover that many of their expectations aren't going to be realized. Wives and husbands who've been married for decades often complain that they're bored or that long-term differences have become too hard to live with. Like their younger counterparts, they weigh the possibility of divorce in the hopes of finding a more fulfilling life with a new partner.

In this chapter, we help you take a clear-eyed look at your marriage, and help you determine whether your long-term interests are better served by leaving or staying with your spouse. We also show you what to do if your partner is the one who has decided to divorce you. We then discuss various alternatives to divorce, and help you use them to keep your marriage together.

Deciding if Your Marriage Is Worth Saving

Divorce is the future tense of marriage.

— Milton Berle, comedian

We believe in marriage — but we also believe that divorce can sometimes be a couple's best option. If a marriage is no longer healthy or viable for one or both partners, ending it may be the better alternative. However, it's hard to turn back after you've initiated a divorce, and spouses who give up on the relationship without first considering all of the consequences often wind up regretting their decision.

Around half of all married couples wind up divorced, and that number probably won't go down very much in the foreseeable future. Women and men both have life expectancies approaching 80 years. That means people who marry in their early twenties are likely to wake up next to each other for the next sixty years. Keeping a marriage together for that long is a tall order, even for the most satisfied and devoted couples. The situation becomes far more difficult when wives and husbands have unresolved problems and serious differences.

Divorce is never a pleasant process, and it can sometimes have devastating effects — even on your health! Consider the following statistics:

- Divorced men are twice as likely to die prematurely from cardiovascular disease than married men — and are almost seven times more likely to commit suicide.

- Divorced women die earlier than their married counterparts and lose 50 percent more time from work as a result of various illnesses.

- Divorced people of both genders are more likely to abuse alcohol and drugs than are married people.

Excuse me Reverend, do you mean those words literally?

"'Til death do us part" is a commitment that people make on their wedding day. But can anyone understand what that really means?

Imagine what would happen if the bride or groom said something like: "Wait a minute. How am I supposed to know how I'm going to feel five, ten, or twenty years from now? 'Til death do us part' is too big a chunk of time to think about. Let's just say that I'll give this marriage my best shot."

There are, of course, religious people who are quite literal about taking their vows. Most religions frown on divorce, and some absolutely

forbid it. Some individuals may not be particularly religious, but believe that commitment is a sacred bond — you do something because you said you'd do it, despite how you feel.

It's not our place as therapists to question anyone's religious or moral judgments. We respect couples who've committed themselves to staying together for life — as long as neither spouse is being physically or emotionally abused. We also believe that divorce can be a reasonable option, even when the circumstances are not so extreme.

These health risks alone are reason enough to ask yourself the following question: Is it likely that splitting with your spouse will lead to a happier, healthier, and more rewarding life than you'd have if you could find a way to stay in the marriage?

Evaluating your investment in the marriage

When considering divorce, the amount of time that you've been married makes a difference — and so does your age. Some wives and husbands who've been married for a short time soon realize that they've made a mistake. The decision may be mutual, though more often, only one of the spouses wants out of the marriage.

The younger you are and the less time you've been married, the easier it is to divorce — but that doesn't necessarily mean the breakup will be a piece of cake. Still, a couple in their twenties who has been married a year or two can often make a clean break and walk away relatively unscathed. It's different, though, for midlife couples who have a lot of shared history together. They may have children and sometimes grandchildren, as well as complex financial ties and social networks to consider.

Make a list of what you'll miss if you choose to divorce. Even if you're no longer in love with your spouse, you may find all sorts of elements of the marriage that are difficult to replace if the two of you split up. They include the following:

✔ You've invested in your life together as an intact family. If you split up, you'll probably see your children less — and certainly under different circumstances.

✔ You know each other's quirks — even though some of them may drive you crazy. After living together for years, you've grown accustomed to each other's ways. You've gotten used to your husband's offbeat sense of humor. He knows just how you like your morning coffee, and always prepares it for you. These and a hundred other little things are easy to take for granted when you live with someone. Yet these are often the very things estranged spouses talk about missing most, years after the divorce has been finalized.

✔ You've built social ties as a couple. If you've been together for a number of years, you've probably developed friendships with couples who share common interests. These relationships are often hard to maintain after you divorce.

Your married friends may not want you around after your breakup. Divorced women, in particular, are often abandoned by their married friends — who may consider them to be a threat.

> ✔ You're emotionally involved with each other's families in unique ways. You may enjoy some of your in-laws, and may even be friends with them. No new partner will have the relationship that you did to your spouse's parents, because you knew them when you all were young. This is an especially important factor if your parents or your spouse's parents have passed away. That link between the two of you and the older generation is an irreplaceable part of your personal and shared history.

The decision to divorce requires a kind of cost-benefit analysis. The less you have invested in the marriage, the more likely it is that divorce will be a reasonable option.

Recognizing the problems that are driving you to leave

Happiness in marriage is entirely a matter of chance.

— Jane Austen, author

One of the most common complaints that we hear from wives and husbands who want to divorce is, "I'm no longer happy." Although this may be an accurate statement, it doesn't necessarily mean that a divorce is the answer to the problem.

There may be many reasons for your unhappiness that have little or nothing to do with your spouse or your marriage. You may feel frustrated about your lifestyle, work, or your financial status. You may be unhappy about your health or appearance. You may have an undiagnosed biochemical depression. These things may have little or nothing to do with your spouse.

Before you start taking steps toward a divorce, ask yourself if you've done everything you can to solve those personal problems that are more about you than your spouse or your marriage. We've seen too many people make the mistaken calculation that changing partners will make them happier. They often find out that the grass really isn't greener with someone else. (For specific techniques on developing a realistic view of marriage turn to Chapter 2.)

Small improvements can make a big difference in your relationship. When you and your spouse first fell in love, everything seemed great — even perfect. Now that you have some problems, you may begin to see your entire marriage as horrible. Your once-thoughtful wife suddenly seems more selfish than you ever could have imagined. Your formerly kind-hearted husband has morphed into a totally insensitive jerk. In reality, people usually don't change that much. At best, no marriage is ever perfect, and when things seem to be falling apart, marriages often aren't as bad as disgruntled spouses make them out to be.

What often happens is that things have slipped below the margin — that invisible line that separates good-enough marriages from those that aren't good enough. In many cases, it only takes a small improvement to move the relationship back above that critical dividing line.

Work at creating a net profit on your marriage balance sheet. Start by picturing your relationship as if it were a business. Imagine a store that's making a small profit. The owners probably wouldn't describe their situation as great. Still, it may be good enough to hang in and keep trying.

Now, picture what would happen if that same business began faring just a little bit worse. Instead of a net profit, there's a small net loss. The actual margin of difference between the small profit and small loss may be minimal in terms of dollars. However, if a store continues to lose money, it will eventually fail. But, if the owners can come up with a few relatively minor improvements, they can often turn that small loss back into a modest profit. Then at least they're still in business.

Most wives and husbands aren't looking for their partners to be perfect. More often than not, a small improvement will suffice. Consider the following example: If you've been uptight because your husband often acts crude and insensitive, would it impress you if he improved his table manners and expressed a little more interest in your concerns? You're probably resigned to the fact that he's not some storybook prince who's going to carry you away on a white horse. A show of effort and a small improvement is often enough to make a meaningful difference.

Recognizing your ability to live on your own

I've never thought about divorce. I've thought about murder, but never divorce.

— Joyce Brothers, psychotherapist and TV personality

Before you go ahead with a divorce, ask yourself the following question: How are you at being alone? Some divorced spouses find it gratifying to establish independent lives, and actually enjoy the solitude. However, many more divorced people find that they miss their former spouse's companionship and have trouble coping on their own.

Don't automatically assume that you're going to find another relationship, at least not very quickly. Some people jump into a divorce, figuring that someone better is waiting on the horizon. But more often than not, it takes months or years to find another lasting relationship. Some divorced women and men never find one. And around two-thirds of those estranged wives and husbands who do remarry wind up divorcing again.

Your decision about whether or not to divorce is no reflection on your personal character. Wives and husbands who choose to divorce are no better or worse than those who stay in their marriage. Some people take every commitment they make quite literally, while others are willing to find extenuating circumstances. On the other hand, many wives and husbands who decide to stay in a flawed relationship get down on themselves for not having the courage to go through with a divorce.

How good are the chances of replacing your spouse?

Before you consider a divorce, we encourage you to consider the following statistics:

✔ Women seek divorce more often than men. However, the remarriage rate for men is three times as high as that for women.

✔ Men tend to marry younger women — which makes the odds of finding a new husband even tougher for a middle-aged divorced woman.

✔ Only ten percent of wives and husbands who leave their spouses in the midst of an affair wind up marrying their lovers. And three quarters of those marriages end in divorce.

✔ Over 75 percent of wives and husbands who divorce because of an affair wind up regretting the decision to divorce.

Some of those feelings come out of a sense of disappointing the friends and relatives who've been urging them to stay in or get out of the marriage. We strongly encourage you not to dwell on these counterproductive emotions. Your need for companionship, fear of loneliness, or financial insecurity are not signs of weakness or a lack of courage. Rather, they indicate that you've given careful thought to your decision.

Understanding the impact of divorce on children

It would be hard to find any other group of children — except, perhaps, the victims of a natural disaster — who suffered such a rate of sudden serious psychological problems [as the children of divorce].

> — Judith Wallerstein, author and marriage researcher

Most kids [are resilient] in the face of divorce and remarriage.

> — Mavis Heatherington, author and marriage researcher

Everyone agrees that divorce is rough on children. The real debate centers around whether children are worse off when their parents divorce or when they stay together in a bad marriage. There's no easy answer to this question because you always have to take the following factors into consideration:

✔ How bad a particular marriage is

✔ The ways in which the marriage is bad

✔ The coping abilities of the child or children

✔ The quality of the parenting

✔ The child custody arrangements and whether or not they include both parents

In a home where children witness or experience physical or verbal abuse, profound mental illness, or serious substance problems, children are often better served when their parents split up. Beyond that, each situation must be evaluated on a case-by-case basis.

If you have children and are considering divorce, answering the following questions can help you predict how well your children will react:

✔ **How old are your children?** In general, preschool kids do better than school-age children and young adolescents, who often have great difficulty making the adjustment. There is some evidence that college-aged young adults who have recently left home also have a hard time accepting the divorce.

✔ **How much conflict are your children exposed to?** We know families where young children were better off after their parents divorced, especially where the parents were either constantly at war or had almost no communication. However, in many other cases, marital problems didn't seem to have an especially negative impact on the children — even though one or both spouses complained that they were very unhappy.

✔ **Can you and your spouse be effective co-parents?** Even the strongest critics of divorce admit that children do well when the parents are able to interact in a civil way, and not involve the kids in their battles. We know children who are doing better since their parents divorced because they have less conflict in their lives. The estranged parents may still be at war, but at least they're physically separated, and the children are out of the direct line of conflict.

✔ **What are the projected living arrangements for the children?** Most children don't like change. Young kids often find moving to a new house (or back and forth between two houses) stressful — even when if it's a bigger house in a better neighborhood. The prospect of living in a home without both parents is bound to be a difficult adjustment for any child. However, families can help children successfully negotiate this rough transition — especially if the parents live nearby and have frequent contact with them.

Ultimately, you may have to act in your own self-interest in leaving a marriage, even if your children are totally opposed to your actions. The timing of the decision (should you do it now or wait until after high school graduation?) and the post-divorce planning for the children are critical.

How do kids feel about divorce?

Research shows that kids tend to have a much less tolerant view of divorce than their parents. In one study, 700 junior high school students were asked to rate a number of life events in terms of the amount of stress. The results were as follows:

✔ Students rated divorce as being the most stressful life event, next to the death of a parent or sibling.

✔ The separation of their mother and father was given a higher stress ranking than the death of a friend, being seriously injured, feeling that nobody liked them — even higher than being "physically hit" by a parent.

It's clear from this study that, if these kids could vote, they'd probably abolish divorce. Of course, children have almost no voice in making this decision.

In most divorces, primary custody is awarded to the mother, while the father receives visitation rights. However, many shared-custody arrangements have become popular in recent years. These include the following:

✔ **Sole custody with liberal visitation:** One parent is temporarily or permanently awarded exclusive legal and physical custody of a minor child, but the other parent is granted liberal access during the week, on holidays, and on vacations.

✔ **Joint legal custody:** Wherever the child lives, both parents have the right and responsibility to make major decisions for the child — such as schooling, religious upbringing, and health care.

✔ **Joint physical custody:** The child lives with the father part of the week and with the mother part of the week, according to a schedule approved by both parents or the court. Some joint physical custody is strictly 50-50, but there is no limit to the creativity and ingenuity of the arrangements. The child can spend the week with Mom and weekends with Dad. He or she can spend most of the week with Mom, but major holidays and long vacations with Dad, and so on.

✔ **Joint legal and physical custody:** Both parents share decision-making and caring for the child.

✔ **Split custody:** Siblings are split up between the parents. For example, the brothers reside with Dad, and the sisters live with Mom.

The purpose of all these arrangements is so that both parents remain closely connected to their children. Children need to see their mothers and fathers, and many divorced parents miss having regular contact with their kids. Even more important, research on joint custody shows that the more involvement the child has with both parents, the better he or she is likely to fare.

The success of any custody arrangement depends mostly on the willingness of the concerned adults to work cooperatively.

Winning Back Your Mate

Come back baby/Let's talk it over/Just one more time.

— Traditional blues lyric

When a wife or husband wants a divorce, she or he has some control over the situation. However, the spouse who is being rejected is forced to assume a defensive posture. In some cases, the rejectee is shocked to hear that his partner is considering a divorce. He may be aware that there are problems in the marriage, but doesn't realize that they've gone this far.

Your spouse's announcement that he or she plans to divorce you doesn't mean that it's a done deal. The following techniques are very powerful in tilting the scales back in your favor:

✔ **Keep the dialogue going.** When a marriage starts to crumble, it's hard to have meaningful conversations. A spouse who has decided to leave may not want to discuss the situation with you, fearing that he or she may invite criticism or provoke a drawn-out fight.

Don't use sex as a substitute for talk. Some couples experience a complete sexual shutdown in the face of marital problems. Others actually start having more sex than ever as a way of avoiding more constructive ways of dealing with their problems. We hesitate to discourage any married couple from making love, but under these circumstances, sex can actually wind up preventing couples from dealing with more serious underlying issues.

Getting your mate to talk openly is a key strategy. You may find that you're better off keeping *your* mouth shut. However, it's important to motivate him or her to keep on talking — even if it means enduring a barrage of complaints without counterattacking. At least you'll find out more about what your partner is thinking.

✔ **Highlight what's good about the marriage.** All marriages are a combination of bad and good. Before a person can feel comfortable about leaving a marriage, he or she first has to maximize the negative and minimize the positive. If that person spent much time dwelling on the good points in the marriage, he or she may find it too hard to break away. In order to get your partner to stay, you want to slow down the process long enough to create doubt. Hopefully, she'll start to wonder if she's making the right choice.

Most wives and husbands who seek a divorce have mixed feelings about the marriage. You want to make your case by countering every negative view with a positive one. If, for example, she complains that you never have fun anymore, remind her of all the things you enjoyed doing together in the past. Acknowledge your spouse's feelings, and then come up with a concrete plan to resume at least one or two of your favorite activities.

✔ **Avoid walking on eggshells.** If your husband has said that he wants to leave, it won't help to hide in a corner or make yourself invisible. There's nothing you can say that will permanently strengthen his resolve to leave you; there's no single thing that you're going to do that will cause him to walk out.

The more proactive you are in trying to convince your spouse to remain in the marriage, the better your chances of success. Think of it like a TV commercial. You keep hearing the same message until you're fed up — but you end up buying the product anyway. Even if it doesn't work, what have you lost?

✔ **Buy as much time as you can.** Convince your spouse to give you time to try and change his or her mind. Ask your spouse to give you a year. If he or she refuses, ask for six months — or even three months. It's important to prevent your partner from leaving in the heat of the moment, which will make your position considerably weaker.

Time can be your greatest ally in persuading your spouse not to walk out the door. With time, you may convince him or her that you're willing to change. By then, the two of you will have had a chance to cool down and to gain a better perspective on the situation. Then you can explore what each of you has to do to make the relationship work.

✔ **Don't be a pitiable case.** Your spouse's decision to split is bound to leave you feeling hurt and rejected. Under the circumstances, you may begin to cast yourself as a victim or martyr. However, your spouse is more likely to leave if you present yourself as an object of pity. At first, he or she may feel sorry for you, but pity will soon be replaced by contempt. You may win some points among your same-sex friends, but even they will start avoiding you if you continue to act like a victim.

Some desperate spouses play the ultimate card by threatening to commit suicide. This may delay things for a while, but in the long run, it is more likely to ensure the end of the marriage.

The last thing you want is for your mate to see you as a pitiable case. Your spouse will then be more convinced than ever that his or her best interests lie elsewhere.

The rejecting partner always has the final say about whether he or she will stay or go. It's important to recognize that your spouse may ultimately leave you — despite all your best efforts. In that event, you'll know that you did what you could to save the marriage. Beyond that, the ultimate outcome may be out of your control.

At the end of the day, you have to go on with your life — whether or not your partner decides to leave. You need to own up to the reality that your marriage didn't work out — and recognize that, even though the marriage failed, you're not a failure.

Reframing Your View of a Flawed Marriage

It wasn't exactly a divorce. I was traded.

— Tim Conway, comedian

If you compare the wide-eyed expectations that couples have when they first marry with the disappointments of their day-to-day life after ten or twenty years, it's remarkable that even more wives and husbands *don't* end up divorcing. And yet, many people seem to realize that the realities of divorce can be a lot worse than the frustrations of staying together.

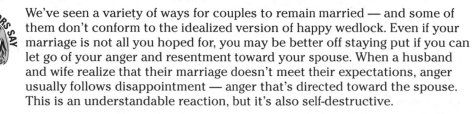

We've seen a variety of ways for couples to remain married — and some of them don't conform to the idealized version of happy wedlock. Even if your marriage is not all you hoped for, you may be better off staying put if you can let go of your anger and resentment toward your spouse. When a husband and wife realize that their marriage doesn't meet their expectations, anger usually follows disappointment — anger that's directed toward the spouse. This is an understandable reaction, but it's also self-destructive.

Most husbands and wives don't set out to fool their partners. If you're disillusioned with your marriage, the chances are good that your partner is also disappointed that things didn't turn out as you'd both hoped. Constructive anger can be a useful emotion if you're planning to divorce. Anger is counterproductive for people who live in the same house because it only winds up making both of you more bitter.

In order to let go of your anger, we recommend that you do the following:

✔ **Grieve for your disappointment.** It's tough to come to terms with the fact that many of your expectations haven't been met and that the life you have isn't the one you wanted. On the other hand, it's quite possible that many of those expectations were unrealistic to begin with. (See Chapter 1 for a complete discussion of the marriage myths that people often buy into.)

✔ **Don't use anger as a substitute for grief.** The loss of your dreams and expectations can be as hard to accept as any other misfortune. If you approach these losses by lashing out at your spouse, it will be next to impossible to avoid becoming embittered.

If you're going to move forward, you need to accept the fact that your marriage doesn't meet your expectations, and that it may be too late ever to achieve those expectations. However, this doesn't mean that you can't have new dreams to pursue — even if you'll need to fulfill them outside of your marriage.

✔ **Don't think of your spouse as the enemy.** If you look at your spouse and take inventory of his or her faults, you may begin to see that person as someone who has completely messed up your life. Pretty soon, he or she becomes your most bitter enemy. This thought process isn't likely to lead to anything positive. Furthermore, it probably isn't true.

Even if your spouse has turned out to be a major disappointment in many respects, he or she can still be valuable in the following ways: a friend, a companion who shares your interests, a parenting and grand-parenting partner, or a compatible roommate.

Even if you have regrets, forgive yourself and work toward detaching from your spouse. Invest your energies in shaping a future based on choices that are likely to bring you more fulfillment.

✔ **Don't blame yourself.** As you think about all that's wrong with your marriage, you may be tempted to ask yourself: "What's wrong with me? Why don't I have the strength to leave?" Yet leaving doesn't require any more strength than finding a different way to make it work.

✔ **Don't let the expectations and opinions of others drive your choices.** All of us are shaped by the many voices trying to tell us how we're supposed to live: the voices of our families and friends, and messages we get from movies and the advertising industry. If you're not careful, this overbearing chorus can drown out your own internal voice that's trying to tell you where your best choices lie.

✔ **Diversify your emotional portfolio.** After you accept the fact that you're going to stay in your imperfect marriage, begin reinvesting your energies in different activities and people. This means that you'll have to create more distance between you and your spouse.

Your attempt to diversify won't succeed as well unless your spouse makes an effort to do the same. If you start making new friends and doing things on your own, while he sits at home and broods, the two of you will have a hard time co-existing.

One technique we use to help married couples reframe their relationships is to encourage them to begin looking at their husbands and wives more like friends or acquaintances than like lovers. You may tolerate annoying habits and quirks in your friends that you'd never accept in your spouse. For example, you'd never scream at a friend for watching television or reading the newspaper, even if you want to talk to him.

Creating the Kind of Marriage That Works Best for You

If you made a list of reasons why any couple got married — and another list of the reasons for their divorce, you'd have a lot of overlapping.

— Mignon McLaughlin, journalist and author

We believe that you don't have to end a marriage just because you aren't particularly happy with your spouse. You can find many good alternatives to divorce — alternatives that may well address your long- or short-term needs. Before you decide to divorce, take a look at some of the choices available to you — they're listed in the following sections.

When you choose a lifestyle that redefines the terms of your marriage, you're essentially telling each other that the relationship is no longer as important to both of you as it once was. This implies that you no longer have the same kind of expectations of one another — or the marriage. And that's not necessarily a bad thing, because it means that you won't be so easily disappointed.

Agree to live as friends or compatible roommates

This arrangement often works for what we call low-sex, low-conflict couples. If the sex has all but gone out of your marriage, but you basically get along, you may want to consider the following options:

✔ **Friends with shared interests:** Even if there is no longer passion in your marriage, you may still have enough in common to continue living together as friends. The terms of that friendship must be negotiated: Some couples continue to do most things together, while others agree to have mostly separate lives. The details of how each couple handles such an arrangement depends on what kinds of things they enjoy and how much they like to be together.

Claire and Jim have two grown children. They enjoy taking trips in a group with three other couples. They enjoy their children very much, and both like to participate in church activities. However, they do nothing else together. When they go on trips, the other couples have no idea that Claire and Jim are leading largely separate lives.

Some couples get more joy out of a great concert or dinner party than from a night of sex. Others share an enjoyment of films or fine art. Still others have developed a valued network of friends and social contacts. One or more of these shared interests may be enough to keep a husband and wife together, depending on their needs and values.

✔ **Strictly roommates:** We know couples who are not necessarily good friends on any level. Nevertheless, they've decided to continue living as roommates who share expenses. For such a situation to work, couples can't have a great deal of open conflict.

After 30 years, Linda and Arnie both acknowledged that they no longer had anything in common and were on the verge of getting a divorce. But, after talking it over, they decided that divorce would be too disruptive, both financially and emotionally. So they agreed to continue living together as roommates. Linda and Arnie almost never coordinate their comings and goings, and each leads a totally separate social life. Neither cooks, but they sometimes go out to dinner together. Both of them occasionally sleep with other people — but never in the condo that they jointly own and share. That would be a violation of their arrangement.

Make family your main priority

Divorce can have a shattering effect on relationships with the extended family. Estranged parents and grandparents may have to negotiate separate visits with their children and grandchildren, and this can be upsetting to all concerned.

You can, of course, find many cases in which divorced people maintain good relations with both sides of the family. However, older couples who love extended-family activities may find divorce a painful and lonely option. These couples sometimes opt to stay together as friends or roommates, where the primary or even sole function is that of parents and grandparents.

Recast your marriage as a business partnership

If you and your spouse have built (or have the potential to build) a successful business enterprise, this may provide a good basis for staying together. Couples who've taken years to establish a business often find that it's far more practical to stay in the marriage than to divorce. This kind of arrangement can work for husbands and wives who don't sleep together, have few fights, and maintain good communication in limited areas, such as financial matters.

Have a low-risk extramarital affair

This is definitely the most controversial of the divorce alternatives — and many people find it objectionable. However, the reality is that couples — especially those who've stopped having sex — are sometimes able to keep their marriage together if one or both partners finds sex outside the marriage.

These affairs must be discreet and tactful. They can be explicitly acknowledged, but both parties must establish certain ground rules. For example, both spouses may agree never to be out in public with another person, or not to allow the affair to interfere with family activities or rituals.

Usually, the fundamental understanding in these kinds of affairs is "don't ask; don't tell." Where there is little or no sex in a marriage, a husband and wife may assume that the other partner has an outside lover. Even though it's never verbalized, both spouses may accept a limited amount of "discreet cheating."

Recognizing When Divorce Is Your Best Option

> *I guess the only way to stop divorce is to stop marriage.*
>
> — Will Rogers, actor and comedian

When you've tried the techniques and alternatives that we explore in this chapter, and you still feel that there's no way to keep the marriage together, divorce may indeed be your best option.

Marriage isn't for everybody. Furthermore, not all marriages are meant to last forever. Some couples are so hurtful to each other that they can't get along even as friends or roommates. Some disillusioned wives and husbands may decide that they'd be better off living on their own — even if they can't ever find someone else to marry.

If you've made the choice to end your marriage, we urge you to think of divorce as the most positive alternative under the circumstances and an opportunity to create a new lifestyle that will work for you. *Divorce for Dummies* by John Ventura and Mary Reed (IDG Books Worldwide, Inc.) is a valuable resource for any couple that's moving in that direction.

Can affairs ever be low-risk or ethical?

We realize, of course, that extramarital affairs are completely unacceptable to some couples on moral or ethical grounds. For other couples, it's a viable alternative, but we ourselves have debated just how these liaisons should be conducted:

Sue: I believe that certain extramarital affairs can be ethical, but only if both partners somehow agree that it's okay.

Steve: That sounds good, in theory. Still, wouldn't you agree that, most of the time, both partners really know what's going on — but choose not to discuss it.

Sue: You're probably right. But in that case, you can't really call them ethical. Not only that, there's the issue of sexually transmitted diseases to consider.

Steve: Okay, but how about if the married couple never has sex? Then what's the risk?

Sue: With many couples, it's not all or nothing. They may have sex three-or-four times a year. And that could be enough to contract AIDS or some other disease. That kind of scenario is low-risk — but it isn't no risk!

Part VI
The Part of Tens

The 5th Wave   By Rich Tennant

"I couldn't find any rose petals, but
I figured corn flakes make more
sense in a milk bath anyway."

In this part . . .

The Part of Tens offers key pieces of useful information. In Chapter 18, we show you some thoughtful ways to put more romance into your marriage. Chapter 19 cautions you about words and expressions to avoid saying to your partner. In Chapter 20, we review the things you should — and shouldn't — do when you and your partner are having an argument. In Chapter 21, we help you recognize problems that require outside help. Finally, in Chapter 22, we end the Part of Tens by offering creative suggestions for spicing up your sex life.

Chapter 18

Ten Ways to Make Your Marriage More Romantic

. . . .

In This Chapter
▶ Recapturing lost intimacy
▶ Making yourself more attractive to your partner
▶ Showing your love through actions and words

. . . .

*R*emember when you were courting? All you could think about was how exciting and romantic it was to be together. Back then, you couldn't do enough to please each other.

As time passed, you got so accustomed to married life that you stopped making special efforts for each other. There were always so many responsibilities and details to take care of, who could think about romance?

Maybe you've been missing those blissful feelings — and you sense that your partner misses them too. This chapter shows you ten ways that you can start putting more romance back in your marriage.

Pay Attention to Your Appearance

There's a saying: Beauty's only skin deep, but ugliness goes right through to the bone. Too often, people who've been married for years no longer feel the need to go through the effort of looking good for their partner.

If your wife doesn't enjoy seeing you lounging around the house in your underwear, or if your husband is bothered by seeing you in curlers and an old bathrobe, don't ignore it. Doing that is a lot like saying: "We're married. Therefore, I don't have to bother putting on any kind of show. You're always going to be there, so I don't have to worry about pleasing you." After you become indifferent to your appearance, your spouse may have a hard time seeing you in a romantic and exciting way.

There's nothing wrong with being comfortable around the house. But do yourself, your spouse, and your marriage a favor by paying attention to your dress and personal hygiene. Show your husband or wife that you care by taking the time to look, feel, and smell good.

Show Your Love Every Day

Show by your actions that you love and cherish your partner through special gestures every day. For example:

✔ **Create rituals that show how much you love your partner.** For example, try giving him or her a five-minute backrub or leaving a sexy note. Frequent gestures like these convey romantic and loving feelings that are impossible to ignore.

✔ **Remember that you don't have to spend much money.** A fresh flower from the garden can say more than an expensive bouquet from a florist. A simple homemade dinner that you take the time to prepare can be more appreciated than an elaborate meal at a five-star restaurant.

The key ingredient in showing your love is that the gestures have special meaning for your partner. That will always be appreciated — even more so if those gestures don't have much meaning for you. For example, think of how good your husband would feel if you surprised him by inviting his parents over for a visit — especially if he's aware that they're not your favorite guests. Think of how appreciated your wife would feel if you bought tickets for a romantic comedy — knowing that it's not the kind of film you'd ever choose to see yourself. These kinds of thoughtful acts show that you're always thinking of your partner's needs — and that has to make him or her feel good.

Use Words of Love

Saying the words "I love you" is always a good idea — as long as they're said sincerely. Everyone appreciates being told how much they're loved and cherished.

Here are some ways to expand that simple three-word phrase:

✔ **Share your hopes, dreams, and secret thoughts.** There are some things that you can only communicate through words. And few things make your partner feel closer to you than letting her in on your most private thoughts and visions.

When your goal is to create more closeness in your marriage, you want to share only thoughts and emotions that are likely to make your partner feel loved and wanted. Save any worries that are likely to generate anger or tears for another time.

✔ **Tell your partner often how much you love being married to her.** Then, talk about the qualities you enjoy most. Is it her terrific sense of humor? The way he greets you at the door when you come home from work? Married couples often spend a lot of time complaining about one another's faults and shortcomings. If you want to stir up the romantic fires in your relationship, try letting her know what she does that pleases you most.

Use a Gentle Touch

The way people touch each other communicates different feelings and provokes different sensations. We often hear wives complain that their husbands only touch them when they want sex. Women seem to like more hand holding, kissing, and gentle physical closeness than men. So, guys, don't wait for bedtime to touch and fondle your wife. Make it part of the way you communicate every day.

The absence of affectionate touching doesn't always mean that there's a problem in the marriage. However, a certain amount of gentle, non-sexual touching enhances closeness and heightens the sense of romance between the partners. This touching can take many forms, like a pat on your partner's face, an arm around her back, or the stroking of his hair.

Research shows that touching doesn't just feel good — it can actually help heal all sorts of emotional and physical wounds. People who are never touched actually die sooner. So imagine how much better a regular dose of tender physical contact can make your partner feel.

Make Time to Be Alone Together

When husbands and wives don't spend enough time alone, they are bound to grow apart. And when a couple already has problems, they often distance themselves from one another by using kids, friends, family members — even groups of strangers — as buffers.

Couples with young children need to make a special effort to find time to be by themselves. Sure, it's not always easy to find a babysitter. It often seems easier to drag the kids along to wherever you're going. That may be conducive to a rich family life, but you need to balance that with time for the two of you.

Make it your business to find at least a few hours each week for the two of you to be alone together. Go to a movie, a concert, a museum, or a ballgame. Some other ways to spend time alone include the following:

✔ **Cultivate a new interest together.** If you're the type of person who does lots of things on your own, consider finding some new hobby or interest the two of you can enjoy together. Consider taking tennis lessons, buying a subscription to a series of jazz concerts, or taking a cooking class.

✔ **Go for walks together.** Whether you take a twenty-minute aerobic walk around the neighborhood three times a week, or an hour-long stroll on the beach, walking is a great way to spend time alone together.

✔ **Meet somewhere for lunch.** Try to make these meetings a regular part of your week. Find a favorite romantic spot and make it your own, or try new places. If possible, choose quiet restaurants that have a romantic atmosphere. And don't forget to wear something special for the occasion.

✔ **Try to get away overnight as often as possible — preferably at least once a month.** This is tough for busy couples, especially those who have young children. Whatever the configuration of your family, a change of scenery can help you forget the stresses and responsibilities that keep you and your spouse apart in the course of your busy lives.

You don't have to go on an exotic vacation — or even very far from home. A night in a nearby bed and breakfast will do just fine.

Simply logging in time together won't make your relationship more romantic. What you need to do is to spend uninterrupted time sharing thoughts, ideas, and activities in a way that gives you pleasure and draws you closer as a couple.

Do All of the Traditional Things — Even if They Seem Corny

There's a reason why certain gestures and environments are considered romantic. They've worked for a very long time! Remembering your partner's birthday, giving a box of candy on Valentine's Day, and holding the door open for your partner may be traditional or expected gestures — but the more of them you can build into your marriage, the more romance you'll generate.

You can also try burning scented candles, selecting soft lighting, and playing sensual music when you're getting ready to make love. But don't limit your use of mood-enhancing techniques to lovemaking. They are just as effective in creating a romantic atmosphere when you're preparing an intimate dinner — or when you're planning to spend some quiet time together reading or talking.

A sensational surprise party

Sue: My last birthday was a great example of the kinds of extraordinary things you do for me. It was a snowy night, and we'd planned to go out to a local restaurant for a quiet dinner. But when I came home from work, there was someone there preparing drinks and food. I soon realized that you were having dinner catered by one of our favorite restaurants. That was great in itself. But a few minutes later, my closest friends started showing up one by one.

Steve: I knew you'd like it that I didn't invite my own friends.

Sue: Right. That's the point. You were doing this for me, and it was great. Instead of walking in and having a bunch of people yell "Surprise," the evening kind of evolved in a most wonderful way. Every few minutes, another one of my close friends walked in — and I was surprised all over again. There were just rolling waves of excitement.

Steve: It was really a thrill that I could do something to make you so happy.

Pay attention to how many restaurants go out of their way to create a romantic ambiance for their patrons. Notice the careful attention they pay to the type and volume of the music, the color and intensity of the lighting, and the aromas in the room. After you find an ambiance you like, try to duplicate it as a way of adding more romance to your marriage.

Do Something Out of the Ordinary

A thoughtful surprise can sweep your spouse off her feet. The key is to plan something different that shows you're attuned to what makes your partner happy and excited.

The unexpected thing you do doesn't have to be elaborate or expensive. You can simply announce that you've hired a babysitter so that you can catch a film your partner has been wanting to see. Or, you can offer to prepare a special meal — a gesture that would be even more of a surprise if it's something you never do. The important thing is that it's something out of the ordinary that has meaning and gives pleasure to your partner.

Play and Laugh Together

When the routines of day-to-day life begin to take over, you may forget that playing together is as important as working together. Few things help you appreciate the good things in life — and in your marriage — than adding a touch of child-like playfulness.

- ✔ **Watch the way children play; the way they seem to take pleasure from each moment.** Adults often let themselves get so loaded down with pressures and responsibilities that they forget how important it is to have fun.

- ✔ **Think of play as any activity that you enjoy together.** It may be taking a drive in the country, going to the zoo, or taking up ballroom dancing. Or stay home, order in a pizza, and rent a couple of videos. Whatever makes the two of you smile and feel light-hearted.

Different kinds of playfulness are appropriate at different times. For example, some play involves the kind of intimate touching most couples would only do behind closed doors — though there are some couples who enjoy fooling around with each other in public. There are also very public kinds of playfulness, like spending time at an amusement park or dressing up for a costume party. Almost anything is fair game if you both find it pleasurable.

In addition, use humor to lighten things up. Some couples have fun joking around with each other — often in a silly way. They find that laughter adds spice to the relationship, and keeps potentially heavy issues in perspective. We ourselves have always enjoyed one another's sense of humor. We consider that to be a great asset to our marriage.

A little well-placed humor can quickly turn a potential argument into a moment of laughter. The next time your partner appears to be tense and an argument seems to be brewing, think of something you can say or do that's likely to make him laugh or put a smile on his face.

The following guidelines can help you use humor in ways that bring you closer together.

- ✔ **Always know what kind of response you're after.** For example, if you're having a very serious discussion, it can help to say something witty to reduce the tension. However, an attempt at silliness or gross humor can make things worse.

- ✔ **Have a laugh at your own expense.** Self-deprecating humor can be an effective way of reducing tension. It works especially well when your humor communicates that you're able to see your shortcomings from your partner's perspective.

✔ **Never make a joke at your partner's expense.** This goes double if you're in the midst of an argument. Making a nasty or sarcastic crack about your partner will either cause your spouse to withdraw or make him or her even angrier.

You don't need a specific reason to use humor. A well-placed joke or humorous remark is almost never out of place. It can help fight boredom, while adding fun and romance to your marriage.

Revisit Your Shared History

Is there a special spot where you used to spend time when you were courting? A certain restaurant near your first apartment where the two of always had Sunday brunch? How long has it been since you've been back to those places?

Return to the locations that have special meaning to you — on a regular basis, if possible. It may not be practical for you to go back to the exotic island where you spent your honeymoon, but what about revisiting that park where you used to stroll together hand in hand, or that beach where you spent a week the summer you first met? Revisiting places that are special to you will help keep the romance alive in your marriage.

Continue to seek out new romantic places and rituals, and add them to the ones you already have.

Your shared history as a couple is ongoing. The special experiences and meaningful rituals that you create over the course of your marriage help you have a richer and more romantic life together.

Chapter 19

Ten Things You Should Never Say to Your Partner

*T*he wrong words can be very hurtful. And after you say them, it's almost impossible to undo the damage. We've known people who still sting from an insult that a spouse may have hurled 30 years ago in a moment of anger. That's one reason why we recommend that you avoid saying hurtful words at all costs.

Some hurtful things that married partners say to one another may not be direct insults. They may use biting or sarcastic words or come out with remarks that signal a dishonest way of avoiding unpleasant tasks and subjects that their spouses bring up. Words of this kind are hurtful because your spouse usually knows that they are essentially dishonest — even though you may not intend to tell an outright lie. Here, then, is our own list of phrases that may cross your mind — but should never cross your lips when you and your partner are together. And, if you happen to slip, be sure to apologize — and mean it!

"You Never" or "You Always"

When you're angry at something your partner does (or doesn't do), it's tempting to exaggerate that behavior by acting as if that sums up your partner's entire personality. This tactic may help relieve your immediate frustration, but it won't do your marriage any good. For example, if you say, "You never help around the house," there's little chance that your partner will react positively. Then again, what else can you expect when you corner someone that way?

You can find exceptions to every rule. So even if you wish your partner would do more housework, keep in mind the times when he or she did his share — like during the week that you had the flu last month.

Try the following tips:

✓ **Compliment your partner for doing something that you appreciate.** This is a much more effective way of getting what you want than accusing your spouse of never doing anything.

Attacking and criticizing your partner is almost always a bad strategy. Even if your criticism is accurate, you're not likely to get what you want by hitting your partner over the head with his or her shortcomings.

✓ **Always express your feelings by starting with the word "I" instead of the word "you."**

• Don't say: "You never do anything" or "You're always watching a baseball game when I need your help around the house."

• Do say: "I'd be free to spend time this afternoon with you and the kids if you could help me out with some chores."

"Yes, But . . ."

Everyone wants to be heard — especially your spouse. When he or she says something, it's important to make it plain that you understand the meaning behind those words — particularly if you're going to disagree.

For example, if your partner says, "I'm unhappy with the way you're handling the household finances," it would be a mistake on your part to answer by saying, "Yes, but you never put the bills on my desk, so I don't know when they're due."

On the surface, "yes, but" seems like a simple, offhanded remark. More often than not, it's an underhanded way of saying, "I don't really care about what you're saying. I'm not listening." It would be better to come right out and say that you totally disagree with the remark. That's more honest, and it may generate some constructive dialogue.

If you disagree with something your partner has said, make sure he or she knows that you've been listening. Then disagree in a way that's likely to create an atmosphere of cooperation. For example, you may say something like: "I can see that we're having a problem coordinating our bill paying. Let's talk about finding a better way to handle it."

"It's All Your Fault"

People usually say this when they're feeling guilty about something they did or forgot to do. The car runs out of gas in the middle of a highway, and the husband screams at his wife: "You should have reminded me to gas up before we left. This is all your fault."

When something goes wrong, forgive yourself — and your partner. Most everyday mishaps are nobody's fault. Besides, everybody messes up once in a while. Those are times when we need our husband or wife to let us off the hook.

Try to find some humor in the situation. Five years from now, you'll probably laugh at the mishap, if you even remember it at all.

"Are You Getting Fat?"

Most people are sensitive about their appearance, especially in areas where they feel vulnerable. So, if your partner has put on weight, don't even think about raising that issue — especially if you're in the middle of a fight.

Think before you talk! An attack on your spouse's physical appearance is likely to be an underhanded way of venting your frustration and anger. When you attack your partner's weight, hair, or any other aspect of how he or she looks, try to think about what's behind those hurtful words.

If you're genuinely concerned about your spouse's weight, use diplomatic and positive ways to raise the issue without being insulting. Consider approaching the weight issue in one of the following ways:

- ✓ I've been reading about the benefits of healthy eating. Let's try to get into a more healthful diet together.

- ✓ Wouldn't it be great if we could take a long walk together each night after dinner?

- ✓ I just bought this terrific book on low-fat cooking. Let's try to make some of the recipes.

Even the gentlest hint about good health and weight loss may rattle your partner, especially if he or she is especially sensitive. However, you do have a right to express your concerns, as long as you do so in a constructive way — and in private.

Don't sweat the little things

Steve: Remember a few years ago, I went for a walk around the neighborhood and I didn't take my wallet. Instead, I put five 20 dollar bills in the pocket of my shorts. When I got home, that money was gone.

Sue: You were driving yourself crazy — mostly because you were feeling so guilty about messing up. You must have spent an hour re-tracing your steps, but you never found that money.

Steve: I sometimes shop for the best price to save a few dollars on computer equipment and other stuff I buy. But to lose a hundred bucks so carelessly — I felt like a complete idiot.

Sue: Oh well, at least you didn't say it was all my fault for not making you carry your wallet.

Steve: Actually, what you did say was: "Stop beating yourself up over this. Everyone loses things sometimes. Nothing is worth giving yourself an ulcer — certainly not that money. Why don't we just forget about it?" I can't tell you how much better that made me feel.

"That's Not My Job"

We see marriage as the ultimate cooperative venture. That means husbands and wives should be willing to pitch in whenever possible. Even if one partner contributes more in a particular area, the other should be ready to assume a greater role at a different time.

When you respond to your partner's request by saying, "That's not my job," you're really saying, "I'm not fully committed to making this marriage work." Responses like, "I can't do it," or even "You do it so much better than me," amount to the same thing.

There's a big difference between not having much experience at doing something and not being able to do it. For example, some husbands have never been called on to cook, clean, and change diapers because they've been brought up to believe those are "a woman's job." Still, the plain fact is that men are perfectly capable of doing all of the jobs.

Husbands and wives who are rigid about what they will and won't do endanger their marriage. For example, what if a wife became ill and couldn't take care of the house for a period of time? In a marriage where the partners had flexible roles, the husband would jump in and do his best to pick up the slack. The same principle applies to wives who are fulltime homemakers. What if a working husband became disabled, and he was no longer making a salary? Imagine what would happen to the family if the wife said: "Earning money is a man's job, so I refuse to pitch in!"

Divide responsibilities in ways that reflect your strengths and choices — instead of outdated gender stereotypes.

The more role flexibility you build into your marriage, the easier it will be to deal with day-to-day living — and with unexpected setbacks.

"Why Can't You Be More Like . . .?"

This is a backhanded way to criticize your partner. It's also an ineffective strategy of trying to get what you want. For example, if you'd like your spouse to be more sociable, it would be insulting to say "Why can't you be more like Bob Jones?" Or, "I wish you were more like Bob Jones."

If you want your partner to do something, use a direct, but non-confrontational approach. For example, if you'd like him to be more sociable, say: "I'd really like it if we could go out with friends more often." Or, "You've got so many interesting opinions, I really enjoy it when you share them with our friends."

Don't compare your spouse to someone else on the basis of what you perceive to be a single negative trait. People aren't defined by any one aspect of their personality. For example, your husband might not be as sociable as Bob Jones, but he may be far more intelligent and considerate.

People often look better from the outside — especially when they're married to someone else. It's both unfair and a distortion of reality to reduce your partner to a single caricature. What's even worse is to then compare the thing you like least about your partner with what appears to be someone else's greatest asset. If you had to live with that other person, you may soon realize how lucky you are to be married to the man or woman you're with.

"I'll Try"

More often than not, saying "I'll try" is a non-confrontational way of saying "no." For example, if your husband asks you to go to the bank and you say, "I'll try," that's only one notch better than saying, "I'll think about it," or "I'll keep it in mind." If you simply said no, you'd at least be putting your cards on the table.

Using words like "I'll try" is a form of passive resistance. When you keep responding to your partner's requests that way, there's a good chance that he'll eventually give up and do it himself. This may, in fact, be what the partner who's using the passive resistance is trying to achieve. But, in the long run, this kind of approach generates anger and bad feelings.

If your partner asks you to do something you'd rather not do, tell her how you feel. Then, either agree to do what she asks, or discuss ways to come up with an alternate plan for how you're going to handle the request.

For example, if your wife wants you to clean the table and wash the dinner dishes and you hate that particular task, present her with the following alternative: "I'll do most of the cooking if you do most of the cleaning after dinner. Once in a while, we can switch off."

If your partner accepts the suggestion, follow through with your commitment to switch tasks occasionally. If she doesn't care for that arrangement, work together at coming up with something more acceptable.

"Forget It, I Don't Want to Fight"

This is an ineffective and phony way to deal with conflict. It's the same as saying: "Leave me alone. I'm not interested in how you feel." People who use this expression sometimes act as if they're giving in. Actually, they're not conceding a thing.

Some spouses try a somewhat more passive variation of the same theme by simply ignoring their partner's complaints and burying themselves behind a newspaper or in front of the TV set.

Ultimately, there's no way of avoiding unpleasant issues that matter to your partner. You can try to tune out his or her complaints, but they're bound to flare up again.

It's okay to postpone a discussion. However, if you say, "Let's talk about this later," you need to define what "later" means. For example, you may suggest that the two of you discuss the issue after the kids go to bed or after you come home from work. The important thing is to acknowledge that your partner wants you to deal with something specific, and to let her know that you plan to attend to it at a specific time.

"I'm Getting a Divorce"

When you're in the midst of the same argument you've had a thousand times, you may be tempted to say the following words to yourself: "What do I need this for? I should get out of this marriage." On the other hand, actually threatening your spouse with a divorce is the emotional equivalent of punching him or her in the mouth. An only slightly less-toxic variation of this theme is to throw up your hands and say, "If you think I'm so terrible, why don't you get a divorce?"

When you threaten to leave your spouse — or invite him or her to leave you — you're messing with the cement that holds the foundation of a marriage together. In general, people can control the words that come out of their mouths, even if they can't always control the thoughts that run through their heads.

Unless you've given the matter a great deal of thought and have decided that you truly want a divorce, it's a major mistake to ever utter those words.

Chapter 20

Ten Ways To Have a Fair Fight

In This Chapter

▶ Keeping your arguments focused

▶ Finding cooperative ways to work out your differences

▶ Making sure neither of you feels like a loser

Married couples argue for all sorts of reasons and in lots of different ways. Arguing can be a positive force in a marriage — or it can be a sign of serious problems. It all depends on *how* a couple argues.

Some couples claim that they never argue. That's next to impossible in marriages where both partners feel free to express their differences. Other couples have frequent arguments that sometimes get very loud. However, the volume and frequency of fights aren't very telling — nor are the issues that a couple fights about. The most important question is: Are the fights fair?

Every boxing match has a referee to make sure the boxers follow the rules of the ring. In marriage, you and your spouse have to referee your own disputes without help from a third party, so you need to hammer out rules and limits that work for you. You and your partner can set flexible boundaries that suit your individual personalities and your marriage — as long as you follow the rules of fair fighting.

Understand What's Really Going On

When you sense that a fight is about to erupt between and your partner, try to scope out the underlying cause of the argument:

- Are you or your spouse just letting off steam?
- Is there something specific that you want your partner to do?
- Are your angry words an expression of serious differences or conflict in your marriage?

Different strategies are effective for handling different kinds of arguments. The following techniques can work well, depending on the situation:

- ✔ If your partner is just blowing off steam, it's sometimes a good idea to say nothing and let him or her cool down.

- ✔ If you want your partner to do something, a direct approach often works best.

- ✔ If your arguments are part of an ongoing pattern that leaves one or both of you feeling bad, consider seeking out professional help.

Stick to the Issues

You're more likely to get your partner to see things your way if you avoid personal attacks and concentrate on what you're trying to accomplish.

For example, if you're upset because your wife is late, don't say, "You have absolutely no consideration for other people." Instead, try saying: "I feel more relaxed and have a much better time when we get to places a few minutes early. Can we do it that way next time?"

Your partner is likely to respond to your needs if she doesn't feel attacked and forced to defend herself.

Listen Beyond the Literal Words

When two people live together, they often become the brunt of each other's frustrations. For example, your husband may be angry at another driver who cut him off on the way home from work. He may be even angrier that he has to deal with rush hour traffic every morning and night.

Your husband has no easy way to fix that problem, so he picks an argument with you because you forgot to buy the magazine he asked for that morning. Instead of responding to his angry words, take a step back and try to figure out the real frustrations behind your partner's need to snap at you.

Even if an argument starts out being about something outside the marriage, the focus can shift quickly — especially if hurtful words are used. Keep fights from spinning out of control. Many arguments start out with a thoughtless remark or criticism, and then they escalate. Spouses know each other's most vulnerable spots, so they can easily assault them. The natural temptation is to counter that biting remark and to initiate a major battle.

Give your partner the benefit of the doubt. Many arguments don't start with bad intentions on anyone's part. But things can get out of hand quickly if you assume that your partner is an adversary who's out to get you. Instead, try asking, "What's really bothering you? Is your boss still pressuring you about that project at work?" You may be surprised to find that what's upsetting him has little or nothing to do with you.

Look at Both Sides

It's natural in the course of an argument to focus only on your own point of view and to tune out what your partner is trying to get across. Doing that is the equivalent of having a conversation with yourself, and it virtually guarantees that you won't be able to resolve the argument in a way that's satisfactory to both of you.

Try switching places. See if you can convincingly argue your partner's position. If you both do that, you'll know that you truly understand each other's viewpoint.

Try thinking of your arguments as struggles for better cooperation. We live in a competitive world, where people often have to defeat others in order to win. For example, politicians attack their opponents on all sorts of irrelevant issues in order to win elections. Athletes sometimes revert to dirty tactics to score points. Businesses will sometimes use unfair tactics to get a leg up on their competitors.

Marriage is supposed to be the ultimate cooperative venture. But too often, husbands and wives mimic the competitive model that they see all around them. The skills you need for a successful marriage are often the opposite of those you need to succeed in the marketplace or business. Forget cut-throat tactics, and make your marriage a safe place for both of you.

Look for Ways to Bend without Breaking

In a successful marriage, both partners must be able to compromise and negotiate. Sometimes, the two of you can find a middle ground. If, for example, you want to spend your two-week summer vacation at the shore and he wants to spend it at a resort with a golf course, you can work it out in several different ways:

> ✔ You can both spend a week at the shore, then a week at the golf resort.
>
> ✔ You can each spend a portion of your vacation time apart.
>
> ✔ You can agree to go to the shore this summer, and to the golf resort next summer.

Figure out what's at stake for each of you — and defer to the partner whose needs are stronger. For example, if your wife has had a particularly stressful year, and you know that she finds spending time near the ocean relaxing, consider taking the kind of vacation she wants this summer.

In the long run, it's most important that the outcome of your disagreement doesn't leave one of you feeling like a loser. If you yield on an issue that's important to your partner, it's likely that your partner will do the same for you on another occasion.

Use Strategic Timing

Be sensitive to your partner's shifting moods. Is your husband rushed and frazzled most mornings? If so, don't raise difficult issues when you wake up, especially if they're going to require a long discussion. Instead, pick a time when he seems more relaxed and positively disposed.

For example, suppose you've just told your cousin, whom your spouse doesn't especially like, that you'd like him to stay for a week. It's not a good idea to break that news when your husband's feeling rushed or exhausted. However, if you make that same request when your spouse is relaxed and doesn't feel pressed, you're likely to have a much different kind of conversation.

Timing your request doesn't mean that you're walking on eggshells or that you're afraid to speak. It simply means that if your partner is in a negative frame of mind, he may say no to something that he'd agree to at another time.

Don't Garbage-Bag

When people get into an argument, they often start with one issue, segue into another, and wind up throwing in everything but the kitchen sink. They then bring up a host of past grudges and resentments.

Discuss only one issue at a time. If you're arguing about household finances, don't throw up her tendency to be late, or that he burned the chicken when preparing last night's dinner. When you do that, you're sure to wind up fighting about personalities — not issues.

Don't try to fix your partner. Marital arguments often give husbands and wives an excuse to practice a little dime-store psychology. They'll say things like, "The problem is that you're just like your mother," or, "We're not going to get anywhere until you get over your neurosis." Your spouse needs to feel loved and respected for who he or she is!

You are not your spouse's therapist. It's not your job to fix his or her personal problems. Trying to do so is an especially counterproductive strategy when you're in the middle of a fight.

Don't Go for the Jugular

When arguments between married couples become heated, a common strategy is to throw up the one thing that's sure to hurt your partner's feelings. For example, if a husband knows his wife is insecure about her skills as a mother, he may attack that vulnerability in the middle of an argument about housework.

Attacking your partner's weak spot in the middle of a fight is one of the worst things you can do. These attacks generate a lot of bad feeling that can last long after the immediate argument ends.

Don't Take the Moral High Ground

When married partners have an argument, the issue at hand often gets buried beneath a battle about who is a better, kinder, more considerate human being.

Unless you or your partner is trying to win an election, it's not important to sort out who the better candidate is. Chances are, both of you do your share in creating problems.

Nobody wins when the focus of a fight shifts from a specific issue to a battle over whether the husband or wife is morally superior.

Make Sure Both of You Can Live with the Outcome

There are different resolutions to marital fights. Some arguments lend themselves to compromise. Others wind up being resolved in ways that favor one spouse over the other. Still others have no clear outcome — and are likely to be repeated again and again.

When one partner feels crushed in the wake of an argument, the long-term health of the marriage suffers. Even if you give in, neither of you should feel bullied or manipulated by your spouse.

Husbands and wives who are committed to each other and their marriage understand that neither partner truly wins if the other walks away feeling like a loser. Both of you have to be able to live with the outcome of your disputes, or someone will wind up feeling angry and resentful.

Chapter 21

Ten Signs That Your Marriage Is in Trouble

*M*ost married couples experience a certain amount of stress and strain just about every day. However, that doesn't mean the marriage is in trouble — or that one or both partners need outside help.

The rough patch that you and your partner are experiencing may be a function of the natural ups and downs of marriage — and of life. For example, you may be having career-related stresses, financial problems, or arguments over differences in personal style. Two well-adjusted people in a solid marriage can usually handle these hurdles by themselves — especially if they use the techniques that we explore in this book.

There are also stressful events that are expected parts of the life- and marriage-cycles, like childbirth, aging, illness, kids leaving home, and parents dying. These life events can affect wives and husbands in adverse ways that temporarily block out positive aspects of a marriage. Still, unless these changes become unusually stressful or disruptive, most couples handle them — and sometimes even use them to strengthen their marriage.

Any change or disruption can start a marriage on a downward spiral, especially if it's very painful or long-lasting. However, the following are sure signs that a marriage is in trouble.

One Spouse Is Physically Violent

Actual or threatened physical violence is the worst thing one partner can do to another. If your spouse hits you, you may consider taking steps to get out of that relationship. At the very least, you need to find a safe way to physically remove yourself from the situation. If you want to ensure your safety, don't return to a physically abusive marriage until the battering spouse gets help. Keep in mind that patterns of abuse are extremely difficult to change.

Although you can find exceptions, most physical abuse is perpetrated by men against women. Most batterers were themselves abused as children.

One Spouse Is Verbally Abusive

Words can be used as weapons that intimidate and threaten — even if there is never any actual physical violence. In general, insults and sarcasm are negative communications in the context of a marriage. Most couples can deal with this kind of behavior if it only surfaces occasionally. However, when partners engage in a pattern of hurling insults and put-downs at each other, that's usually a sign of trouble. What's more troubling are emotionally abusive relationships in which one partner is always on the giving end and the other is on the receiving end of the insults.

Verbal abuse can be even harder to stop than physical abuse, because it's easy for verbal abusers to claim that they were only joking or that their partner is over-sensitive. It's often difficult to convince verbal abusers that the partner who's being insulted is the one who gets to decide what is and isn't abusive.

One Spouse Is Abusing Alcohol or Drugs

Alcoholism can be hard to identify, because taking a drink is so acceptable — and even expected. What can be more natural than having a beer at a ballgame, a glass of wine with dinner, a cocktail before dinner, or a tropical drink on a hot afternoon at the beach?

Drinking is considered a natural part of the enjoyment in any of these contexts. The question is, where do you draw the line between social drinking and problem drinking? If you suspect that your spouse is an alcoholic, there's a good chance that he or she has a problem. Keep in mind that many alcoholics never appear to be drunk, and often deny that there's anything wrong.

Alcohol is often present in cases of spousal abuse. Many abused wives report that their husbands are fine when they're sober — and become abusive after a couple of drinks.

Drug problems are a lot like alcoholism, but there are some important differences. Drugs like cocaine and heroin are illegal — and using them can get you arrested. Illegal drugs also cost a lot more than alcohol, and addicts often lie and even steal to get enough money to buy drugs.

Your husband's or wife's drug habit is a danger to you and your family. Spouses of drug users can be held criminally liable if drugs are found and can lose ownership of a house or a car.

One Spouse Has a Problem with Compulsive Gambling or Compulsive Spending

Gambling can be an addiction — much like alcoholism or drug abuse. The average person can have a glass or two of wine with dinner and never be a problem drinker. Similarly, most people can place an occasional bet without ever becoming a problem gambler. In a way, society encourages compulsive gambling because it perpetuates the fantasy of getting rich quickly. Every day, we see another multi-million dollar lottery winner on TV. It's not surprising that people ask, "Why not me?"

The compulsive gambler always thinks that he's one bet away from reaping his fortune. What he can't accept is that he's hooked — just as surely as any drug addict.

A compulsive gambler can run through a family's assets in a relatively short time. He can end up losing everything the family owns. Yet he still tries to scrape up the money to make the one more bet that's sure to turn his luck around.

Compulsive spending is similar to compulsive gambling — though it hasn't been researched as well. However, studies show that some people can't control their urge to buy things that they don't need and can't afford — even though the behavior may cause them to neglect their spouse and family responsibilities.

As with most compulsive behaviors, there's a fine line between a person who enjoys spending and a compulsive spender. As long as there isn't an excessive drain on family finances, compulsive spenders aren't likely to be seen as addicts. The problem usually comes to light in the wake of a financial setback. At that point, the non-spending partner may begin to scrutinize expenditures and ask, "Where did all our money go?"

One Spouse Is a Workaholic

Most people have been brought up to believe in the value of hard work. Some people, however, drown themselves in work as a way of distancing themselves emotionally from their spouses and children.

You may hear a number of ready excuses for workaholism: Commitment to building a career and the need for money are the two most common and reasonable-sounding ones. However, research shows that workaholics are literally addicted to work.

Working long hours is usually seen as a virtue. However, some people can't stop thinking about work — even during those rare times that they're actually with their families.

Spouses of workaholics sometimes feel caught because of the good money and fancy lifestyle that can result when work is their partner's only passion. Nevertheless, these marriages are at high risk for divorce — and a true workaholic may not be especially bothered if his spouse leaves.

Research shows that workaholism can have a devastating effect on children. One study found that children of workaholics can suffer similar problems, such as anxiety and depression, as those experienced by children of alcoholics.

One Spouse Is Having an Affair

A secret relationship outside the marriage almost always signals problems inside the marriage — especially if it's a long-term liaison that includes lots of lying and deceit.

Husbands and wives have extramarital affairs for many reasons. Marital cheating can take place when a couple is having problems with closeness or sex, or when the partners feel starved for attention or friendship. Or, it can be the result of personal problems that have nothing to do with the marriage but get heaped onto it.

There are different kinds of extra-marital affairs. Some husbands or wives have a one-night stand at some point in the marriage but are faithful otherwise. Others have a discreet secret relationship with the same lover for years. Still others are philanderers, who regularly cheat with different partners.

Once a spouse finds out that his or her partner has been cheating, both of them must take definite steps to control the damage and start rebuilding.

The cheating partner needs to do the following:

- ✔ Identify the conditions that precipitated the affair, and make a commitment to deal with these conditions differently in the future.

- ✔ Take responsibility for the deception, even if the other partner played a part in bringing about the circumstances that led to the cheating.

- ✔ Apologize for the pain the deceived partner has suffered, and allow enough time for healing.

The betrayed partner needs to do the following:

- ✔ Understand the problems in the marriage that led to your spouse's cheating, and your contribution to those problems.

- ✔ Be aware of danger signs that the same problems may be resurfacing or that new ones are arising.

- ✔ Try to forgive. If the cheating spouse demonstrates that he or she is truly sorry, you should be prepared to forgive, or the marriage will not survive.

With effort, a marriage can survive — and even grow — after an affair.

One Spouse Is Depressed

Sadness is a natural emotion — especially in the face of a loss. That loss can be the death of a family member or friend, the loss of a job — even the end of a dream. These losses can change your view of the world. They can also make everyday functioning more difficult — in your personal life, your career, and your marriage.

Most people eventually recover from their losses and depressed feelings. The amount of time to recoup depends on the type and severity of the loss, the level of support from family and friends, and differences in resilience and personal strength.

You may not even know that you're depressed, and yet, you're distracted at work, experiencing changes in your eating and sleeping patterns, or losing interest in sex. If grief appears to be unending, or if you or your spouse begins experiencing profound changes in motivation and mood for no apparent reason, the problem may be caused by clinical depression.

Doctors have a number of effective treatments for depression — including psychotherapy and anti-depressant medication. If you suspect that you or your spouse is depressed, schedule a complete physical checkup to eliminate the possibility that the problem is based on a physical ailment or a medication that you're taking, ask your doctor for a referral to a mental-health professional.

Depression left untreated can wreck even a strong marriage. Depressed men and women often develop substance-abuse problems and sometimes attempt suicide.

The Two of You Disagree About Having Children

Disagreements about having children is one of the hardest conflicts to resolve. A couple may differ about family structure or issues concerning infertility or adoption. However, the question of whether or not to have a child is something couples ought to discuss before they get married — even though one or both may later have a change of heart.

Don't automatically assume that your partner shares your views on having children. Young couples sometimes fail to explore this matter before they marry. Or one of the partners may tell the other that he doesn't want to have kids — and the other partner figures that she will be able to change his mind. This problem often comes up in second marriages, with an older husband who has children from a previous marriage.

If one spouse can't visualize a life without kids and the other has decided that he doesn't want to shoulder the responsibilities, a compromise may not be possible. One or the other partner will have to prevail, and it won't be easy to find a solution that doesn't leave someone feeling bitter or cheated.

You and Your Partner Have Stopped Having Sex

A totally or virtually non-existent sex life spells trouble for a marriage. Fortunately, problems with sex can often be corrected in an otherwise solid relationship.

Most couples find that the frequency of sex begins to decrease after a few years of marriage. Studies show that this decrease in desire is as normal as the intense sexual high many couples experience early in their relationship. Husbands and wives may accept this downward curve of desire, but still begin to doubt their virility or attractiveness.

The most troubling sexual problems occur under the following circumstances:

✔ When one partner feels a great deal more desire than the other.

✔ When a husband or wife is experiencing some kind of sexual dysfunction.

✔ When one partner wants to engage in sexual activities that the other is opposed to.

There are many effective ways for couples to deal with sexual difficulties — some of which require medication or the help of a qualified sex therapist. But before you seek professional help, consider the following:

✔ **Make time for lovemaking.** Research shows that one reason so many people have low sexual desire is that they are simply too busy and stressed to think about sex.

Good sex requires energy, creativity, and a certain amount of planning. After a long day of juggling work and family responsibilities, many husbands and wives are simply too pooped to pop.

✔ **Make your partner feel wanted and special.** Instead of jumping into bed and expecting sparks to fly, spend as much time as you can playing with, talking to, and becoming more intimate with your partner.

The less often you and your spouse make love, the less intimate and sexual you're likely to feel toward one another, and the more likely it is that things won't go smoothly the next time you decide to make the effort.

You and Your Partner No Longer Enjoy Being Together

Couples who come into therapy often complain that they no longer have much in common, that they don't enjoy being together, or that they can't recall the last time they laughed. These couples may keep up appearances by attending family functions and celebrating holidays together, but these token gestures don't hide the emptiness in their relationship.

Excessive computer use can be dangerous. During the past few years, we've talked with a growing number of wives and husbands who complain that their partners are addicted to the Internet. People who spend hour after hour online are effectively tuning out their partners and hurting their marriage — even if they're not looking to meet someone else online.

Partners in viable marriages often maintain separate interests and even separate friends. However, after a husband and wife stop being good friends and enjoying the time that they do spend together, the relationship is in danger of becoming an empty shell.

Chapter 22

Ten Ways to Have a More Exciting Sex Life

*R*emember how excited you felt when you and your partner first began making love? Your fantasies of passionately kissing each other and going to bed were only surpassed by the real thing. Then you got married, and your sex life seemed to get a little less passionate year by year.

It may or may not make you feel better to know that this downhill arc is par for the course. At the beginning of a relationship, you feel a sense of fantasy, adventure, and risk that form a powerful aphrodisiac. Marriage, on the other hand, provides safety and security, which plays against those hot, passionate feelings that the two of you shared at the beginning.

Now for the good news: Sex between married partners is potentially deeper and more satisfying than any other kind. It may be tantalizing to fantasize about having sex with someone new — even a complete stranger. However, you have a far better chance of having truly exciting intimacy with your spouse — and to continue making sex especially fulfilling as you discover more about yourselves and each other.

Make Sexual Contact Part of Your Everyday Life

Sexual contact doesn't have to take place in the bedroom only; nor do you have to take off your clothes. There are all sorts of small, erotic gestures that can turn you both on, including the following:

- An unexpected, stolen kiss

- A soft, gentle touch on the neck or shoulder

- An arm placed around your partner's waist

These sensual touches can be very enticing, because they communicate your feelings in subtle and unexpected ways.

Find the sensuous communications that please your partner most. Everyone has certain "hot spots" where a touch is especially enticing. Maybe he likes being petted on his neck as the two of you hug. Perhaps she likes it when you rub her back at the base of the spine.

Studies show that sensuous touching raises the level of *endorphins,* chemicals in the body that block out pain and increase the body's pleasure potential.

Expand Your Sexual Horizons

Married couples often get into a kind of comfort zone — which, after a number of years, can disintegrate into a boredom zone. You may be surprised at how much spice the following simple changes can add to your sex life:

- **Change the time and place.** For example, if you always have sex in the bedroom, try it on the couch or the living room floor. If you generally make love at night, try doing it in the morning or in the middle of the afternoon.

- **Change the sensory environment in the following ways:**

  - If you always turn off the lights when you make love, try it with the lights on in front of a full-length mirror.

  - Try experimenting with different kinds of scented candles or aromas to find out which kind is most pleasing to you both.

  - If you and your mate have enjoyed great sex while a certain song was playing, make that your special song, and play it when you're making love. Or, play music that releases both of you.

  - If your spouse was turned on when you wore a particular piece of lingerie, wear it again soon.

- **Experiment with different positions.** Couples often use only one or two positions when they make love. Doing it in different ways adds variety and provides an opportunity for increased stimulation. There are a wide variety of books and videotapes that demonstrate the various lovemaking positions. It's fun trying new methods to make love, and you can wind up adding exciting pleasures to your sexual repertoire.

Anything goes in marital lovemaking — as long as it's pleasing and acceptable to both partners. That doesn't mean that you should do things that you find offensive. Still, there is no safer place than a loving marriage to experiment and extend the boundaries of your sexuality.

Tell and Show Each Other What Pleases You

Unless you and your partner are mind readers, you both have to be specific about what you want and need your partner to do when you make love.

It's natural to feel somewhat hesitant about revealing your desires to others — even to the person to whom you're supposed to feel closest. However, if you truly want to have a more exciting sex life, you have to be willing to stretch yourself beyond your comfort zone.

- **Talk in spite of your fear.** You have it within you to share your thoughts and feelings with your partner, no matter how afraid you might feel. The only way you can conquer this fear is by making your desires known.

  Whenever you take a chance, there's always a chance of rejection. Still, anything worthwhile requires a certain amount of risk — and that includes creating a more exciting sex life.

- **Always use "I" statements in letting your partner know what you need.** This is a fundamental rule of all good communication because it avoids blame and lets the other person know what you're thinking and feeling.

  In the context of lovemaking, using "I" statements gives your partner an opportunity to respond to your needs. For example, if you want to be touched in a certain place, try saying: "I love it when you rub my thigh." If you want your partner to use a softer touch, try saying: "I get so turned on when you gently stroke my chest."

  Positive feedback almost always works better than criticism — especially when making love.

- **Show your partner what you mean.** After you've asked your partner to touch you in a certain place or in a certain way, make sure your message has gotten through: Stroke him or her in the exact way you want to be stroked, or demonstrate by touching yourself.

- **Encourage your partner to let you know what he or she feels.** The best way to do this is to take the lead in making your feelings known, and to let your partner know how interested you are in giving him or her pleasure.

Unleash the Power of Fantasy

Imagination is a safe, cost-free tool that all men and women can use to enhance sexual pleasure. We think of fantasy as a kind of vacation from the realities of everyday life. In lovemaking, fantasies generate excitement and help keep your worries at bay.

✔ **Allow your mind to run free.** If you have a recurring erotic daydream or a sexual fantasy, don't hesitate to call on it when you're making love to your spouse. The mind is the most powerful erogenous zone.

Fantasies — including those about someone other than your spouse — are your own personal mind adventures. They are not signs that you don't enjoy making love to your partner.

Nothing destroys the joy of lovemaking like guilt. Any attempt to censor your feelings automatically ruins your pleasure. Even if the movie in your mind is X-rated, you're the only one watching it. So enjoy!

✔ **Exchange or discard fantasies as you wish.** One of the great things about fantasies is that you can switch them mid-reel or shut them down when you no longer want or need them.

Take Advantage of Pornography

Many people enjoy looking at or visualizing others having sex. Studies show that men like to look at pictures and videos of attractive women or exciting sex acts. Women tend to enjoy reading stories focusing on romantic relationships, and visualizing the action in their minds.

At its best, pornography contains an imaginative story line, as well as visual images of people having sex. At its worst, pornography is exploitive — and it can be highly offensive to some people.

Every person has to make his or her own aesthetic and moral decisions. We would never presume to influence you in this area. Our goal is helping you create more sexual pleasure in your marriage.

Some couples enjoy erotic materials together. At the same time, it's important for each of you to respect each other's right to entertain his or her own fantasies. In the long run, you'll probably come out ahead if you don't interfere with your partner's private thoughts.

Make Special Time for Sex

The whole notion of scheduling sex runs counter to the myth that good love-making always has to be unplanned and spontaneous. Yet many modern couples are so busy with careers, children, and household duties that they're often too exhausted to have sex.

- ✔ **Make sex a high priority.** When couples let sex become too low a priority, it often disappears completely from their marriage.

- ✔ **Make a date for sex.** This kind of planning increases the fun and excitement because you have something to look forward to.

- ✔ **Stick to the schedule.** When you and your partner schedule special time for lovemaking, keep that commitment — even if you don't feel like it at the moment. After you get started, you're may soon find that you're totally in the mood.

Become an Artful Kisser

Kissing is a neglected and underrated sexual art. Many couples find kissing to be even more intimate and pleasurable than intercourse. Becoming an artful kisser can enhance other aspects of your sex life, but as with any skill, you have to keep practicing.

Don't let kissing fade from your sexual repertoire. Married couples sometimes stop kissing as they settle into a marriage. This can often be the beginning of a downward spiral in their sex lives.

Kissing is a powerful technique for increasing passion. The following are some of the ways to use it to enhance your and your partner's sexual pleasure:

- ✔ **Kiss with your eyes open.** Lovers in films always seem to kiss with their eyes closed — as if their thoughts are elsewhere. When you and your partner kiss or make love with your eyes open, it helps you focus on the excitement of the moment and adds novelty to the experience.

- ✔ **Kiss your partner in different ways.** When you're alone making love, take your time as you lock lips. Kiss your partner with different levels of intensity. Does she like it when you softly bite her lip? Does he get turned on when you gently caress his tongue with yours? Find out what he or she likes — and stay with that.

Don't Focus Just on the Orgasm

One of the most effective ways to improve your sex life is to take the emphasis off having an orgasm. When we tell people this, they sometimes ask: "What's the point of starting if you're not going to finish?"

That kind of response underscores the problem. When the sole focus of sex is having an orgasm, the emphasis is narrowed to a one-dimensional goal of performance.

Sex at its best includes love, intimacy, friendship, mutual exploration, and fun. If these elements have gone out of your sex life, the following techniques can help you recapture them:

✔ **Concentrate on kissing and touching each other — as though you were on a first date.** This may seem like a limited approach to sex. Actually, taking the emphasis off of the orgasm can free you to expand your sexual horizons.

✔ **Forget about time.** When a couple focuses primarily on achieving orgasm, it's as if the clock is running. You may not actually be in a hurry. However, the sense that you must accomplish a specific goal may cause you to feel unnecessarily pressed.

✔ **Agree that neither of you is going to have a climax the next time you go to bed.** This technique helps take the pressure off and frees you up to simply enjoy one another. It is especially useful when one or both partners is having trouble reaching orgasm.

When we suggest that couples try this technique, we ask them to promise that they'll do everything in their power *not* to have an orgasm. Experience has shown us that this is a wonderful piece of reverse psychology. More often than not, we'll get a call from the husband or wife the next day saying, "Sorry Doc, we had to break our promise. Both of us wound up having orgasms!"

Talk Sexy

Talking sexy or "dirty" to your partner can be a real turn-on, as long as you know the right words to say. For example, some people are turned on by sexually explicit or X-rated words. Others get aroused when their partner talks about the things they're going to do in bed that night.

You can use sexy talk in almost any place or at any time. Consider trying the following:

- Leave your partner a sexy or romantic message on her private e-mail, voice mail, or answering machine.

- Slip an erotic note in his brief case or lunch box.

- Put a naked picture of yourself or the two of you on her desk — with a caption that reads, "Thinking of you."

- Use phone sex when you're apart. If one of you is traveling and you can't be together, the phone can be a great tool. Use it either to heighten anticipation about seeing each other again or to help one (or both) of you masturbate while you're apart.

Have Sex With Someone You Love — Yourself!

Contrary to what you may have heard, most men and the majority of women masturbate — and marriage doesn't put an end to the practice.

Masturbation is an important and routine part of adult sexuality — not just something teenagers do on the sneak. It's common for married people to masturbate — even if some wives and husbands don't want to admit it to their partners. Masturbation is a good way for one or both partners to get started. As the lovemaking continues, masturbatory fantasies can be integrated into a reciprocal sexual experience between the two of you.

Think of masturbation as an appropriate and healthy activity for you or your partner under any of the following circumstances:

- When the two of you are not having sex.

- As a way to get aroused before lovemaking.

- As a way to enhance orgasm.

- As a way of enhancing sexual pleasure at any time.

If you are masturbating but not being sexual with your partner, that is something you need to talk about with each other — and possibly with a therapist.

In general, men don't need anything more than their own fantasies to masturbate — although some men like to use explicit photographs or videos to enhance those sexual thoughts. Some women enjoy using vibrators and other kinds of props to enhance masturbation.

Maintain your sense of humor. Certain comedians have made masturbation a favorite topic — and some aspects of it really are funny. Betty Dodson is a sex educator who has written extensively on the topic of masturbation. She tells stories about accompanying a number of women clients to a grocery store to select zucchinis and other vegetables to use for self-pleasuring. Not only were the vegetables just as effective, more natural, and cheaper than mechanical or electric vibrators, they added some humor to a topic that's often taken much too seriously.

When you talk about masturbation — or any form of sexual activity — keep in mind that you're not dealing with brain surgery. The whole point of masturbation is to have fun, enjoy your body — and hopefully, share that joy with your partner.

Appendix A

References

• •

*T*his appendix lists the sources for most of the research that we cite and quotations that we've used throughout the book. A complete bibliography follows the references.

Chapter 1

Research on married couples who lived together first is summarized in "The Relationship of Cohabitation and Mental Health: A Study of a Young Adult Cohort." *Journal of Marriage & the Family* (May, 1998).

Research on the health benefits of marriage is summarized in "Marital Status and Happiness: A 17-Nation Study." *Journal of Marriage and the Family* (May, 1998).

Chapter 2

Howard Markman's research demonstrating that time spent playing together is an "investment in the relationship . . ." is cited in "The 9 secrets of happy couples" by Rebecca Rice.

Chapter 4

Deborah Tannen's theories about the different communication styles of women and men are explored in her book, *You Just Don't Understand: Men and Women in Conversation*. The material in this chapter is drawn from interview material in "Men. Women. Talk. Talk. Talk. Talk. Talk. Hear? No." by Barbara Gamarekian.

"Recent research" on marital communication is based on materials in *Good Marriage: How and Why Love Lasts* by Judith S. Wallerstein and S. Blakeslee.

The principles of win-win negotiation are detailed in *Getting to Yes: Negotiating Agreement Without Giving In* by Roger Fisher and William Ury.

Chapter 5

Dave Barry's quote is from *Dave Barry's Guide To Marriage and/or Sex.*

"Optimism is a skill you can learn . . ." is the subject of *Learned Optimism* by Martin E. P. Seligman.

Chapter 6

Betty Carter discusses her ideas about workaholism and sex in "When Young Married Couples Don't Make Love Anymore" by Susan Squire.

Dee Barlow, coauthor of *Resiliency: How to Bounce Back Faster, Stronger, Smarter* (New York: Master Media, 1995) is quoted in Squire, Susan, *ibid.*

"Research shows that married couples are happier when husbands share in housework and childrearing." Cited in *Halving It All: How Equally Shared Parenting Works* by Francine Deutsch, and in a Brown University study cited in "Striking A Balance" by Mary Amorose.

"The more highly educated a woman is, the more likely she is to masturbate." Statistic reported in The Janus Report on Sexual Behavior, a study published in 1993, and cited in "Be your own best sex teacher (masturbation)." by Catherine Eaton.

"There are a lot of wonderful dimensions to sex besides just huffing and puffing . . ." from *The Guide To Getting It On!* by Paul Joannides.

"A woman lets a man enter her — she lets him in." Ona Robinson, PhD is quoted from a 1991 co-author interview.

Lonnie Barbach suggests that "women enhance their enjoyment of intercourse. . . ." Barbach's ideas about sexuality are explored in *The Erotic Edge: Erotica for Couples.*

"There's usually more to a good sexual experience than the simple hydraulics of sticking hard into wet. . . ." *The Guide To Getting It On!* by Paul Joannides.

The orgasmic crescent is described in *Are We Having Fun Yet? The Intelligent Woman's Guide to Sex* by Marsha Douglass and Lisa Douglass.

Chapter 7

The effect of various diseases and medications on male sexual dysfunction is explored by Dr. Sidney Wolfe, director of the Public Citizens Health Research Group in *"Worst Pills, Best Pills."* The quote is from an interview on *Good Morning America*, March 3, 1999.

"Sex is like a language. . . . "David Schnarch is quoted in his article "Joy with your underwear down (human sexuality)."

"Studies show that women's sex problems aren't nearly as well understood as men's. . . ." Boston University urologist and researcher Irwin Goldstein is cited in "Viagra might work for women, patients and researchers say" by John Hendon.

"Studies show that women who masturbate regularly achieve better vaginal lubrication," cited in Lonnie Barbach's "The Pause — A Closer Look At Menopause and Female Sexuality."

The scientific study of sexual dysfunctions was pioneered by Dr. William H. Masters and Virginia E. Johnson, who published the book, *Human Sexual Response*.

"Lonnie Barbach finds that women who never enjoyed sex very much in the first place sometimes use menopause as an excuse to abandon sexual activity altogether. . . ." cited in "The Mature Woman: Sex After Menopause."

"There's room in a marriage for different speeds and styles of lovemaking . . ." is discussed in *Men are from Mars; Women are from Venus: A Practical Guide to Improving Communication and Getting What You Want in Your Relationships* by John Gray.

June Reinisch's views on premature ejaculation and other sexual dysfunctions can be found in *The Kinsey Institute New Report on Sex; What You Must Know to be Sexually Literate* by June Reinisch with R. Beasley.

Chapter 8

An important source of information on the first year of marriage is *Intimate Partners: Patterns in Love and Marriage* by Maggie Scarf.

Chapter 9

Department of Agriculture statistics are cited in "The Cost of Children: Bottom line on kids: $1.45 million," *The Atlanta Journal and Constitution* (March 23, 1998).

The Whirlpool Foundation study on the financial contributions of working mothers is cited in "Working moms and their children — still ambivalent about their roles" by Maggie Jackson.

Sociologist Arlie Russell Hochschild's research demonstrating that many wives and husbands would much rather work than spend time with their families is detailed in her book *The Time Bind: When Work Becomes Home and Home Becomes Work.*

Chapter 10

"Many truisms of middle age appear to be false" statistics in sidebar were revealed by a 1999 MacArthur Foundation survey.

"If you have to be somewhere, middle age is the place to be," *ibid.*

Research on women's sexuality after menopause and estrogen replacement therapy is cited in "The Pause — a Closer Look At Menopause and Female Sexuality" by Lonnie Barbach.

Daniel Levinson quote is from his book *The Seasons of a Man's Life.*

Margaret Mead on menopausal zest is cited in: *Secret paths: Women in the New Midlife* by T. Apter.

Differences in men and women at midlife are explored in *In Our Fifties: Voices of men and women reinventing their lives* by W. H. Bergquist, E. M. Greenberg, and G. A. Klaum.

Men's midlife problems are detailed in "Components of a man's well-being at midlife," T. Julian, P.C. McKenry, and M. McKelvey.

Chapter 11

Research shows that partners who've been together for between 20 and 30 years are at high risk for divorce is cited in *My turn: Women's Search for Self After Children Leave* by P. G. Shapiro.

"Research shows that many mid-life couples who've launched their children have happier marriages and enjoy life more than those of the same age whose children continue to live at home . . ." data cited in *My Turn: Women's Search for Self After Children Leave* by P. G. Shapiro.

"Research shows that parents who have positive relations with their children are best able to cope with this transition . . ." data cited in "Emptying the nest and parental well-being: An analysis of national panel data" by L. White and J. N. Edwards.

"Research shows that if you don't stay close to your children after they leave, the pain of missing them continues to linger . . ." data cited in "Emptying the nest and parental well-being: An analysis of national panel data" by L. White and J. N. Edwards.

Chapter 12

"One out of every three Americans is a member of a stepfamily" data provided by the Stepfamily Association of America, and cited in "America's Stepfamilies: Here They Are At A Glance" by Keith Goldschmidt.

Over 70 percent of those relationships don't work out. . . . Statistic cited in "Rebuilding a marriage after adultery is a tough task, but many couples succeed" by Mark Curnutte.

The idea that a prenuptial agreement can serve some of the same purposes as premarital counseling is forwarded in *Loving and Leaving: Winning at the Business of Divorce* by Bernard Rothman.

Research on remarried women's and men's views on housework is cited in a study called "Entitlement, Obligation, and Gratitude in Family Work," published in *The Journal of Family Issues* (January, 1996).

Attorney Bernard Rothman is quoted in *Loving and Leaving: Winning at the Business of Divorce.*

"Research shows that people who have never been married have the hardest time adjusting to the rigors of a stepfamily . . ." cited by Benjamin Schlesinger in "Instant Stepparents," in *Stepfamilies.*

"Hold regular family conferences." This section draws from concepts cited in "Families, Take a Meeting — Confabs Help Families Communicate, Listen to Reactions of Others," by Darryl E. Owens.

An additional resource used for this chapter is "Twenty Major Issues in Remarriage Families," *Journal of Counseling & Development* (July/August 1992).

Chapter 13

"It's the puddle that drowns you, not the flood" quoted from Alexander Solzhenitsyn in *First Circle*.

"Research shows that one of the best ways to reduce stress is to communicate with a close friend at least twice a week. . . ." data is from a poll conducted by Princeton Survey Research Associates, cited in "Communicate With a Close Friend," *Jet* (May 13, 1996).

"There are three specific ways that stress has a negative effect on marriage. . . ." quote is from *Marriage Partnership Magazine* (Winter 96, Vol. 13 Issue 4).

"When a computer memory is full, it shuts down. . . ." is quoted from Susan J. Kraus in "Mommy panic (working mothers)."

Physical pain is one of the most common symptoms of red-zone stress. . . . Dr. John Sarno's theories on stress and back pain are detailed in his book *Healing Back Pain: The Mind-Body Connection*.

"Happiness is the ability to receive. . . ." Mark Epstein is quoted from his article, "Opening up to happiness."

Chapter 14

The problems men sometimes have when their wives earn more money is detailed in, "Battle of the bucks (how the improving earning power of women affects their relationships)" by Christy Casamassima.

Betty Carter's research on "the impact of each partner's financial contribution to a marriage — and the resulting power battles . . ." is explored in her book, *Love, Honor, and Negotiate: Making Your Marriage Work*.

Chapter 15

Divorce statistics based on 1996 data from the U.S. Office for National Statistics.

Statistics on marital cheating among people of various age groups is detailed in "The Baby Boom Turns 50," *American Demographics* (December, 1995).

"Research shows that women are far more likely to forgive their unfaithful husbands than husbands are to forgive their unfaithful wives. . . ." This tendency is pervasive in many cultures, as pointed out by Dalma Heyn in "The Affair: What to do When You Get Caught."

"Research shows that 70 percent of couples who divorced because of infidelity come to regret that decision. . . . " Statistic cited in "Rebuilding a marriage after adultery is a tough task, but many couples succeed" by Mark Curnutte.

Chapter 16

Marianne Walters' quote is from "Couples Therapy: It Could Be Just What You Need," by Joanmarie Kalter.

Marian Bentancourt quote is from *What To Do When Love Turns Violent*.

Information in sidebar on safety plans draws from information in "Why don't you just leave him?" by June Sheehan Berlinger.

Chapter 17

The health risks of divorce are cited in "Deadly divorce: Divorce Can be Hazardous to Your Health" by John J. DiIulio, Jr.

"How good are the chances of replacing your spouse?" The statistics in the sidebar are cited in *Triangles: Understanding, Preventing, and Surviving Affairs* by Lana Staheli.

"How do kids feel about divorce?" Statistics in sidebar are cited in "Divorce's Toll on Children," by Karl Zinsmeister.

The information on the various types of custody arrangements is drawn from *Divorce For Dummies* by John Ventura and Mary Reed (IDG Books Worldwide, Inc.) and *Loving and Leaving: Winning at the Business of Divorce* by Bernard Rothman.

Chapter 22

The problems of children of workaholics is detailed in *Chained to the Desk: A Guidebook for Workaholics, Their Partners and Children, and the Clinicians Who Treat Them* by Bryan Robinson.

Sources of Quotations

The Oxford Dictionary of Modern Quotations. Edited by Tony Augarde. Oxford, NY: Oxford University Press, 1991.

Berle, Milton. *More of the Best of Milton Berle's Private Joke File.* Edison, NJ: Castle Books, 1996.

The Penguin Thesaurus of Quotations. Edited by M.J. Cohen. New York: Penguin Books, 1998.

The Oxford Dictionary of 20th Century Quotations. Edited by Elizabeth Knowles. Oxford, NY: Oxford University Press, 1998.

Magill's Quotations in Context. Edited by Frank N. Magill. New York: Salem Press, 1969.

Bibliography

Amorose, Mary. "Striking A Balance." *The Bergen Record* (May 20, 1999).

Apter, T. *Secret Paths: Women in the New Midlife.* New York: W.W. Norton, 1995.

Barlow, Dee. *Resiliency: How to Bounce Back Faster, Stronger, Smarter.* New York: Master Media, 1995.

Barbach, Lonnie. *The Erotic Edge: Erotica for Couples.* New York: Dutton, 1994.

Barbach, Lonnie. "The Mature Woman: Sex After Menopause." *Contemporary Women's Issues Database* (April 1,1995).

Barbach, Lonnie. "The Pause — a Closer Look At Menopause and Female Sexuality." *Contemporary Women's Issues Database* (Vol. 21, June 1, 1993).

Barry, Dave and Jerry O'Brien. *Dave Barry's Guide To Marriage and/or Sex.* Emmaus, Pennsylvania: Rodale Press, 1987.

Bentancourt, Marian. *What To Do When Love Turns Violent.* New York: HarperCollins, 1997.

Berlinger, June Sheehan. "Why don't you just leave him?" *Nursing* (Vol. 28: April 1, 1998).

Bergquist, W. H., E.M. Greenberg, and G. A. Klaum. *In Our Fifties: Voices of men and women reinventing their lives.* San Francisco: JosseyBass, 1993.

Bolton, Robert. *People Skills: How to Assert Yourself, Listen to Others, and Resolve Conflicts.* New York: Simon & Schuster, 1986.

Bolton, Robert and Dorothy Grover Bolton. *People Styles at Work: Making Bad Relationships Good and Good Relationships Better.* New York: AMACOM, 1996.

Brown, Emily M. *Patterns of Infidelity and Their Treatment.* New York: Brunner-Mazel, 1991.

Carlson. Richard. *Don't Sweat the Small Stuff . . . And It's All Small Stuff.* New York: Hyperion, 1997.

Carter, Betty and Joan K. Peters. *Love, Honor, and Negotiate: Making Your Marriage Work.* New York: Pocket Books, 1996.

Carter, Betty and Monica McGoldrick. *Changing Family Life Cycle*, 2nd Edition. Needham Heights, MA: Allyn and Bacon, 1989.

Casamassima, Christy. "Battle of the bucks (how the improving earning power of women affects their relationships)." *Psychology Today* (March 13, 1995).

Curnutte, Mark "Rebuilding a marriage after adultery is a tough task, but many couples succeed." *Gannett News Service* (June 24, 1997).

Deutsch, Francine. *Halving It All: How Equally Shared Parenting Works.* Cambridge, Massachusetts: Harvard University Press, 1999.

DiIulio, John J., Jr. "Deadly divorce: Divorce Can be Hazardous to Your Health." *National Review* (April 7, 1997).

Douglass, Marsha and Lisa Douglass. *Are We Having Fun Yet? The Intelligent Woman's Guide to Sex.* New York: Hyperion, 1997.

Eaton, Catherine. "Be your own best sex teacher (masturbation)." *Cosmopolitan* (Vol 220: May 1, 1996).

Epstein, Mark. "Opening up to happiness." *Psychology Today* (July 17, 1995).

Evans, Patricia. *The Verbal Abuse Relationship: How to recognize it and how to respond.* Holbrook, Massachusetts: Adams Media, 1996.

Fisher, Roger and William Ury, *Getting to Yes: Negotiating Agreement Without Giving In.* New York: Penguin Books, 1983.

Gamarekian, Barbara. "Men. Women. Talk. Talk. Talk. Talk. Talk. Hear? No." *The New York Times Book Review* (June 19, 1991).

Goldschmidt, Keith. "America's Stepfamilies: Here They Are At A Glance." *Gannett News Service* (September 1, 1994).

Gottman J. and N. Silver. *The Seven Principles for Making Marriage Work.* New York: Crown, 1999.

Gottman J. and N. Silver. *Why Marriages Succeed and Fail; and How You Can Make Yours Last.* New York: Fireside, 1993.

Gray, John. *Men are from Mars; Women are from Venus: A Practical Guide to Improving Communication and Getting What You Want in Your Relationships.* New York: HarperCollins, 1990.

Heitler, Susan M. *From Conflict to Resolution: Skills and Strategies for Individuals, Couples, and Family Therapy.* New York: Norton, 1990.

Hendon, John. "Viagra might work for women, patients and researchers say." *AP Online* (April 30, 1998).

Heyn, Dalma. *Marriage Shock: The Transformation of Women Into Wives.* New York: Villard Books, 1997.

Heyn, Dalma, "The Affair: What to do When You Get Caught," *Cosmopolitan* (August 1, 1995).

Hochschild, Arlie Russell. *The Time Bind: When Work Becomes Home and Home Becomes Work.* New York: Metropolitan Books/Henry Holt & Company, 1997.

Imber-Black, Evan, *The Secret Life of Families: Truth-Telling, Privacy, and Reconciliation in a Tell-All Society.* New York: Bantam Doubleday Dell, 1998.

Jackson, Maggie. "Working moms and their children — still ambivalent about their roles." *AP Online* (June 6,1998).

Joannides, Paul. *The Guide To Getting It On!* West Hollywood, California: The Goofy Foot Press, 1999.

Julian, T., P.C. McKenry, and M. McKelvey. "Components of a man's well-being at midlife." *Mental Health Nursing* (13.285-298).

Kalter, Joanmarie. "Couples Therapy: It Could Be Just What You Need." *Cosmopolitan* (August 1993).

Kraus, Susan J. "Mommy panic (working mothers)." *Redbook* (February 1, 1995).

Levinson, D. J. *The Seasons of a Man's Life.* New York: Ballantine Books, 1978.

Markman, HJ, SM Stanley, and SL Blumberg. *Fighting for Your Marriage: Positive Steps for a Loving and Lasting Relationship.* San Francisco: Jossey Bass, 1994.

Masters, Dr. William H. and Virginia E. Johnson. *Human Sexual Response.* New York: Bantam, 1980.

Notarius C. and H. Markman. *We Can Work It Out: How to Solve Conflicts, Save Your Marriage, and Strengthen Your Love for Each Other.* New York: Perigee, 1994.

Owens, Darryl E. "Families, Take a Meeting — Confabs Help Families Communicate, Listen to Reactions of Other." *St. Louis Post-Dispatch* (September 14, 1994).

Pittman Frank S. *Private Lies; Infidelity and the Betrayal of Intimacy.* New York: Norton, 1989.

Ponton, Lynn E. *The Romance of Risk: Why Teenagers Do the Things They Do.* New York: Basic Books, 1997.

Reinisch, June, with R. Beasley. *The Kinsey Institute New Report on Sex; What You Must Know to be Sexually Literate.* New York: St Martin's Press, 1990.

Rice, Rebecca. "The 9 secrets of happy couples." *Redbook* (February 1, 1997).

Robinson, Bryan. *Chained to the Desk: A Guidebook for Workaholics, Their Partners and Children, and the Clinicians Who Treat Them.* New York: York University Press, 1998

Rothman, Bernard, *Loving and Leaving: Winning at the Business of Divorce.* New York: The Free Press, 1990.

Sarno, John. *Healing Back Pain: The Mind-Body Connection.* New York: Warner Books, 1991.

Scarf, Maggie. *Intimate Partners: Patterns in Love and Marriage.* New York: Random House, 1987.

Schnarch, David. "Joy with your underwear down (human sexuality)." *Psychology Today* (July 1, 1994).

Schnarch, David. *Passionate Marriage: Love, Sex, and Intimacy in Emotionally Committed Relationships.* New York: Norton, 1997.

Schlesinger, Benjamin. "Instant Stepparents." *Stepfamilies* (Spring, 1992).

Seligman, Martin E. P. *Learned Optimism.* New York: Alfred A. Knopf, 1991.

Simring, Sue Klavans and Steven Simring. *Compatibility Quotient.* New York: Fawcett, 1990.

Shapiro, P G. *My turn: Women's Search for Self After Children Leave.* Princeton, New Jersey: Peterson's, 1996.

Solzhenitsyn, Alexander. *First Circle.* New York: Harper, 1968.

Squire, Susan. "When Young Married Couples Don't Make Love Anymore." *Cosmopolitan* (October 1, 1996).

Staheli, Lana. *Triangles: Understanding, Preventing, and Surviving Affairs.* New York: HarperCollins, 1997.

Tannen, Deborah. *You Just Don't Understand: Men and Women in Conversation.* New York: William Morrow, 1990.

Van Pelt, Nancy. *How to Talk So Your Mate Will Listen and Listen So Your Mate Will Talk.* New York: Revell, 1989.

Ventura, John and Mary Reed. *Divorce For Dummies.* Foster City, California: IDG Books Worldwide, Inc., 1998.

Wallerstein Judith S. and S. Blakeslee. *Good Marriage: How and Why Love Lasts.* New York: Houghton 1995.

Weber, Eric and Steven Simring. *How to Win Back The One You Love.* New York: MacMillan, 1983.

Weiner-Davis, Michelle. *Divorce Busting: A Revolutionary and Rapid Program for Staying Together.* New York: Fireside, 1993.

Weil, Bonnie E. *Make Up, Don't Break Up.* Holbrook, Massachusetts: Adams Media, 1999.

Westheimer Ruth. *Sex For Dummies.* Foster City, CA: IDG Books Worldwide, Inc., 1995.

White, L., and J. N. Edwards. "Emptying the nest and parental well-being: An analysis of national panel data." *American Sociological Review* (55, 1993).

Zinsmeister, Karl. "Divorce's Toll on Children." *Current* (February 1, 1997).

Appendix B

Resources

● ●

*I*n this appendix, we list a variety of resources that can help you improve your marriage.

Premarital Counseling

The following is a sampling of types of premarital programs available:

- ✔ Coalition for Marriage, Family, and Couples Education, phone 202-362-3332, Web site www.his.com/cmfce/.

- ✔ Practical Application of Intimate Relationship Skills program, phone 888-PAIRS-4U, e-mail info@pairs.org.

- ✔ Premarital Relationship Enhancement Program, phone 303-759-9931 or contact John Heverin at 516-538-6642.

- ✔ Saving Your Marriage Before It Starts, Center for Relationship Development, Seattle Pacific University, Seattle, WA 98119, phone 800-286-9333.

- ✔ Takes Two (designed specifically for African-American couples), phone 301-439-0024.

Other services are offered by therapists and through religious institutions.

Therapy and Counseling

The following professional associations can provide referrals for and information about marriage therapy and counseling:

- ✔ American Association for Marriage and Family Therapy, 1100 17th St. NW, Washington, DC 20036, phone 202-452-0109. This organization publishes its own helpful *Consumer's Guide for Marriage and Family Therapy*. It also provides online referral and other information through its Web site, www.aamft.org/faqs/DirPub.htm.

- American Association of Pastoral Counselors, 9504A Lee Highway, Fairfax, VA 2201-2303, phone 703-385-6967.

- American Association of Sex Educators, Counselors, and Therapists (AASECT), 435 N. Michigan Avenue, Suite 1717, Chicago, IL 60611, phone 312-644-0828.

- American Mental Health Counselors Association (provides referrals to professionals in your area), phone 800-326-2640.

- American Psychiatric Association, 1400 K Street NW, Washington, DC 20005, phone 202-682-6000.

- American Psychological Association, 750 1st Street NE, Washington, DC 20002, phone 202-336-5500.

- Mental Health Directory (a comprehensive listing of outpatient mental health clinics, psychiatric hospitals, mental health centers, and general hospitals with separate psychiatric services), Superintendent of Documents, Washington, DC 20402, phone 202-783-3238.

Infertility and Adoption

Resolve, Inc., a national organization based in Belmont, Massachusetts, provides information on infertility, adoption, high-tech pregnancies, and insemination. The organization runs support groups and seminars, and provides references to support groups and physicians who specialize in treating infertility, phone 617-643-2424.

Sexual Difficulties

Contact the following groups for assistance with sexual difficulties:

- The Impotence Information Center provides information on the causes and treatments of male sexual dysfunction, phone 800-843-4315.

- The Male Sexual Dysfunction Institute offers a hotline to answer questions about medical sexual problems, phone 312-725-7722.

- The San Francisco Sex Information Line answers questions about all aspects of sexuality and reproductive health. It also provides referrals to other medical and counseling resources, phone 415-621-7300.

- Sexaholics Anonymous, a self-help group in California, provides information on and therapy for addictive sexual behavior, phone 805-581-3343.

Stress

Try the following agencies for help in dealing with stress:

- ✔ The American Institute of Stress in Yonkers, New York, provides information on stress and stress management as well as referrals to experts in your area, phone 212-410-9043.

- ✔ Stress Management Publications, Superintendent of Documents, US Government Printing Office, Washington, DC 20402.

Retirement

The American Association of Retired Persons (AARP) can be an excellent resource. Contact them at P.O. Box 199, Long Beach, CA 90848-9983, phone 800-515-2299, Web site www.aarp.org.

Mental Illness

National Institute of Mental Health (NIMH) conducts research and provides information on depression and other mental disorders. Contact NIMH at 5600 Fishers Lane, Room 15C05, Rockville, MD 20857, phone 301-443-4515.

Alcoholism and Other Addictive Behaviors

Many 12-step programs are listed in your local phone book and newspaper. For additional help and information, contact the following organizations:

- ✔ The Alcohol Abuse Emergency 24-Hour Hotline provides information on treatments available for alcoholics, alcohol detox programs, and referrals to local treatment facilities and support groups, phone 800-252-6465.

- ✔ The Alcohol and Drug Helpline, sponsored by the American International Hospital Services, offers referrals to alcohol and drug dependency units, phone 800-821-4357.

- ✔ Children of Alcoholic Families National Clearinghouse on Alcohol Information, P.O. Box 2345, Rockville, MD 20852.

- ✔ Elderly Alcohol Abuse Information Center, National Institute on Aging, 2209 Distribution Circle, Silver Spring, MD 20910, phone 301-495-3455.

✔ The Cocaine Hotline, sponsored by the Psychiatric Institute of America and Fair Oaks Hospital in New Jersey, provides information on the health risks of using cocaine and offers referrals to local counseling services, phone 800-262-2463.

✔ The National Clearinghouse for Drug Abuse Information Helpline at the National Institute of Mental Health in Rockville, Maryland, offers programs, information, and referrals on drug abuse, phone 301-468-2600.

✔ The National Drug Information and Referral Line, sponsored by the National Institute of Drug Abuse, provides phone counseling and referrals to support groups and treatment programs, phone 800-662-4357.

Domestic Abuse

Take domestic abuse seriously! Contact any of the following resources:

✔ National Hotline for Battered Women, phone 800-799-SAFE, Web site www.famvi.com\htlines.htm.

✔ Wife Beating and Elder Abuse Help Center Clearinghouse on Family Violence, P.O. Box 1182, Washington, DC 20013, phone 703-385-7565.

✔ Center for the Prevention of Sexual and Domestic Violence, 936 N 34th Street, Suite 200, Seattle, WA 98103, phone 206-634-1903, fax 206-634-0115.

✔ Children's Defense Fund 25 E Street NW, Washington, DC 20001 202-628-8787.

✔ Health Resource Center on Domestic Violence, Family Violence Prevention Fund, 383 Rhode Island Street, Suite 304, San Francisco, CA 94103-5133, phone 800-313-1310, fax 415-252-8991.

✔ United Nations Development Fund for Women (UNEFEM), 304 E. 45th St., New York, NY 10017, phone 212-906-6400.

Divorce

The following helpful Web sites are among those suggested in *Divorce For Dummies* by John Ventura and Mary Reed (IDG Books Worldwide, Inc.):

✔ Divorce Helpline: www.divorcehelp.com

✔ Divorce Info: www.divorceinfo.com

✔ DivorceNet: www.divorcenet.com

✔ Divorce Online: www.divorce-online.com

✔ Divorce Support: www.divorcesupport.com

You may also want to contact the resource Center on Child Custody and Child Protection, National Council on Juvenile and Family Court Judges, P.O. Box 8970, Reno, NV 98507, phone 800-527-3223.

Index

• *G* •

Notes

Notes